D0983866

THE SHAKER ADVENTURE

THE SHAKER
ADVENTURE

By MARGUERITE FELLOWS MELCHER

PRINCETON UNIVERSITY PRESS • PRINCETON
LONDON : HUMPHREY MILFORD • OXFORD UNIVERSITY PRESS
MCM XLI

TO F. G. M.

PREFACE

THERE are many people I should like to thank for help received in the writing of this book—writers known and unknown, most of them not living now, who took the trouble to record for future readers their contemporary impressions of the Shakers. There are scholars like John Patterson MacLean of Ohio and Edward Deming Andrews of Massachusetts, who have spent years of study in this field, and librarians like Mrs. Nellie Pierce of Enfield, New Hampshire, who have painstakingly collected and preserved local newspaper articles by and about the Shakers. Then there are such libraries as the New York Public Library and the Dartmouth College Library which make their carefully gathered and efficiently catalogued collections of Shaker material easily available to the public. I should also like to thank the Montclair Library which has never yet failed me when I have asked for its help. Further thanks are due to public-spirited citizens like Clara Endicott Sears of Harvard and Boston, Massachusetts, who has organized a Shaker museum where Shaker workmanship may be seen and studied.

Then there are private individuals who have taken time and pains to unearth certain obscure facts for me, or who have made it possible for me to see Shaker buildings which are now owned by "the world." I should like to mention John Rudd and Robert Barnes Rudd of Tyringham, Massachusetts; C. Lambert Heyniger, headmaster of Darrow School at New Lebanon, New York; Father Versailles of La Salette at Enfield, New Hampshire; Brother Salvius of Notre Dame Institute at Alfred, Maine; the warden of the State Prison Farm at Enfield, Connecticut, and—most gratefully of all—the Shaker sisters themselves at Sabbathday Lake, Maine, New Lebanon, New York, and especially at Canterbury, New Hampshire. If I did not feel that they would prefer not to be designated—knowing that the Shakers have always chosen to sink the individual in the community—I should like to give their names.

Thanks also are due to my mother and to my aunts who knew my Shaker great-aunt Zelinda and my Shaker great-uncle Elias, and some of the other Enfield, New Hampshire, Shakers. Thanks also to my husband for his sympathetic interest and advice. Last of all, my appreciation to Joseph Brandt who is, it seems to me, the ideal publisher to work with.

M.F.M.

CONTENTS

PART ONE

THE ADVENTURE BEGINS

I. TOAD LANE TO NEW LEBANON

T HERE is, in a poem by Robert Frost, the line: "What to make of a diminished thing."

This is the problem facing anyone who tries to tell the story of the Shakers and to explain the meaning of their strange adventure. For it was an adventure in all senses of the word: a voyage into the New World of the American colonies, an experiment in human brotherhood, an attempt to chart that hardest of all realms to enter, the realm of the spirit. Above all, the Shakers were spiritual adventurers. So far as most—perhaps all—of their members were concerned, their spiritual adventure was successful; but in the eyes of the world it was a failure. The Shaker religion seems to have left little or no imprint on the religious thinking or feeling of these times. It was conceived in the ecstasy of emotional exaltation; it was born amid the pangs of struggle against bigotry, misunderstanding, and even fear, which this strange new religion aroused; it grew in strength and dignity and confidence; and it began to diminish, until now it has dwindled almost away. The early fire is burning low; the confidence of the middle period has been undermined by attacks from without and betrayals from within.

Few if any new recruits to Shakerism are found today. There is no one to whom to hand on the torch, even if that torch were still bright. Soon, in all probability, the sect will be extinct. What interest can it hold for us in this age? It drew comparatively few of the "world's people" even at its zenith. And now, when its sun is setting, "what to make of a diminished thing?"

If the Shaker aim, fantastically impossible to most people, was once able to attract members in sufficient quantity to build up those well-organized, self-supporting family communities, why and at what point did it falter? Was it perhaps that those of its members who really attained the perfection for which they were struggling found nothing further to work toward? All nature, and all inventions of man, too, seem to show that in perfection are the seeds of death. The full-blown rose has already begun to die—as a rose. The day of the clipper ship was over just when it attained the utmost rightness and beauty of line. Were the Shakers aiming so high that, granted it was possible for a few to reach the goal, they found nothing further toward which to journey? Or was the diminishing only a sinking back into the common lot and accomplishment of mankind? In any case, what, if anything, did the Shakers bring back from the heights for the rest of us? Even a report of a view would be something.

They did bring back the report of a view, and wrote it down for the "world's people" and for posterity. But the description of an emotional experience, however faithful and inspired, never wholly catches the rapture of the experience itself. A listener can always doubt the truth of the report. The sight of one's own eyes is another thing. If we cannot share, or even wholly credit, the spiritual adventure of the Shakers, we can see its results in the work of their

4

hands: their plain, perfectly constructed buildings, furniture, and tools; and we can examine the orderly, workable economic system they built in a confused world. Although beauty was not a part of their creed, they left a legacy of beauty to the world: the beauty that follows order, the beauty that comes unsought when the lines are right. And beauty does not diminish.

Everybody asks two things of life: adventure and security. · The proportion of these two ingredients determines the nature of the individual. Or perhaps it is the other way around. But it is impossible to imagine a satisfactory life that does not hold a measure of each. The Shakers achieved a perfect balance between the two—perfect, that is, for their purposes and from their point of view. The adventure which meant the most to them was in the realm of things spiritual, where, paradoxically, their souls also found security and peace. The earthly security that the world noted and often envied was physical and economic, and only achieved after much hardship. The spiritual adventuring sprang from inner dissatisfactions and cravings that united the Shakers in a kind of quest of the Holy Grail. The economic security was developed out of their need for a stable, dependable way of living together. The result was a workable scheme of communal life that has lasted over a hundred years. And the adventure has left on Shaker faces a contentment so rare in the world today as to attract attention and comment.

The early Shakers came mainly from the lower middle class groups. They were rooted in revolt: revolt against smugness and bigotry in religion, revolt against social and economic evils, revolt against the uglier side of human nature. The Camisards in France, who are usually considered the spiritual ancestors of the Shakers, were the direct result of the Revocation of the Edict of Nantes in 1685.

5

Under the leadership of Jean Cavalier, a young baker, they went about the countryside of the provinces of Dauphiné and Rivarais stirring up men's emotions, and prophesying the coming of God's kingdom on earth. Their meetings bore all the marks of a religious revival in its most extreme form. Although there were only five or six hundred in this Protestant group, the French government felt obliged to restrain them, which it did by persecution, torture, and in many cases death. A few of them escaped with their leader to England at the beginning of the eighteenth century, when they began holding meetings in the neighborhood of London. By 1705 the English group had increased to between three and four hundred "prophets," as they called themselves. But their prophetic ardor cooled on English soil. Perhaps Jean Cavalier had no gift for organizing to match his power of arousing. All adventure and no security could not be endured for long. At any rate, little further is heard of these prophets till 1747 when a Quaker couple, James and Jane Wardley, joined them and brought new fire to dying enthusiasm by announcing the second coming of Christ as near at hand. Even the Wardleys, however, were unable to weld these gatherings of emotional reformers into a purposeful and united group until Ann Lee joined them.

Ann Lee, like most of those who were to become her followers, belonged to the common people. Her father was a blacksmith, as was also her brother William Lee, and the man she married, Abraham Stanley. As a girl Ann worked in a cotton factory, and later was a cutter of hatter's fur. When older, she was employed as a cook in the Manchester Infirmary. With seven other children in the family, any kind of formal education was out of the question. Ann grew up unable either to read or write. She was always "serious

6

and thoughtful, and never addicted to play like other children." Like Joan of Arc, she had visions and prophetic dreams. While it was patriotism and the church with Joan of Arc, it was humanity with Ann Lee: a passion for saving and purifying mankind. She was extremely sensitive to conditions about her, feeling deeply her individual responsibility for bettering these conditions.

When Ann Lee was born in Toad Lane, Manchester, on February 29, 1736, George II was king of England, with corrupt politicians for ministers. From 1739 till 1763, England was almost continuously at war with either France or Spain, until the distress caused by these wars and by the taxation necessary for waging them led to bitter discontent among the people. Manchester was an Anglican bishopric as well as an important center of textile manufacture. The textile workers had accepted the political situation and the taxes because they could do nothing about either. They also accepted the religion that was handed out to them. Religion had become perfunctory, therefore religious persecution had ceased in England. If the eighteenth century was an age of prose in literature, it was even more so in religion, because religious leaders had forgotten that emotion is a part of all true religious experience. The time was ripe for a resurgence of religious emotionalism. It is perhaps not wholly a coincidence that those two masters of the emotional appeal in religion—John Wesley and George Whitefield—followed close after Jean Cavalier and his "prophets." Both Wesley and Whitefield found waiting audiences hungry for their message. The religious revival with its doctrine of conversion came to be an important phenomenon both in England and America. It was out of the union of religious revivalism and economic need that Shakerism was born. Ann Lee repeated many times during her life, "Put your hands to work and your heart to God."

As Ann grew up in the sordid surroundings of an eighteenth century industrial town, she was deeply impressed by the "depravity of human nature and the odiousness of sin." She spent many hours in prayer, often agonizing all night over her own sinful state. Very early she felt great repugnance toward all physical manifestations of sex. In spite of her feelings in this matter, however (with which Ann's mother appears to have sympathized before her death in Ann's youth), Ann's father insisted on her marriage to Abraham Stanley, by whom she had four children. All of these died in infancy or early childhood. Ann's previous convictions kept returning to her, reinforced by the thought that the death of her children was a judgment on her for having been led away from her beliefs. She found no peace anywhere and "often spent whole nights in laboring and crying to God for deliverance from sin." She became so weak at times that she could hardly stand. It was at this period that she met the Wardleys. In the twenty-third year of her life, September 1758, she united with the society under their care. "The light of these people led them to an open confession of every sin which they had committed, and to a full and final cross against everything which they knew to be evil: hence they were endowed with great power over sin; and hence Ann found that protection which she had so long desired, and which, for the time being, was answerable to her faith."

The Wardleys welcomed Ann as a promising and helpful disciple. Ann Lee impressed everyone with her devoutness and her honesty. She had a warm, magnetic personality that drew people to her. No one could see or hear her without believing that she was wholly sincere. The Wardleys, like the Camisards, had been teaching that Christ's second coming was imminent. It was a comforting thought for poor confused souls—something good to look forward to. James and Jane Wardley had come to have a deep conviction that His second coming would be in the form of a woman. Hence they were waiting and watching for her who might seem to fill the requirements. They became increasingly sure that Ann Lee was the woman. The passion Ann brought to her longings and labors for the pure and sinless life was unquestionably real. Her agonized struggles to find and understand the will of God and to conform all her actions to it were no common manifestations of the work of the spirit, even in that group of emotional revivalists. All of them were fanatics; most of them were mystics as well. Ann was practical in her fanaticism and her mysticism. One might almost say she used the scientific method of analysis. Searching for God, she was seeking also for the springs of human nature. Why did men sin? She observed people closely; she learned to read the thoughts and motives behind their acts. "A good tree cannot bring forth evil fruit," was a favorite phrase. She looked about her in Toad Lane and saw that man's ungoverned natural impulses: greed, pride, sex—caused most of the ugliness found in human life. It seemed to her that sex was the root of all. And since sex was responsible for so much that was bad, it must in itself be bad. She was over a hundred years ahead of Freud in this analysis of the springs of human conduct. And she was practical and direct in her use of it. "If your eye offend you, pluck it out." She cut the Gordian knot and did away with sex altogether.

Thus Shakerism was announced to the world. It was a way of life leading to spiritual perfection over the dead body of man's physical nature. It was a great adventure in that conquest of self which is more difficult than the conquest of cities. It was another proof that self-denial can bring greater ecstasy than self-indulgence. Its four foundation principles were confession of sins, community of goods, celibacy, withdrawal from the world. The first, and in large degree the second of these, were practised from the start. The third and fourth had to wait for complete fulfillment till the Shakers were established in their own communities in America. But the Shaker way of life proved to be a workable one. It worked so well that it lasted over a hundred years.

All of this did not happen in a moment. For nine long years Ann labored in constant travail of spirit and body before Shakerism could be born. At times she became so weak from sleepless nights and weary days that she was unable even to feed herself. At other times, she was restored miraculously to radiant vigor and a strength-giving confidence that buoyed up the hopes and spirits of her companions. Her vivid presentation of the heavenly visions and divine revelations that had come to her gave her face a more than earthly beauty, causing her eyes to exercise a strange power over all observers. Her days of soul-searching and agonizing were ended by the famous vision which signalized the birth of Shakerism. This vision came to Ann while she was in prison on some charge of disturbing the peace. She saw Adam and Eve in the Garden of Eden committing the act that resulted in their expulsion from the Garden and in saddling mankind with a heritage of sin. It was revealed to her that she was the anointed successor to Jesus—the mother incarnation of the word of God again to be given to man in this second coming of Christ. She was Mother Ann: Ann the Word. The Wardleys were convinced beyond a doubt that she was the one they were waiting for. Ann became filled with serenity. Her days of seeking were over; she had found the truth and truth had set her free; she knew now what God wanted her to do. Having attained spiritual peace for herself, she could turn her whole attention toward helping others along the road that God had pointed out to her.

The Wardleys now acknowledged Ann Lee as the spiritual head of their Society. As reports spread of her words and acts, the Society began to increase rapidly. Many people were starving for just such spiritual bread; many drab lives were brightened by these glimpses of spiritual glory; many simple men and women longed for a gentler, kindlier way of life than any they had known; all these found comfort in the sincerity and strength and goodness that Ann Lee radiated. But growth in numbers brought a corresponding danger. This strange sect of shaking, dancing fanatics began to be regarded as a menace to the peace of the community. Some of the new members "fell away," lacking courage to face the persecution that followed. The handful that remained was strengthened by adversity, both in loyalty to one another, and in the firmness of their convictions.

It is possible that the Shakers would have been left unmolested in the exercise of their disturbingly emotional religious rites if they had been willing to keep their religion in one compartment and their daily practice of living in another. But like her who became their leader, and like Jesus of Nazareth whose name they always coupled with hers, they thought of religion as something to live by; they actually practised what they preached. After making honest public confession of their sins in meeting, they went back into the world determined to sin no more. This was hard for the average citizen to endure. It made the neighbors uncomfortable when a fellow dweller in Toad Lane claimed that she could give the keys to Heaven to all who would turn away from the normal pleasures and relationships of human life. Friendships were ended by this new religion; families were broken up. To be sure, there was New Testament authority for this. "He that loveth father or mother more than me is not worthy of me." But what had that to do with Toad Lane? Besides, men fear what they do not understand. It was as easy to believe the shaking and the twitching and the frenzied dancing of the Believers came from the devil as that it came from God. So the persecutors, like all persecutors past and present, looked about for an excuse to justify their deeds.

Sabbath-breaking and blasphemy were the crimes of which Ann Lee, like Jesus, was accused. A Sunday meeting in her father's house was broken up on the pretext that the Shaker dancing and singing were a profanation of the Sabbath. The worshippers were roughly handled and dragged off to prison, later to be released. There followed other similar attempts to discourage Shaker zeal. The most serious of them was an actual plot against Ann's life. She was seized and confined in a stone cell not large enough to lie down in, and kept there fourteen days without food. At least that was the intention of her jailers. But young James Whittaker, a devoted follower who was later to become one of the leaders of Shakerism in America, found a way to feed her. Somehow, he gained access to the door of her cell, and by means of a pipe whose stem he passed through the keyhole, he fed her with milk and wine. At the end of the two weeks her jailer came to open her door expecting to find her dead. Her enemies were not only surprised, but confounded when she walked out alive and apparently as vigorous as when she went in. They were a little frightened at this evidence of supernatural protection; and some of them began to question the advisability of persecuting her further. Her following was increased by this seeming miracle, and her power strengthened.

There were other persecutions in England, mostly at the hands of irresponsible mobs. The blasphemy charge seemed to be justified when Ann claimed to be the incarnation of the second coming of Christ: the female element that supplemented Jesus and thus completed the revelation to the world of a father-and-mother-God. She affirmed this claim by visions and proved it by a convincing interpretation of Bible prophecies. When, however, her persecutors brought her before a tribunal of four ministers of the established church with the demand that her tongue be bored through with a hot iron, "these men, being desirous to hear her own testimony, gave her liberty to speak for herself. Accordingly she spoke, and manifested such evident power of God, that they thought proper to dismiss her; and admonished her accusers to let her alone, and not abuse her." Her disappointed persecutors decided to take the law into their own hands and to stone her to death as a blasphemer. Four of the Shaker brethren—her own brother, William Lee, James and Daniel Whittaker and James Shepherd—insisted on going with her. The five Shakers were conducted outside the town and made to stand in a valley whence Ann's persecutors could conveniently stone them from the side of the hill. In spite of repeated attempts with the "sufficient quantity of stones, suitable for their purpose" which they had collected, the men on the hillside failed to hit any of them except Daniel Whittaker, whom they wounded slightly on the temple. They fell to quarrelling, as those who are unsuccessful in nefarious undertakings often do, and finally gave up. Mother Ann, in relating the affair said, "While they were throwing their stones, I felt myself surrounded with the presence of God, and my soul was filled with love.

I knew they could not kill me, because my work was not done; therefore I felt joyful and comfortable, while my enemies felt distress and confusion." A footnote to this account adds that Daniel Whittaker, the only man at all inconvenienced by this experience, "afterwards fell away."

Eventually the persecutors of the Shakers tired; or as a Shaker historian puts it, "In consequence of the sudden and untimely death of some of her most bitter persecutors, and the conversion of others, these cruel abuses finally ceased. Her enemies saw that she was evidently protected and supported and her life preserved by some interposing power, notwithstanding all their attempts to destroy it; and hence, for more than two years previous to her leaving England, she and her little band enjoyed their faith in peace." During this period, while resting on their oars, deciding what to do next, they heard talk about the English colonies in America. It was just before the War for Independence; and ideas of democracy and freedom were being discussed even in Toad Lane. Mother Ann was at length "by a special revelation, directed to repair to America; and at the same time, she received a divine promise, that the work of God would greatly increase, and the millennial church would be established in that country." Many individual members of the Society told of signs, visions, etc. that confirmed this plan. On May 19, 1774, therefore, they set sail from Liverpool for New York on the ship *Mariah*, with Captain Smith of New York. The Wardleys remained behind. Their part in the great adventure was finished. Like John the Baptist, they had only prepared the way for a greater one who was to come after them.

The Shakers had been fortunate in having two sponsors able to give them financial help when they needed it most. The first, John Townley, belongs to the Wardley period. He was a well-to-do brick-layer living in Canon Street, Manchester, and his wife was an ardent member of the Wardleys' Society. John Townley had contributed much toward the support of these early Believers, even taking the Wardleys into his own household to live and allowing them to hold many of their meetings in his home. His wife's brother, John Hocknell, who was also a man of property, living in Cheshire twenty-four miles from Manchester, followed his example by inviting a number of the poorer members of the Society to make their home with him. This John's wife, however, was not so coöperative in her attitude toward the Shakers as was his sister's husband. John Hocknell's interest in this wild new sect "at first displeased Hannah his wife, and her natural relations (the Dickins family), who were wealthy and high spirited people; whereupon three of her brothers, with the assistance of a magistrate, had John put into prison at Middlewich, four miles from his own house. He was tried and released, and soon after, Hannah became a member of the Society and continued through all the increase of the work, till she departed this life (in America) sound in the faith."

When the Shakers left for America, John Townley and his wife remained behind in England; but John Hocknell followed Ann Lee to the New World. It was he who arranged for the voyage to America, paying a large share of the passage money; it was he who negotiated the purchase of the wilderness tract of land near Albany, New York, where the Shakers first found a real home of their own. He is described, in what sounds like understatement, as "a man of very meek deportment . . . greatly gifted in visions and prophecies . . . a very honest, conscientious and upright man." This picture gives no hint of magnetism and warmth such as Mother Ann possessed; nevertheless, John Hocknell must have been a great comfort to the penniless adventurers.

The eight who accompanied Mother Ann on the voyage to America, after having settled their affairs in England, were her husband, Abraham Stanley, her brother, William Lee, her niece, Nancy Lee, James Whittaker, John Hocknell, Richard Hocknell, son of John, James Shepherd and Mary Partington. The captain was not overpleased at the prospect of carrying a group of fanatics on the long journey across the stormy Atlantic, though he was somewhat reassured when Mother Ann promised him that he "should not have whereof to accuse them, except it were concerning the law of their God." When, however, in the course of the passage, they "went forth, in obedience to their inward feelings, to praise God in songs and dances," the captain felt that he had been deceived and threatened to throw them overboard if they did not behave themselves.

Mother Ann apparently felt that it was safer to obey God than the captain, so the Believers "went forth again," and thereby angered the captain to such an extent that he prepared to carry out his threat. Whether or not he would have done so will never be known, for a severe storm sprang up at the crucial moment, and the ship, which was old and not too seaworthy, opened a leak. All hands had to be called to the pumps and the Believers did their share valiantly. Nevertheless, the water came in faster than they could bail it out, and the captain almost gave up hope. Mother Ann, however, did not lose confidence in her God, but spoke words of encouragement to the captain. "Captain," she said, "be of good cheer; there shall not a hair of our heads perish; we shall all arrive safe to America. I just saw two bright angels of God standing by the mast, through whom I received this promise." She inspired the sailors to renewed efforts, and she and her followers helped them with efforts as well as words. Suddenly a wave miraculously struck the loose planks which had been causing the trouble, and drove it back in place. The leak stopped, and the ship was saved. The captain was so impressed with Mother Ann's power that he gave her permission to worship as she pleased during the rest of the journey; and they all reached New York, safe and happy on the sixth of August, 1774. The captain generously gave entire credit to the Shakers for the success of the voyage.

In this manner, the English founder of the new religion that was to save the world reached the land of her visions. She and her eight faithful followers might have been considered stormy petrels. They left stormy days behind them in England; their crossing of the ocean was marked by storm; they landed in New York in a stormy period of American Colonial history—obscure English immigrants to a land whose people were turning against England. It was only two years before the outbreak of the American Revolution; it was one month before the assembling in Philadelphia of the first Continental Congress. The Believers had no friends or acquaintances in America, no place to go, no means of livelihood except by the work of their hands. Probably at that, they felt very little less secure than they had always felt in England. Abraham Stanley and William Lee had their trade of blacksmith; James Whittaker was a weaver. Mother Ann, always practical, advised them to separate for the time being, and earn their separate livings as best they could. She herself remained in New York, finding lodging with a family named Smith for whom she did washing and ironing. Her husband got work with Mr. Smith who, providentially, was a blacksmith. William Lee and John Hocknell went up the Hudson to Albany looking for a suitable place to settle. They took an option on a piece of land near Niskayuna (later Water-vliet), which, though only "eight measured miles North-west from the center of the city of Albany," was an uncleared wilderness, and seemed sufficiently remote from settlements and the public eye to afford security and a chance for spiritual growth. John Hocknell returned to England to fetch the rest of his family, and "to make further arrangements for the settlement of the society in this country"; which in plain terms meant raising enough money to complete payment on the land. He was at that time seventy years old.

While waiting for John Hocknell to come back from England, William Lee and some of the others found work in Albany; they and Mother Ann exchanged visits from time to time to keep up their morale. Before the time of waiting was up, however, Mother Ann came very near starvation. Her husband, Abraham Stanley, was taken so seriously ill as to require Mother Ann's whole time and attention for nursing him. This meant that neither was earning anything; they were alone in a strange city without any means of support. Ann nursed her husband devotedly, never sparing herself. At one time "her only shelter from the inclemency of the weather was a small uncomfortable room, without bed or bedding, or any other furniture than a cold stone for a seat, and her only morsel was a cruse of vinegar, and as she afterwards testified, she sat down upon the stone, without any fire, sipped her vinegar, and wept." Abraham recovered; but instead of showing gratitude to Ann for her devoted care, he began immediately to backslide from Shakerism. Apparently he had never been as ardent in the faith as the others; but he had conformed, at least outwardly. Now he deliberately turned away from all that Mother Ann held most precious, urging her to give up her convictions and enter once more into the marriage relationship with him.

When she refused he left her, returning later with a woman of the streets whom he threatened to marry unless Ann would yield. She stood firm in her refusal, however; and this was the end of Abraham Stanley so far as the Shakers were concerned. It is not unthinkable that Abraham acted from the best of motives. He had backed up his wife thus far in what must have been a trying situation for a husband. Possibly he really loved her and was trying to force her hand in order to save her from the consequences of her fantastic adventure. But in the eyes of the Shakers he "fell away," and was a traitor to the cause.

Late in December of 1775, John Hocknell returned, bringing his family and also John Partington with his family. They landed in Philadelphia, whence they proceeded to New York to report to Mother Ann. In February 1776, he and the newcomers went by land to Albany where they visited the other members of the little band, and became actual owners of the wilderness tract which they "leased in perpetuity" from Stephen van Rensselaer, Esq. It was midwinter; they grew impatient waiting for spring when they could start work together in their own domain. As soon as the river was open for travel, Hocknell went again to New York, returning with Mother Ann and such earthly possessions as had been left behind. The Believers were reunited, after nearly two years of separation and hardship in a strange land.

During the summer of 1776, they all worked at Niskayuna, draining and clearing the land, putting up buildings, preparing the soil for crops, that they might become a self-sufficient community. The courage and industry of this little band of artisans from an English factory town made up for their lack of knowledge of frontier agriculture. In September 1776, less than two months after the signing of the Declaration of Independence, Mother Ann and her followers took up their permanent residence on their new property in the future state of New York. They were established as land owners in what was to become the United States of America. For the next three and a half years they worked and worshipped in a peace that seemed like a heavenly interlude between the persecutions and hardships they had left behind in England and the future trials that awaited them in America after the beginning of their real work in this new land of freedom.

At first they were occupied with the immediate problems of subsistence, content in their new home, working for themselves and for each other, holding their services of worship unmolested, savoring a security they had never found in England. Soon, however, some of the members began to grow restless, fearing that their mission had come to a dead end since no new members came to join them. Mother Ann was not worried; she counseled patience, promising that the testimony would be opened in the New World in the fullness of God's time. In prophetic visions she saw multitudes drawn to Niskayuna in search of the Shaker gospel. "The time is near at hand," she said, "when they will come like doves." The Believers curbed their impatience and waited, trusting her who had never failed them. At last the signs for which they had been waiting came. Mother Ann was right, as always.

In the spring of 1779, New Lebanon, New York, became the center of a series of religious revival meetings such as were common in the American colonies during the latter half of the eighteenth century. It is claimed by some ecclesiastical writers that these revivals, begun by the English John Wesley and George Whitefield, and the American Jonathan Edwards, were a result of reaction from the tendency toward deism which had swept both countries. While revival leaders doubtless had this in mind, it seems unlikely that their congregations—rough pioneers in frontier country, as much of colonial America was—wasted many thoughts on theological distinctions. Pioneer conduct is black and white; wartime conduct is the same. Neither has room nor time for subtleties. New Lebanon was pioneer country, the edge of a wilderness. The year 1779 was wartime, the middle of our Revolution. Revivalism is one form of hysteria; and all hysteria, whether of religion or of war, springs from fear and unfulfilled desire. This world is hard and terrible: how can I escape from it; what must I do to be saved? Men desire passionately to be able to look forward to a better world than this present world they know. Hence they invent heavens and utopias. One of the brightest prospects has always been the second coming of Christ, and this was the theme of the New Lebanon revival sermons. An amazing number of people dwelling in towns on either side of the border between New York and Massachusetts were seized with conviction of sin and revulsion against the shortness and general unsatisfactoriness of human life. They were filled with an agonizing desire to make terms with an eternity that might promise more. The revival lasted all summer. All sorts of people attended the meetings: young, old, middle-aged; Methodists, Presbyterians, Baptists; men and women from poor and ignorant families, college graduates. The whole district was like one great revival meeting.

The New Lebanon Revival was not dissimilar to the meetings held by the Wardleys in England. Some who attended confessed their sins aloud, crying for mercy; some went into a trance-like state in which they saw visions and received prophecies of Christ's imminent second coming. Others shouted and danced for joy because they believed that the day was at hand for wars to cease and God's kingdom on earth to begin. Many who had been church members and believed themselves to be Christians were impressed with the emptiness and the falsity of the established churches. They were ready to make any sacrifice, to follow anyone who could lead them to a fuller, truer way of life. But as the summer wore on and nothing happened, they saw the brightness of their visions fading, felt the warmth of their ardor cooling. Many sank back into the disillusionment from which the Revival had temporarily lifted them. Church members returned empty to their churches. The worldlings turned their backs once more on the illusion of religion. "Even the Revival leaders and speakers sat in silence with their heads bowed down. . . . The spirit and power of God, which had been so copiously showered down upon the people, seemed now at an end."

There were, however, a few earnest souls who found it impossible to forget so easily the glimpses they had had into a better world. These kept together through the winter, encouraging each other, trying to hold the visions they had received, waiting, watching, praying for something that should seem an answer to their prayers and their desires. Their patience was rewarded in the spring, when word came to them of "a strange people living above Albany, who said they served God day and night, and did not commit sin." Singly and in groups they went to the wilderness tract at Niskayuna to see for themselves what manner of people these were. They were welcomed as expected guests. The opening of the gospel in America had begun.

II. OPENING THE TESTIMONY
IN AMERICA

IT was early in the year 1780 that the disappointed but still ardent revivalists turned their steps toward Niskayuna. As Mother Ann's little community numbered not over ten or a dozen men and women, its resources for hospitality were scant. Nevertheless, the Shakers succeeded not only in making the strangers feel at home while there, but also in sending them back to their several dwellings strong in the new faith. Husbands and wives together often embraced the new gospel and went home to found little centers of Shaker influence in their own communities. Sometimes whole families joined at a time.

Although the first converts came from nearby, soon people in distant towns began to hear rumors of this strange new sect and came to learn about them at first hand. From Massachusetts, Connecticut, New Hampshire and Maine they came, returning home to practise and to impart what they had learned. After a time members of the Niskayuna group began making journeys into the other states to visit the new converts in their home towns. On the way they would stop with families whom they knew to be sympathetic to the Shaker teachings. At every house so visited, meetings were held with songs and dancing and the "shaking" that had given the sect its name. More converts were added to the growing numbers. And the travellers from Niskayuna were sure wherever they went, of a joyous welcome from these enthusiastic fellow-Shakers.

With the "world's people" along the route it was different. At first they regarded this queer sect with contemptuous amusement; later their jeers changed to something more sinister. As in England, friends were separated and homes sometimes broken up by the coming of the Shakers into a community. Persecutions began, increasing in intensity. On one trip made by Mother Ann and the elders between Niskayuna and Harvard, Massachusetts, hostile mobs formed in almost every town. There is no doubt that the injuries inflicted on the Shakers by many of these ruffians shortened the lives of the original members of the little band. William Lee and Mother Ann both died very shortly after their return to Niskayuna from this two-year missionary journey into Massachusetts and Connecticut.

The persecutions started nearer home, however. It is perhaps not strange that the townspeople of New Lebanon should resent Mother Ann's easy capture of two New Lebanon ministers in 1780: the Baptist Joseph Meacham, who had been one of the leaders of the Revival, and Samuel Johnson, a Presbyterian. And these two were only a beginning. Though most of the joiners were poor, uneducated, and in their early twenties or younger, enough men of weight and substance were attracted to the Shakers to cause alarm and resentment in their communities. And they were not all of them in the first flush of reckless youth. Joseph Meacham was a man of forty, born in Enfield, Connecticut, in 1740. Samuel Johnson was a Yale graduate of the class of 1769, with an A.M. degree to boot. When he joined the Shakers his wife, Elizabeth, joined also. Daniel Goodrich of Hancock, Massachusetts, was the son of a deacon in the Baptist church. Most of the early converts who have left written records of their lives before and after joining the Shakers were sons and daughters of New England churchgoers, brought up in the fear of God and the devil (in the tradition of Jonathan Edwards) , agonizing over the state of their souls, finding no comfort in the religion which their parents had taught them. As the Shaker sect grew, it became practical to form communities which could practise their own way of life and conduct their own peculiar form of worship. The persecutions made this increasingly necessary. But it was not till three years after Mother Ann's death that the Shakers did "gather into society order." Just before she died she told her followers, "The time will come when the church will be gathered into order, and then it will be known who are good believers. But that is not my work; it is Joseph Meacham's work; my work is nearly done."

All the written accounts of Mother Ann's work and words were made some years after her death. In this circumstance, the Shakers saw another similarity to New Testament history. Christ's words and deeds were unrecorded in writing until long after his death. This leaves many chances for errors to creep in. Yet there is much unanimity in the reports set down by Ann Lee's followers. According to all of them, she was "a woman rather below the common stature of woman; thickset, but straight and otherwise well proportioned and regular in form and features. Her complexion was light and fair, and her eyes were blue, but keen and penetrating; her countenance was mild and expressive, but grave and solemn. Her natural constitution was sound, strong and healthy. Her manners were plain, simple, and easy; yet she possessed a certain dignity of appearance that inspired confidence and commanded respect. By many of the world, who saw her without prejudice, she was called beautiful; and to her faithful children, she appeared to possess a degree of dignified beauty and heavenly love, which they had never before discovered among mortals.

"She possessed remarkable powers and faculties of mind in nature, which were greatly enlarged and strengthened by the gift of God. At times, when under the power and operation of the Holy Ghost, her countenance shone with the glory of God, and her form and actions appeared divinely beautiful and very angelic. The power and influence of her spirit, at such times, was great beyond description; and no one was able to gainsay or resist the authority by which she spoke."

Her enemies described her quite differently: "lewd, vile, debauched" were some of the terms they hurled at her. Yet these epithets sound more like the angry mouthings of a rowdy mob than a dependable description. Besides, the mobs had to justify themselves somehow for their brutality to a small group of defenseless worshippers, however fanatical. And certainly, if Ann Lee had been what they said, there were easier paths open to a woman of low character than the one she chose to follow. The Shakers, furthermore, did not neglect to point out that Christ himself was characterized in somewhat similar terms by his enemies among the Jews and the Romans.

A quite obvious reason for some of the persecutions was the fact that the Shakers were recent immigrants from England; the country with which the American colonies were at war. What were these English men and women doing here, living by themselves in a secluded spot not too far from Canada, and enticing good Americans away from friends and families to join them? It sounded suspicious, and it made a plausible pretext for mob action. The transportation to Niskayuna of various kinds of foodstuffs for feeding the many disciples who were converging there gave color to the rumor that these Shakers were in the pay of the British army, supplying them with food and ammunition and serving them as spies. In July 1780, as David Darrow was on his way from New Lebanon to Albany, driving a flock of sheep intended for the Niskayuna community, he and his sheep were seized by a mob of suspicious men who took David off to Albany to be tried by the commissioners and divided the sheep among themselves. Joseph Meacham went along with David to help him.

The two were brought before the commissioners and asked to swear obedience to the laws. The Shakers were opposed on principle to taking any oath, and were furthermore unwilling to pledge themselves blindly to anything, so they refused to do so. David Darrow, Joseph Meacham and John Hocknell were put in prison, and shortly after Mother Ann herself, William Lee and James Whittaker were also arrested and imprisoned at Albany. It was quite evident that this was done with the object of getting rid of the Shakers. The commissioners at Albany, however, seemed to be kindly disposed toward the Believers; and many liberal-minded Americans expressed open disapproval of methods that smacked of the kind of tyranny they thought had been left behind in Tory England. Even at that disturbed period there were citizens ready to raise their voices in defense of civil liberty when they saw it denied to a defenseless minority.

While in prison, however, Mother Ann managed to attract and hold a crowd of listeners. Through the grates of the prison she preached to large assemblies and made many new converts. Soon she was separated from the others with the idea of being banished to the British army at New York. She was taken as far as Poughkeepsie where she remained imprisoned till December when Governor Clinton released her. The other Shakers were likewise released without any formal trial, and allowed to go back to Niskayuna. "Nor was any persecution ever raised against them, but by means of that false religion and spirit of oppression, which had long been established in the British dominions, and whose despotic influence had not yet ceased in America."

The Shakers, usually given to understatement, have left what sound like remarkably calm and unexaggerated accounts of some of the many persecutions they were obliged to endure at the hands of the "world's people." In their quest for perfection they have always tried to be fair and to "judge not." And always they avoided recourse to law unless forced to it by their enemies. Yet their story of the founding of these first New York and New England communities contains one harrowing tale after another of the brutality of man to man. In May of 1781, Mother Ann and the Elders left Niskayuna to visit "the distant parts, from place to place, where the gospel had been received; and in all the principal places which they visited, they were resorted to from the adjacent parts; and their ministry being everywhere accompanied with the gifts of the Holy Ghost . . . many more were added to the faith." They went first to Harvard, Massachusetts, in late June 1781. Harvard was already the home of a small group of religious fanatics whose leader, Shadrack Ireland, had recently died. Mother Ann said this was the place she had seen in her visions in England; she said the faces of the people were familiar to her, for she had seen them all before. She remained there some months, living in the "Square House" where Ireland had lived, and visiting the towns around: Shirley, Littleton, Woburn, and Petersham. In December, when she and the Elders were in Petersham, the first Massachusetts mob attacked them, dragging Mother Ann feet first out of the house, throwing her into a sleigh "with as little ceremony as they would the dead carcase of a beast, committing at the same time acts of inhumanity which even savages would be ashamed of." James

Whittaker, William Lee, and others were badly beaten and bruised. It was decided to go back to Harvard where they felt safer.

Soon, however, people in Harvard began muttering and whispering suspicious tales about the Shakers. Again the rumor began to circulate that they were English spies. It was reported that they had stores of ammunition hidden in the Square House where they were making their home. On petition from a number of Harvard citizens, the town militia entered the house to make investigations. No ammunition was found, but the New York Shakers were warned to leave town. They were at first unwilling to do so; but when they heard that another mob was getting ready to attack them, they departed during the night. In the morning the mob made its appearance, as expected, and put the remaining Shakers through the equivalent of a "third degree"; but they were unable to learn from them in which direction Mother Ann and the Elders had gone.

The next place visited was Enfield, Connecticut. The travellers arrived at David Meacham's house in March 1782, after a journey continually interrupted by threats and abuse. And no peace awaited them in Enfield. They had hardly been there a week when a mob of about two hundred men came to the house to order them to leave town, following them for eight miles to make sure they complied. The Shakers crossed the Connecticut River, proceeding to West Springfield, Massachusetts, then recrossed the river at Springfield, going from there to Kingston, Granby, Belchertown, Montague, Sunderland, and Ashfield. Here they remained through April and May, finding the rest and retirement that they sorely needed. During this stay they kept pretty much to themselves, save for one visit Mother Ann made to Jonathan and Aaron Wood at Shelburn.

Toward the end of May they felt sufficiently restored to leave Ashfield and journey back to Harvard, where they remained through most of the summer, visiting the Believers in towns around about, and receiving visits from many new converts who were drawn to Harvard from various distant places by reports of Mother Ann and the Elders.

In July more mutterings were heard from the Harvard townspeople against the Harvard Shakers in general and the New York visitors in particular. It seemed wise for Mother Ann to retire to Littleton and Woburn for a few days. On August 19, those Shakers who had remained in Harvard suffered brutal treatment at the hands of the most ferocious mob they had yet encountered. The attackers gathered in front of the Square House early in the morning before light. Word of this was carried through the neighborhood to the many scattered Believers who hastened to the rescue of their beleaguered brothers and sisters. They found a rapidly growing crowd armed with whips, clubs, or whatever they had been able to lay hands on. It was estimated that there were three hundred of them. The Shakers inside the house were on their knees praying for God's protection. The mob outside, hearing their raised voices, began the attack and burst open the door. They dragged out the Believers one by one— by the hair, the collar, the throat. When they were all out, the hostile mob surrounded them and ordered the local Shakers to return to their homes.

The out-of-town Believers were given one hour to make ready for their departure from the town. At the end of the hour, they were commanded to march and were driven ten miles along the rough country road toward Lancaster and the western part of the state. They were handled as all mobs handle their victims—clubbed, lashed, shaken, pounded. At the end of the day they were dismissed with threats of what would happen to them if they ever returned, and of future violence toward the Harvard Believers, many of whom had insisted on accompanying the New York Shakers in spite of the mob. There were sober Harvard citizens who deplored these acts of violence and sympathized with the Shakers, but either they were in the minority or unorganized. Every attempt to remonstrate with the mob met with threats of more violence.

Undoubtedly the Shakers were most exasperating in their reactions to the mob's abuse. They insisted on praying for their assailants, offered their own backs to stop the blows intended for their fellows and turned the other cheek generally. As one old Shaker record puts it, "Such genuine marks of Christianity were too much for the seed of Cain to endure." The Shakers, like the Quakers, were quite sincere in their aversion to the use of force. Never in the course of their history did they abandon their consistent pacifism. It would have been impossible, however, to accuse them of cowardice, for they walked open-eyed into situations of danger whenever it seemed their duty to do so; and they sacrificed themselves gladly to save their brothers and sisters. They seemed truly to "love their neighbors as themselves." An interesting footnote to the mob doings of the day just described is the fact that many of the mob leaders, "who were men of respectable standing in the town of Harvard, and in affluent circumstances, fell under judgments—ran out of their estates, and came to poverty and beggary." This retribution was so marked that men of later years were often heard to say, "Those Shaker drivers are all coming to nothing."

The mobsters were not yet through with the Shakers, however. For a time they left them alone, possibly being a little ashamed, or more likely afraid, of the results of their unlawful act. Mother Ann and the Elders came back unmolested to the Square House, and remained there during the fall and winter, preaching, holding services, carrying on the work of spreading the Shaker gospel. Mother Ann apparently had premonitions of her approaching death, for she made statements and plans from time to time about the future work, adding, "You may live to see it, but I shall not." This was the time when she said that Joseph Meacham would be the one to gather the church in gospel order. She prophesied the starting of the Shaker communities in Kentucky and Ohio, saying, "The next opening of the gospel will be in the Southwest; it will be at a great distance; and there will be a great work of God." She had many visions which she reported to her followers; all her acts were guided by the inspiration she received from these visions or other "gifts of the Holy Ghost." However risky an undertaking might seem, she felt herself obliged to follow these revelations. Accordingly, when she had a call to go to hold a meeting in Shirley in June 1783, she disregarded all warnings of danger from another mob and set out to obey the call. Stories of mob violence are all pretty much alike and not pleasant reading. The proceedings of the Harvard mob were repeated in Shirley. Elder James Whittaker and William Lee were cruelly whipped. Many of the Shaker women also were beaten.

It now seemed evident that a continued stay of Mother Ann and the Elders in the vicinity of Harvard would only call down new persecutions. Early in July 1783, therefore, they left the Square House for good, taking a touching farewell of all their loyal friends in Harvard. At Petersham where they went for a short farewell visit they were again mobbed. This was the occasion on which Elder James read the rabble an article on the Bill of Rights, as a preamble to reasoning with them. During the twelve days that the New York Shakers remained in Petersham there was hardly a night when they were left undisturbed by hostile gatherings. Finally they started westward, crossing the Connecticut at Sunderland and visiting in Cheshire, Richmond, and Hancock, where another mob awaited them on August 4. Here a warrant was served on the Shakers and their local supporters to appear before the Board of Justices of the Peace in Richmond. The Shakers were fined twenty dollars as disturbers of the peace, and ordered out of the state. They paid their fine but decided to remain in Massachusetts. "As to leaving the state, they chose to obey God rather than man." Thereupon their friends were put in the Barrington jail, where Mother Ann and the Elders visited them, saying, "We have come to see Christ in prison." Then they returned via West Stockbridge to Hancock. On August 22 they were attacked by another mob, led by a Pittsfield man; and on August 23 they crossed the state line into New Lebanon.

The arrival at New Lebanon was like coming home. Mother Ann and the Elders visited the houses of many old friends where they were received with loving welcome. Even here, however, they were not safe from threats of violence. While staying at the home of George Darrow (the spot where the Mount Lebanon meetinghouse now stands), another mob attacked them in a repetition of the ten-mile Harvard attack. They were driven seven miles along a rough road, beaten, and not permitted to stop anywhere for food although they passed the houses of many Believers. They were rescued finally by a tavern keeper named Ranny, who was apparently man enough to stand up to the mob and disperse them. After a night spent in a nearby house and barn, the Believers returned to the home of Nathan Farrington in New Lebanon. Once again they were mobbed. This time Nathan's oldest son, John, prevailed upon the leaders to go away and come back in the morning when they would be given a chance to talk to Mother Ann. This interval of time gave the mob a chance to cool off to such an extent that only six or eight appeared in the morning, looking sheepish and finding very little to say.

That day at ten o'clock, however, the much beset little band of religious adventurers started for Niskayuna—that wilderness tract seven miles northwest from the center of Albany where they had found their first home in America. Even the one night spent on the way, though in the home of friends, was marred by a visit from rough men who prevented them from eating or resting, although they actually refrained from further physical violence. In the morning Mother Ann and her companions set out on the last lap of their journey. As they reached the ferry across the Hudson near Albany, a band of Indians met them. They hailed Mother Ann with friendly enthusiasm, shouting, "The good Woman is come! The good Woman is come!"

At about eleven o'clock on the night of September 4, 1783, she and her followers arrived safely at Niskayuna. They had been away two years and four months. They had started on their missionary journey in the spring of 1781— the darkest period of the American Revolution; they finished it the day after the signing of the treaty of peace which established America as victorious. They had taken no part in the Revolution. They had kept a single mind on their goal. They had founded the Society of the United Believers (commonly called Shakers) in the new-born republic of the United States of America.

There is some confusion in the records of early Shaker settlements between the date of the founding and that of the "gathering" of the different communities. The date of founding or starting was somewhat indefinite, since it might mean only the meeting together of two or three converts. Usually these early Believers worshipped in private houses or even out of doors. There was as yet no attempt at formal organization even in centers like New Lebanon and Harvard; and the members continued living with their own "natural" families. "Gathering," however, or "gathering into gospel order," meant joining together in communal living. It also included the signing of a covenant. None of the societies were "gathered" in this sense until 1787, three years after the death of Mother Ann; but a good many were founded in the four years of her ministry between 1780 and 1784. Niskayuna and New Lebanon in New York, Enfield in Connecticut, Hancock, Harvard, Shirley, Tyringham in Massachusetts—all these knew Mother Ann in the flesh, for she visited most of them many times.

The New Hampshire and Maine communities, however, though actually founded nearly as early as the others, never had the benefit of her presence. Some of these sections were visited by others of the original group from Manchester, England; many individual members travelled to Niskayuna to see Mother Ann, but she herself never got as far north as the New Hampshire Enfield and Canterbury, or Maine's New Gloucester and Alfred.

In spite of this disadvantage, northern New England Shakerism was soon burning as brightly as any, and was to last longer than most. The New Hampshire and Maine groups came out of a revival similar to the New Lebanon Revival. About 1781, there was a great religious awakening in New Hampshire, Vermont, and the western part of the state of Maine. The leaders were mostly Freewill Baptists. One of the centers of this revival in New Hampshire was Boscawen, which adjoins Canterbury and is not far from Enfield, New Hampshire. The Maine revivalists were particularly active in the region about Gorham and Alfred. The singing and dancing indulged in by the participants was so frenzied and unconventional that doubting spectators dubbed them Merry Dancers. Other names were New-Lights, Come-outers, etc. The revivalists themselves chose to be known as New Light Baptists since they believed they had individually received new inspiration from God. It was at this psychological moment, in the summer of 1782, that the New Lebanon Shakers sent "two messengers of Christ" to Enfield and Canterbury, New Hampshire.

In Enfield the New Lebanon Shakers found welcome reception from James Jewett and Asa Pattee, both ardent New Lighters, who opened their homes to the strangers and their hearts to the Shaker teachings. This new gospel satisfied their longings for a better life and filled them with enthusiasm for the work of converting their neighbors. At Canterbury it was Ezekiel Morrill and Benjamin Whitcher who started the work. To Canterbury and Enfield came John Cotton, another zealous New-Lighter, on his way across New Hampshire from Gorham, Maine, with the intention of buying a farm in Vermont whither many of his friends were migrating. He chose to break the journey by stopping with his fellow religionists in Canterbury and Enfield, and was pleased and surprised to find them both "much changed for the better."

James Jewett, who entertained him hospitably in his home on what was later to be known as "Shaker Hill" in Enfield, soon acquainted John with the reason for this change. He was so persuasive in his presentation of the Shaker gospel that John Cotton also was converted. One morning after breakfast, as he and James Jewett were conversing, John had one of those peculiar experiences of which Shaker history is so full. "The power of God came upon me," he says, "filling my soul and controlling my whole being. It raised me from my chair and under its influence I turned around swiftly, for the space of half an hour. The door of the house was open. I was whirled through the door-way into the yard among the stones and stumps, down to the shore of the Mascoma Lake, some rods distant. On reaching the shore of the lake, that same power that led me to the water whirled me back again in like manner, and I found myself in the same chair that I had been taken from. This was a seal to my faith and a baptism of the Holy Spirit, and I promised to obey it to the end of my days." John gave up his thoughts of a Vermont farm and went back to Gorham and Alfred to preach the gospel tidings. James Jewett remained in Enfield, converting his neighbors, and preparing the soil for the planting of the Shaker community that was to take root some few years later on the opposite shore of Mascoma Lake.

John Cotton reached home June 1, 1783, and in another month he had arranged for a meeting there of three out-of-town Shakers: James Jewett of Enfield, Ebenezer Cooley of New Lebanon, and Eliphalet Comstock of Hancock, who "were received as the ambassadors of Christ." They held meetings in towns around about, as Mother Ann and the Elders had done in Harvard, Massachusetts, and made many converts to the Shaker faith. Benjamin Barnes of Alfred opened his house as general headquarters for the Believers. Shortly after, he donated his property as a nucleus for the communal domain which began to increase as other converts followed his example. The work went on with unabated enthusiasm after the departure of the three visitors.

After the initial voyages across the Atlantic, the Shakers in America were an inland group. The Maine Shakers gave the one maritime touch to the Shaker adventure. In August 1784, the year following John Cotton's successful proselyting venture, some of the Gorham and New Gloucester Believers decided to go to Niskayuna to visit Mother Ann and the Elders. They chartered *The Shark*, a small twenty-eight ton vessel belonging to Greenfield Pote of Portland, and thirteen brothers and twelve sisters set forth under the captaincy of Samuel Brown.

Many of the men were good sailors. They saw to it that their craft was adequately manned and was well stocked with provisions for the return voyage as well as the voyage out. They also picked a good sailing wind for the start from Portland harbor and had a smooth and successful journey to New York, although the sisters were somewhat worried about the passage through Hellgate, having heard that it was apt to be rough and dangerous. The tide was with them, however, and they came in safety into New York Harbor. Here they had to wait a while for a favorable wind to bear them up the river to Albany. A good deal of tacking and beating had to be done before they reached their destination, but those not actively engaged in sailing the boat spent their time fishing. They packed away most of their catch in barrels for presentation to their coreligionists at Niskayuna, for whom they had brought other supplies also from Maine.

After they finally reached Albany, they divided into two groups of which one walked to Niskayuna while the other remained in charge of the vessel. The Maine Believers had sent no word of their coming, and were therefore much surprised to find themselves received as expected guests. Mother Ann had been informed of their visit in a vision and had already directed that preparations be made for their entertainment. The food they had brought with them was doubtless very welcome, since many of the visitors that flocked to Mother Ann came empty-handed. After a short visit, they went back reluctantly but conscientiously to relieve the group who had stayed with the boat so that they, in turn, might have the pleasure and inspiration of seeing Mother Ann and the Elders. Mother Ann was at this time very feeble as a result of her treatment at the hands of the various mobs; but she insisted on meeting and talking personally to all these Believers who had come so far to see her. As always, the sight of her strengthened and uplifted them and sent them back to their homes with renewed courage.

The return journey was not so smooth. Almost as soon as *The Shark* had left New York a terrible storm arose. It was the evening of September 7. By morning nearly all on board were expecting momentarily that the vessel would be wrecked. They were on their knees praying when one of the sisters, Dana Thombs, saw a vision of Mother Ann "who looked calm and smilingly upon her and with uplifted hand breathed peace to the troubled sea." The Believers were re-assured and laid aside their fears. The storm began to lessen; all gave thanks with singing and prayer for their deliverance from danger. But after they had sailed safely into Portland Harbor early on Sunday morning and had separated to go to their different homes, they learned the sad tidings of Mother Ann's death on September 8—just six hours before the vision on shipboard.

The other company of Maine Shakers, who went to Niskayuna by horseback from Alfred were not so fortunate as their New Gloucester brothers and sisters. They had left Alfred early in September; they were met in Albany by Father James with the sad news of Mother Ann's death. In spite of their disappointment they pressed on to Niskayuna to visit the Elders, returning home by way of New Lebanon whence they went to Harvard, Massachusetts, visiting many of their fellow Shakers. The following summer, 1785, Father James Whittaker returned their visit. He was the only member of the original English band to set foot in Maine. He was received with great cordiality, entertained, according to a contemporary account "by all the best people in the place—and urged to accept the hospitality of their homes." In both Maine and New Hampshire the Shakers seem to have met with far better treatment than they were accorded in New York state, Connecticut or Massachusetts. Perhaps the fact that Maine and New Hampshire were a little farther removed from the center of the fighting in the Revolution may have had something to do with it.

The death of Mother Ann marks the end of the first phase of the Shaker adventure in America. As long as she lived the adventure was still in the future; the eyes of the adventurers were ever watching for wonderful sights to unfold around the next corner, over the next height, beyond the horizon. Always they had perfect trust in their leader. She had proved to them time and time again that she saw things hidden from their sight. She knew where they were going; she was confident of the road. Though it might be rough and painful, it led with certainty whither they wanted to go. There was never confusion at any crossroads. A proof of Mother Ann's outstanding qualities of leadership was the fact that even after her death this feeling of confidence in the leaders remained. She had trained well those who were to follow her in the ministry; she had prepared the minds of the rank and file for this change. There was great sorrowing when she died but no faltering. The work went on.

Yet it could not continue in quite the same manner. A part of the adventure was over. No matter how far and how fervently the Believers might travel, they had left behind forever the glorious days of radiant comradeship and ecstatic sacrifice with their beloved Mother Ann. The human system cannot endure radiance and ecstasy overlong. And whereas before her death the Shakers had no past but only a future, now they had a past of endurance and achievement to point to, a tradition to cherish proudly. A tradition has a steadying effect; it is something to be guarded and conserved. One travels less recklessly with a tradition to protect than one does when the tradition is still to be won. The work went on without faltering, but it had now reached a state where organization became necessary. This was left for Father James Whittaker to begin and for Joseph Meacham to finish.

William Lee, Ann's brother, died a few weeks before her, although he was four years her junior. When he left England ten years earlier, he had not yet reached the prime of life, and was "a commanding figure, rather above middling height, thickset, large limbs and strong body." His return to Niskayuna showed him broken in strength and health, though not in spirit. It is reported that the faithful Believers who were waiting joyfully to welcome the travellers home to Niskayuna found their joy changed to tears when they saw how wasted and feeble their leaders had grown. Sorrowfully they listened to the tale of the hardships and physical injuries experienced on that trip through Massachusetts. William and Ann were never really well again after their return. William's "work of suffering continued to the end of his days; nor did he appear to die by any natural infirmity; but seemed to give up his life in sufferings." He was only forty-four years old. When at a later period, his bones were disinterred to be reburied in the little Shaker cemetery at Watervliet beside his sister and the other English Shakers, it was found that his skull had been badly fractured. Just before he died he asked one of the brothers to sing for him. And thus he passed into that world of the spirit which always seemed nearest to the Shakers when they were singing. He was the first of the original English

41

group to go; his death was felt keenly by all the others and particularly by his sister Ann.

As Ann Lee realized that her days on earth were drawing to a close, she felt more and more the importance of leaving her followers equipped to go on without her. Her attitude toward them was that of any loving and conscientious mother toward her children. She kept thinking of things— little and big—that she needed to tell them before she went away. The little things were the practical ways of human living: care and treatment of children, family relationships, household management, manners, etc. The big thing was the importance of the spiritual work which together they had undertaken, and the responsibility for its success that would be theirs alone after her death. Even when she became so weak that every movement was an effort, she insisted on talking to all the pilgrims who came to Niskayuna to see her. "She discovered no anxiety for herself; her principal concern seemed to be to encourage her children to persevere in the way of God, to comfort them in their sorrow, and reconcile them to her departure." To Job Bishop who came to see her three days before her death (and who was later to become the father of the Shaker church in New Hampshire), she said, "I shall soon be taken out of this body; but the gospel will never be taken away from you, if you are faithful. Be not discouraged, nor cast down; for God will not leave his people without a leader." Just before she died, she said, "I see brother William coming in a glorious chariot to take me home." And when the breath left her body, Elder John Hocknell, "who was greatly gifted in visions, testified that . . . he saw in vision a golden chariot, drawn by four white horses, which received and wafted her soul out of his sight."

The many accounts of Mother Ann's ministry that have been left by her loyal followers give a unified, consistent picture of a woman who was at once simple and practical in all human relationships and puzzlingly mystical in her spiritual life. There is no doubt that she knew human nature as few men and women do. There is story after story of her uncanny comprehension of the minds of her visitors. She knew instinctively when they were speaking the truth and when falsehood. She had special sympathy for the shy, the inarticulate, the timid.

To the young and to little children she was tender and understanding. She had no patience with the then prevalent doctrine of infant damnation and original sin. "Little children," she said, "are nearer to the kingdom of Heaven than those of riper age. . . . Little children are simple and innocent . . . if they were brought up in simplicity, they would receive good as easy as they would evil." And again, "You ought not to cross your children unnecessarily; for it makes them ill-natured; and little children do not know how to govern their natures." She laid great stress on neatness and order in the household, on industry and thrift; she was at times appalled by the waste of food she saw about her in New England. Food was more plentiful here in the New World than in Manchester; but she grieved to see it wasted, remembering the many who were without it. She was one of the pioneers in equality of the sexes, insisting on recognition of women's rights and abilities. She gave practical advice to young men. "Do all your work as though you had a thousand years to live, and as you would if you knew you must die tomorrow." And over and over again she repeated, "Put your hands to work and your hearts to God."

43

Work was real and apparent to everyone. Yet to her, God and the spiritual world were equally real and apparent. Actually her attitude toward the world of the spirit was as simple and direct as her counsels about daily living in the world of the senses. It was to unbelievers—to the "world's people"—that it seemed confusing and complex. Mother Ann offered her heart to God as naturally as she offered her hands to work. When she spoke of receiving a gift of God she meant it literally, whether that gift were a gift of song, a gift of dancing, or a gift of prophecy. It was real; it was to be shared; why should anyone find it hard to accept? Yet she never made the mistake of picturing the spiritual life as an easy one. Over and over again she stressed its difficulties, its hardships, its sufferings. It is impossible to doubt her sincerity. Nothing that she taught ever profited *her* in the worldly sense; nothing that she preached made life on earth easier for *her*. She put her mission ahead of herself always. Always, too, she put the needs of the humblest of her followers ahead of her own needs. She inspired love and confidence wherever she went among her people. Their testimonies more than overbalance all accusations that were made against her.

John Farrington, one of those early pilgrims whose feet made the wilderness path between Albany and Niskayuna a highway for the questing Believers—the same John who stood off the mob from Mother Ann and the Elders at his father's house that last night in New Lebanon—set down his memories of Mother Ann forty-two years after her death. In them he pays loyal tribute to the founder of the Shaker faith. He says, "Had not Mother Ann brought forth the genuine fruits of righteousness in her own life and example, she never could have wrought in souls such conviction of sin, and turned so many from the ways of iniquity into the pure paths of peace and righteousness, as she has done. . . . But this same Ann Lee, this instrument in the hands of God, by whom so many souls have received life and salvation, is accused of all manner of evil by the enemies of righteousness and purity. Her name is cast out as evil; her character has been impeached by the tongue of slander; she has been called a blasphemer and a lewd prostitute; she has been charged with beastly intemperance and witchcraft, and many other abominations; and all this catalogue of crimes have been alleged against her by those who had little or no acquaintance with her.

"Now let the candid among mankind judge and compare evidences; let them contrast the accusations against her with her uniform testimony and doctrine. Her worst enemies cannot deny that her testimony was as opposite to every evil of which she is accused, as fire is opposite to water. Can any man or woman of common sense suppose that thousands of rational beings born in a land of liberty and civilization, and brought up in the midst of moral and religious principles and instructions, and in the pursuit of a pure and undefiled religion, and who possessed all the propensities of human nature common to other people, would deny themselves of all worldly pleasures and enjoyments, and subject themselves to the dictates of a woman of base character, who lived in direct opposition to those principles which she daily preached to others? . . . I was well acquainted with Mother Ann. . . . Feeling a powerful attachment to her and the Elders with her, I embraced every suitable opportunity to visit them and be in their company. . . . I often visited them at Watervliet [a later name for Niskayuna], and was with them in prison at Albany—I was with them at Harvard, Shirley, Woburn, Ashfield, Richmond and Hancock in Massachusetts, at

Enfield in Connecticut, and here at New Lebanon. I have seen and heard them in many meetings, and was well knowing to their deportment in public and private, and was well acquainted with their manners at home and abroad, and therefore feel fully able to give a true statement of their lives and characters. And I feel it justly my duty to contradict the false reports which have been spread abroad by the tongue of slander concerning them; for in all my acquaintance with them, I have ever observed the same uniform example of temperance, chastity, righteousness, and every gospel virtue.

"I once was young, but now I am old; and through my life have been an attentive observer of the ways and actions of men; but I have never seen the persecutor prosper, nor the vile slanderer rise to honor. When the gospel first opened here in New Lebanon, the little despised flock who first embraced it were mostly people of small property, and in low circumstances; many among us were indeed very poor; and all of us, like the rest of mankind, were bound in sin and iniquity. . . . I have seen a Society of people spring up, and grow and increase in order, beauty and harmony, till they are, in my view, the glory of the earth—a city of refuge—a shining light and a tree of life to the nations. . . . Where now are those proud and malicious persecutors who vainly strove against the work of God here in New Lebanon and its vicinity, in the early days of our faith? Behold, they are scattered to the four winds! Many of them have been swept from the earth by untimely deaths and retributive judgments, till nothing but an empty name is left to their forlorn remembrance. They have received the reward of their doings, and shared the fate of persecutors in every age of the world. . . . Remember the counsel of Gamaliel to the Jewish high priest and his council: 'Refrain from these

46

men and let them alone; for if this counsel or this work be of men, it will come to nought; but if it be of God, ye cannot overthrow it; least haply ye be found even to fight against God.' "

Mother Ann's life was so closely intertwined with the lives of her followers that her own acts and characteristics as an individual merge with those of the group. Her spiritual emotionalism, her courage, her practicality were prototypes of the emotionalism, the courage and the practicality of all the Shakers. She herself would have preferred it thus. The submergence of the individual in the group was what Shakerism wanted. Yet one quality of Ann's was hers alone: her warm, passionate love for humanity, not humanity in the abstract, but little children, puzzled adolescents, worried men and women, who came to her for help. She listened to them, she yearned over them, she showed them that she really cared as a mother cares when her children are in trouble. She was in deed as she was in name Mother to all the Believers.

III. GATHERING IN GOSPEL ORDER

AFTER Mother Ann's death, Father James became the spiritual head of the Believers. This was the same James Whittaker who as a boy had saved Ann Lee's life in the Manchester prison cell by feeding her milk and wine through the keyhole. He had been with the Believers from the earliest Manchester beginnings, having come under the influence of the Wardleys and of Mother Ann when still very young. He had suffered his share of the Massachusetts and New York persecutions, and was trusted by Mother Ann as one who had passed every test and had never failed her. The American converts regarded him as a pattern of all they hoped to be; their attitude toward him was akin to worship.

Whittaker was only thirty-three at the time of Mother Ann's death, yet people of all ages called him Father. The short term of his ministry was an important epoch in Shaker history. In those three years he labored constantly to build up the morale of his followers and to prepare them to withdraw entirely from the world and become wholly self-sufficient and self-supporting. When he began his ministry, the Believers were living in scattered private houses, usually with their own more or less sceptical relatives; two months after his death the New Lebanon Shakers had come together to make a beginning of what was later to be called the most successful of all American experiments in communal living.

Father James had a warm, friendly personality. There was something at once boyish and saintly about his smile and his manner. He combined the spontaneity and candor of a very young man with a gentle and charitable understanding that came from years of kindly forbearance with all kinds of people. His mere presence was an encouragement to any group. Like Mother Ann, he knew how to put the timid and self-conscious at ease. Young people felt at home with him; children loved him. When he was in the room with them, he would go up to them with a smile, saying "Hold out your little hands and say, 'Come, sweet love.' "

He had the kind of eloquence that everyone enjoys listening to. Strangers who were present at meetings addressed by him were often overheard to say, "I like to hear that James Whittaker speak!" His words were so sincere, so evidently from his heart, that when he wept his audience wept with him; when he rejoiced, their hearts also were filled with joy. His one worry during his ministry was that some of the many converts made by Mother Ann might turn back to "the world," missing her leadership. He labored early and late to strengthen all the brothers and sisters in the faith she had taught them so that he might not fail her. He listened sympathetically to the problems and the difficulties that were brought to him; he strove patiently to show how to solve them. Freely he gave his time to all earnest seekers for the truth. But he was inflexible toward dishonesty of every sort, whether pretence or downright lying. The kindly, smiling eyes could change suddenly to steel when they met insincerity. He was charitable to weak human nature groping blindly toward the truth but he showed no tolerance for falsehood and disloyalty.

Father James and John Hocknell (who was also given the, in his case honorary, title of Father) were the last of the original leaders. New leaders, American-born, were in the making. It was Father James's task to search these out in the different scattered groups of Shakers, to prepare

them to go on with the work. With this in mind he undertook to visit all the places where the Shaker gospel had been
preached and received and to emphasize the need for
"gathering into Society Order." The Maine and New
Hampshire groups were a long way from New Lebanon,
but Whittaker visited them all. Wherever he went, he
left behind him not only renewed enthusiasm but stories
about him that were cherished through the years until they
grew into legends.

When he arrived at Alfred, Maine, after a long journey
on horseback, he stuck a willow wand he was carrying into
the ground, where it took root and grew and spread into a
row of beautiful willow trees that were always pointed out
as Father James's willows. In Canterbury, New Hampshire,
the Shakers still recall with pride that James Whittaker was
once within their walls. But however distant Father James's
journeyings in his endeavors to visit all his flock, he returned
always to the home church at New Lebanon, finding the
group there ever ready to help him. They sent their members to keep Father James company on his travels, and
sometimes to be left in New Hampshire or Maine or Massachusetts to aid in the "gathering"; they gave inspiration
and practical counsel to all the scattered families. For
already New Lebanon was assuming leadership of the
whole sect.

Joseph Meacham was now an elder at New Lebanon;
he had been cited by Mother Ann as a future leader. "Joseph
Meacham is my first-born son in America," she had said.
He and Father James were much together when their
duties permitted it. They saw eye to eye on the four cardinal
principles of early Shakerism: confession of sins, celibacy,
separation, and common ownership of property. Confession of sins was required from the beginning; celibacy

was now beginning to seem attainable; and common ownership would be easier after separation. Although the Shakers
had always practised celibacy themselves even before they
were gathered into their own communities, they used some
caution in the early days in preaching it to the "world's
people." "For," said the practical Joseph Meacham, "I see
no way to protect the people in it." So he worked along with
Father James toward the longed-for gathering into communities apart from "the world."

Even when the Believers had taken the necessary steps
toward forming their own withdrawn settlements, away from
their old friends and their "natural" families, it was not easy
to keep their minds free from entangling alliances with "the
world" in which they had grown up. Father James was
obliged to stress this point over and over again. "I warn you,
brethren," said he, "not to be overcome with the cares of
this world, lest your souls lose the power of God, and you become lean and barren. . . . If you give your minds to labor
upon the things of the world, they will become corrupted."
At the time of Shays's Rebellion, some of the Massachusetts
Believers who lived in the vicinity of Springfield, were heard
by him to express partisan views. Like most of the early
Shakers they were poor men, well aware of the grievances
against which Shays's men were fighting and inclined to
sympathize with them. Father James immediately took them
to task for this, saying, "They that give way to a party spirit,
and are influenced by the divisions and contentions of the
world, so as to feel for one political party more than for another, have no part with me. The spirit of party is the spirit
of the world, and whoever indulges in it, and unites with one
evil spirit against another, is off from Christian ground."
Thus, at the beginning, was the isolationist policy of the
Shakers established.

In January 1787, Father James had a premonition of his approaching death, and thought it wise to pass on some of his authority and responsibility to Joseph Meacham. He called the Believers together in the New Lebanon meeting-house, which had been built over a year before, and told them that he was going to leave them. "I feel that my work is done here," he said, "and I do not know that I shall ever see you again in this world; but I leave you with those who are able to teach you the way of God. . . . Do abide faith-ful; those of you that abide faithful will be like a bud in the bloom; but those who do not abide, will be like a falling leaf; and you will remember these words when you cannot see me." After an affecting farewell, he left for Enfield, Con-necticut, where he died the following July.

The Shakers had made few attempts to gain new members during the last two years of his ministry; they had put all their energies toward strengthening themselves and each other in their beliefs and in their organization. And the fol-lowing September the first Shaker community was estab-lished: the New Lebanon Shakers, under Joseph Meacham and Lucy Wright, "the leading character in the female line," were "gathered into Society Order." It all came about as Mother Ann had prophesied and arranged. "It will not be my lot, nor the lot of any that came with me from England," she had said just before she died, "to gather and build up the church; but it will be the lot of Joseph Meacham and others. . . . Cleave to Elder Joseph; he will be your father, and will take care of you."

For the next few years the Shakers did little proselyting. The leaders found it necessary to complete that separation from the world which made the Shaker adventure practical by giving a measure of security to the adventurers. Little by little they came into possession of lands. Next they began to put up buildings; instead of meeting for worship in private houses they raised churches of their own. The habit of living in the households of their more prosperous members, as they had done since the beginnings in England when John Townley and John Hocknell supported many of the needy Believers, gave way to the erection of communal dwelling houses. It was slow progress—not evenly steady, but by 1794 eleven different communities had been "gathered into Society Order."

New Lebanon was the first, in 1787. They had already built their meetinghouse in 1785. Next in order came Niskayuna, or Watervliet, as it was now called, Harvard, Massachusetts, Enfield, Connecticut, Hancock and Tyringham, Massachusetts, Canterbury, New Hampshire, Shirley, Massachusetts, Enfield, New Hampshire, and the Maine settlements at Gorham, Alfred and New Gloucester (later to be known as Sabbathday Lake). The nucleus around which each of these communities developed was usually a parcel of land donated by an ardent and comparatively well-to-do Believer. Benjamin Whitcher of Canterbury, New Hampshire, who had been housing and feeding forty-three of the Shakers in his own home, gave the Society his estate of one hundred acres, valued at $2,150, together with all his other property. Benjamin had joined the Believers in 1782, taking his wife, Mary, and their four children along with him. Benjamin Barnes of Alfred, Maine, was "one of the first to consecrate his property," turning over his house and lands to the cause. Elijah Wilds was the benefactor at Shirley, Massachusetts; the Darrows had donated land at New Lebanon.

Few of the members were able to contribute as much as these few did to the common wealth, but each brought in what he or she could. Peter Ayers, for instance, who came into the Shaker Society at New Lebanon in 1787, brought with him "1 horse, 1 wagon, 1 lot of tackling, 2 cows, 1 2-year-old heifer, 27 sheep, 25 lb. wood, 1 chaise, 60 lb. flax, 130 lb. tobacco, 1 axe, 1 saddle, 1 sleigh, 1 pad-lock, 1 pound worth of pork, 14 bu. potatoes, 1 bed and bedding, 65 bu. wheat, 16 bu. rye, 4 bu. corn, 2 sickles, 4 turkeys, 11 hens, 1 pair of plow irons, 2 chains, 4 dollars worth of fur, $16.00." Samuel Whittemore of Shirley, Massachusetts, contributed $333.33 toward the raising of the church there; Moses Hayward gave a yoke of oxen worth $45.00; Molly Worcester gave $3.00, and Mary Buttrick, $0.90. Thus the communities gradually became possessed of enough property to house their members, to raise crops for food, to live their own lives apart from interference by the "world's people."

The economic difficulties of the early Shakers have probably never been fully reported. The Believers were so used to accepting without complaint the hardships that came their way, and to giving thanks for whatever slight blessings were theirs, that it was a matter of pride to ignore or to understate all deprivations and discomforts. One of the early Watervliet Shakers, however, has left a brief description of living conditions there about 1788. Watervliet was the new name for Niskayuna—the "wilderness tract" that John Hocknell had procured for the Shakers when they first came to this country—their own property; their first American home.

To begin with, the land was a dense forest beside a small, very winding stream along which was a tangled swamp of huge bogs, wild grass, and weeds. One is inclined to suspect the hand of an early real estate promoter in the sale of this land to the Shakers. From the first it was a continuous struggle to make this terrain fit for cultivation, since it required straightening of the stream, constant drainage, endless filling, etc. Everybody worked at it. "Elder John Hocknell seemed to take a pleasure in subduing the bogs and digging out old stumps." Little by little the land was made fit for planting.

As late as 1788, however, about the time of the gathering into gospel order, the Watervliet Shakers nearly starved. It was the year of the famine in the region around Lake George. The principal food was rice and milk, with occasionally fish from the river. The Shaker work was planting, sowing of grain, haymaking, harvesting. "We were so weak we could not have run twenty rods, but we could work!" For breakfast and supper they had small bowls of porridge; for dinner, "a small bit of cake about 2½ inches square which Aaron Wood cut up and gave to us." On Sundays they sometimes omitted dinner, as that was not a working day. The buildings were small and inadequate. They had no beds and very little bedding. They slept on the floor in rows, using the backs of what chairs they had for pillows. In the fall when the crops began to ripen and potatoes were eatable, they lived better. And throughout everything they gave thanks for the little they had and were always ready to share with those who were more needy than they.

While the Shaker men and women were engaged in toilsome cultivation of the land to make their farms produce more than a starvation diet, or in sawing and preparing the trees they had felled for necessary new buildings and more adequate furniture, the elders had the additional task of grappling with the problems of organization. It seemed important to make the membership more binding. A simple, verbal covenant was devised in 1788, to which all who so desired agreed. This was not put into writing till 1795. Another important matter was the personnel of the leaders. Elders and eldresses were shifted about as seemed expedient—sometimes from New Lebanon to Canterbury, as was Job Bishop, sometimes the other way around, as with Henry Clough, who was called from the leadership of the New Hampshire Shakers to become Joseph Meacham's assistant at the home church.

Hancock, Massachuetts, contributed Hannah Goodrich to Canterbury and Enfield, New Hampshire. Her early journeys thither were made on horseback on a saddle presented to her by Lucy Wright. It is reported that Hannah was very sad at leaving her Massachusetts birthplace and all her old friends for the backwoods of New Hampshire. Eleazer Rand and Hannah Kendall were sent from New Lebanon to Harvard and Shirley to superintend the "gathering" of those two societies. Ezekial Morrill was transferred from Canterbury to become an elder at Enfield, New Hampshire. All the elders and eldresses took orders and instruction from New Lebanon. Unity was beginning to come out of diversity and confusion. Even the religious services, which had been extremely individualistic under Mother Ann, began to settle into ordered patterns. There was no abatement of religious zeal, but the characteristic Shaker love of order—a place and a time for everything—grew with the growing communities.

As numbers increased and activities multiplied it became necessary to work, to rest, to worship in unison. And New Lebanon made the pattern for all the other Shaker societies to follow. New Lebanon started the machinery of Shaker government: the system of elders and eldresses, deacons and deaconesses, trustees both male and female, to carry on the religious teachings, the social regulations, the practical business affairs of the Shakers for well over a hundred years. When Joseph Meacham died in 1796, he was succeeded by Lucy Wright, who dominated the "Ministry" at New Lebanon for several years. After her, came a succession of leaders, both male and female, some of such outstanding ability that even the "world's people" were impressed by them.

While all this internal activity was going on in the New York and New England Shaker communities, the "Ministry" was remembering Ann Lee's prophecy about the opening of the gospel in the Southwest. Rumors from the outside world began to reach them of a strange religious revival that was being held in Kentucky, a revival reminiscent in its manifestations of the New Lebanon Revival. But this revival was of much longer duration and much greater extent than the revival of 1779. It was spreading into other states besides Kentucky: Ohio, Indiana, Tennessee. Perhaps this was what Mother Ann had in mind; perhaps the time was now ripe for the fulfillment of her prophecy. In 1805, when the revival was in its fifth year, the Ministry decided to send messengers into Kentucky and Ohio. The three men chosen to go were John Meacham (son of Joseph), Benjamin S. Youngs, and Issachar Bates. They started on the first day of January 1805. They were to travel on foot over a thousand miles of wilderness trails into a land they did not know, in search of something they might not find. They went full of faith and courage, undeterred by such obstacles as winter weather, ignorance of the routes, lack of roads. They carried out the mission on which they were sent; they found what they were looking for—a chance to open the Shaker gospel in the Southwest.

At the beginning of the nineteenth century there took place in the lands of Kentucky, Ohio and Cumberland (Tennessee) one of the most remarkable religious revivals ever recorded. It was border country, the edge of the wilderness. Kentucky was already a member of the Union; Ohio was to be admitted soon—in 1803. Kentucky's white population numbered not over 220,000, Ohio's only about

45,000; but settlers were flocking fast into these newly avail-able lands west of the Alleghanies. The scattered settlements were increasing in numbers and in size. Some of them were beginning to grow into towns. Churches were plentiful; for a large proportion of the early settlers were professed Chris-tians belonging mostly to the Presbyterian, Baptist or Meth-odist sects. There were in addition, of course, an appreciable number of lawless and unbelieving frontiersmen who scoffed at all churches. Logan County, one of the early centers of the Revival near the southern boundary of Kentucky was at one time called "Rogues' Harbor," because most of its citizens were criminals.

The wave of deism that had been sweeping the country and giving great anxiety to the leaders of the orthodox churches doubtless had small, if any, connection with the criminal tendencies of these unchurched border ruffians. Nevertheless, it offered an alibi to the churches for their failure in reaching and converting these sinners. The Presby-terian ministers therefore sponsored a series of camp meet-ings in 1799, in the hope of stimulating the religious life of these frontier communities. Other churches soon followed their example. The meetings started in Logan and Christian Counties, spread in the spring of 1801 to Madison County in the central part of the state, and from there passed like a prairie fire over practically the whole southwest territory.

The Revival lasted five years. Kentucky was almost one vast camp meeting. The leaders of the established churches soon realized that they had set in motion forces they could not control. The manifestations of spiritual workings be-came so violent that the Presbyterian Synod began cau-tiously to disown its child. New sects arose, claiming for themselves the right to receive God's word direct, with no intermediaries such as ordained clergy, creeds, or even the

Bible. Whole congregations went over to these "New-Lights." The results of the Revival were thus tending rather toward the re-examining of old dogmas, and the beginnings of new religious societies than to increased membership in the already established churches. The orthodox leaders somewhat naturally lost interest in the Revival and even went so far as to brand its more extreme manifestations as the work of the devil. It is an interesting commentary on orthodox church historians, by the way, that the New Lebanon Revival which swelled the ranks of the Shakers rather than the established churches, is ignored by most of them, and the Kentucky Revival, in spite of its vast extent and duration, gets scant attention compared with much smaller revivals which fed the orthodox churches.

While the Presbyterians were losing interest in this Revival that had slipped beyond their control, people from other parts of the country became curious to see for themselves these strange phenomena that seemed to give evidence of more than human power. Many visitors to the meetings put their impressions in writing, and their several accounts give a unified impression of something unexplainable, something beyond the comprehension of man. The best-authenticated history of the meetings was written by Richard McNemar, a scholar and Presbyterian preacher from Warren County, Ohio, and one of the early leaders of the Revival. Later on, in 1803, he led his congregation into the New-Light fold; and two years after that he took most of them with him into Shakerism.

Richard McNemar begins his history of the Kentucky Revival by a short summing up of the state of religion in the region west of the Alleghanies at the end of the eighteenth century. He was broadminded enough to see that a pretty good case could be made out for the deists, since their

59

repudiation of the Bible was based on a realistic evaluation of its results in the acts and works of Christians who professed to be guided by it. "What have those churches exhibited which for ages past have claimed the Bible for their foundation?" he asks. "Little else but diversion, animosity, and confusion. . . . The tree is known by its fruit." Even some of the other ministers themselves were discouraged not only about the future prospects for organized religion, but also about the lack of spiritual grace in their own souls. "The generality, however, were still going on, crying out against infidelity, lampooning the deist, treating his cavils with contempt, and laboring each to augment his party; while a distressed few were watching, like the guards of the night, and ready to meet the first dawn of the approaching day."

The dawn came first to individuals, "who had fasted and prayed, and diligently searched the scriptures. . . . It kindled their love to other souls that were lost in their sins . . . they were constrained to cry out with tears and trembling, and testify a full and free salvation in Christ for all that would come; and to warn their fellow-creatures of the danger of continuing in sin, and entreating them in the most tender and affectionate manner, to turn from it, and seek the Lord, in sure and certain hope that he would be found. Under such exhortations the people began to be affected in a very strange manner. At first they were taken with an inward throbbing of the heart; then with weeping and trembling; from that to crying out in apparent agony of soul; falling down and swooning away, till every appearance of animal life was suspended, and the person appeared to be in a trance." After they came out of these trances they often had visions and "gifts of tongues" which enabled them to speak eloquently of these visions.

This religious hysteria was contagious. As it grew the news of it spread, bringing observers from all about. Many who came out of curiosity were caught up in the spirit of the Revival and either remained to participate or went home to spread the gospel among their friends. As there seemed to be no stated time or term for these Revival services, people camped out on the ground for so long as the meeting should last. Newcomers flocked in to join them by hundreds and thousands, "on foot, on horseback, and in wagons and other carriages." The meetings went on continuously for days and nights. They were usually held near some little church in a clearing at the edge of the forest.

There was a rough stage for the speakers and rows of fallen tree trunks and stumps where the listeners sat. The wagons and the tents were ranged about the open sides of the clearing. The meetings lasted far into the night. "Nothing was wanting that could strike terror into minds weak, timid, harassed. The red glare of the camp fires, reflected from hundreds of tents and wagons; the dense blackness of the surrounding forest, made still more terrible by the groans and screams of the 'spiritually wounded' who had fled to it for comfort; the entreaty of the preachers; the sobs and shrieks of the downcast still walked through the valley of the shadow of death; the shouts and songs from the happy ones who had crossed the delectable mountains, had gone on through the fogs of the enchanted ground, and entered the land of Beulah were too much for those over whose minds and bodies lively imaginations held sway.

"The excitement surpassed anything before known. Men who came to scoff remained to preach. All day and all night the crowd swarmed to and from preacher to preacher, singing, shouting, laughing, now rushing off to listen to some new exhorter who had climbed upon a stump, now gathering around some unfortunate who, in their peculiar language, was 'spiritually slain.' Soon men and women fell in such numbers that it became impossible for the multitude to move about without trampling them, and they were hurried to the meetinghouse. At no time was the floor less than half covered. Some lay quiet, unable to move or speak. Some of them talked, but could not move. Some beat the floor with their heels. Some shrieking in agony, bounded about, it is said, like live fish out of water. Others rushed wildly over the stumps and benches and then plunged, shouting 'Lost! Lost!' into the forest."

The first large meeting described by McNemar was held at Cabin Creek near the northern boundary of Kentucky. It began May 22, 1801, and continued four days and three nights. After this came a meeting at Concord, Kentucky, with four thousand present, which lasted five days and four nights; another at Eagle Creek, across the river in Adams County, Ohio, lasted four days and three nights; one at Pleasant Point, Kentucky, where "the Christian minister (so called), the common professor, the professed deist, and the debauchée, were forced to take one common lot among the wounded, and confess, with equal candor, that hitherto they had been total strangers to the religion of Jesus." A meeting at Indian Creek, Harrison County, lasted five days and nights. Another at Caneridge, Bourbon County, lasted a week, with over twenty thousand people attending. No wonder that the news of these strange goings-on travelled even to New York and the New England states.

Many attempts have been made—and have failed—to explain the physical compulsions that were laid on the participants in these meetings. At the beginning, the "falling exercise" was much in evidence, when listeners fell unconscious and remained in that state for hours and sometimes days. Later there were three general types of involuntary activity: the rolling exercise, the jerks, and the barks. Theological writers use the term Charism to indicate this sort of religious manifestations; psychologists call it mass hysteria. Neither designation explains it satisfactorily.

The rolling exercise consisted in "being cast down in a violent manner, doubled with the head and feet together, and rolled over and over like a wheel, or stretched in a prostrate manner, turned swiftly over and over like a log. . . . The Jerks . . . commonly began in the head which would fly backward and forward and from side to side with a quick jolt which the person would naturally labor to suppress, but in vain; and the more any one labored to stay himself and be sober, the more he staggered, and the more rapidly his twitches increased. . . . Such as were seized with the jerks were wrested at once, not only from under their own government, but that of every one else, so that it was dangerous to attempt confining them . . . yet few were hurt, except such as rebelled against the operation. . . . The barks . . . frequently accompanied the jerks. . . . Both men and women would be forced to . . . take the position of a canine beast, move about on all fours, growl, snap the teeth, and bark, etc."

Observers who came to mock were often seized with an inescapable compulsion to join in one or all of these exercises. Then, as if in recompense for such sufferings and humiliations, hallucinations of indescribable ecstasy would come: visions of the Holy City, melodious sounds in the breast, a singular fragrance that permeated everything. "In a word, all nature seemed to be impregnated with a new and spiritual quality, which rendered every object and every transaction presented to the mind, whether sleeping or wak-

ing, susceptible of some signification which respected the
then present work."

Richard McNemar and Barton W. Stone (who was later
associated with Alexander Campbell in founding the Christian Church) were both drawn into this spiritual vortex. As
leading revival preachers, they saw these strange emotional
excitements at first hand. They began to ask themselves why
this new outpouring of the spirit of religion should manifest
itself in this startling form rather than in the ordinary channels of the established church. They began to waver in their
allegiance to the Westminster Confession. Together with
three other Presbyterian ministers—Robert Marshall, John
Dunlavy and John Thompson—they found themselves in
disagreement with their church on the subject of the Revival. They believed that an honest hunger for righteousness,
which the established churches had failed to satisfy, was at
the root of these mysterious manifestations. They held, with
the New-Lights, that divine revelation came direct to each
individual. This was contrary to the Calvinist doctrine.

For nearly three years, however, they kept their allegiance
to the Presbyterian Synod, although "this was a painful
situation to both parties, for the New-Light to be chained
down in silence, forbidden to pray, exhort, or make any noise
or uproar in time of meeting, however clearly he saw the
danger of the wicked or felt his soul overflowing with the
love and goodness of God. And no less painful did it feel to
the expounder and those who contented themselves with
his learned and ingenious labors, to be interrupted by a sudden shout and put to silence by the din which commonly
followed; and worst of all, to hear that system by which he
had all his wealth in this world and the hope of a favorite
interest in a better set at naught by the general proclamation,
whosoever will, let him come and take of the water of life

freely." At last the church felt the necessity of "banishing from the standing community those flaming zealots whom ministerial authority had failed to reduce into subjection."

The dissenters chose to withdraw voluntarily from the Presbyterian fold; they started a society of their own in 1803, which they called the Presbytery of Springfield, publishing an account of the withdrawal in a pamphlet called, "An Apology for renouncing the jurisdiction of the Synod of Kentucky." They made this move with the intention not of establishing a new church, but of "covering the truth from the impending storm and checking the lawless career of imposition." They considered the existence of the societies they set up as "only pro tempore, a kind of asylum for those who were cast out; that they might come forth and be there, like David's father and mother, with the king of Moab, until they would know what God would do for them."

The result was as they had foreseen; many of the revivalists who believed with them that all the Revival manifestations were only a prelude to a greater revelation of God, flocked to join them. They became known as the Schismatics and adopted four simple statements in the place of a creed: first, respect for the Bible as the only rule and standard; second, close connection between elders and fellowship; third, open and public transaction of church affairs; and fourth, a common place to meet and worship. The whole membership voted unanimously upon these. "It was also moved and agreed that the endearing appellation of Brother and Sister be revived among the members." From this foundation sprang both the Church of the Disciples (Christian Church, called Campbellites) and the Shaker communities of Ohio, Kentucky and Indiana.

The three missionaries sent by the New Lebanon Ministry to open the gospel in the Southwest thus found the soil a ready prepared for the planting of the seed. Their coming broke up the friendship between Richard McNemar and Barton Stone. It brought these two fellow travellers to the inevitable fork in the road. Barton went to the right along with Alexander Campbell and other founders of the Christian Church; Richard took the left turn in company with the Shakers. Barton never forgave Richard. Although he and Richard had suffered equally from the intolerance of the Presbyterian church, Barton now grew suspicious and intolerant of the Shakers to such an extent that he was responsible for much of the early persecution they underwent in the Southwest. Richard was deeply hurt by his former friend's about-face. But Richard had seen the dawn for which he had been watching; henceforth the Shaker sun was to be the light of his life.

IV. PIONEERS IN THE "SOUTHWEST"

O N January first of eighteen hundred and five—the year
which saw the beginning of Jefferson's second term as
president of the United States—the three Shakers set out
from New Lebanon on their long journey to the Southwest.
John Meacham, son of Joseph Meacham, had been
brought up from boyhood in the Shaker faith and was now
in his thirty-sixth year. Benjamin Youngs, a scholar and a
theologian, had joined the Shakers in 1794 and was now
thirty-two years old. Issachar Bates, the senior member of the
delegation, counted nearly fifty years of which only four had
been spent among the Shakers. But the Shakers knew sincerity and qualities of leadership when they saw them, and
they made no mistake when they put their trust in Issachar.
He was the unquestioned leader of the expedition, the experienced, resourceful man of quick decisions and prompt
action. When persecutions came, as they did, he knew better
than the earlier, English-born group had how to deal with
the persecutors. It was not for nothing that he was a native-
born American and a veteran of the Revolution. To be sure
he had renounced the use of force and violence when he
became a Shaker, but he knew how to impress and handle
men who did use them. And he knew, also, how to invoke
the protection of the law.

The three fellow travellers started on foot with one horse
between them to carry their luggage. They went by way of
New York, Philadelphia, Baltimore, Washington, D.C., and
Lexington, Kentucky. From Lexington they made visits to
various sections where revivals had been, or were being, held.
At Caneridge they heard Matthew Houston speak and were

67

themselves invited to address the audience, who listened approvingly and said among themselves, "This is what we have been praying for, and now it has come." On March 9, they crossed the river into Ohio, going first to Springfield and the vicinity, where they attended other meetings, and finally to the home of Malcham Worley of Turtle Creek, near Lebanon in Warren County where, Issachar writes, "we found the first rest for the soles of our feet, having travelled 1,233 miles in two months and twenty-two days."

Malcham Worley, a boyhood friend of Richard McNemar's, had been very active in the Revival. He was a man of substance and weight in the community. Both he and Richard had been praying for something to happen, for a sign which would show them the spiritual way to go from the emotional heights to which the work of the Revival had brought them. Malcham was impressed at first sight by the strangers. "Three men prepossessing in appearance, grave and unassuming in their manners, very intelligent and ready in the Scriptures, and withal possessed of great boldness in their faith. Their dress was plain and neat, perfectly uniform and quite old-fashioned—white fur hats, crown five inches deep, rim five-and-a-half wide, grey coats, blue waistcoats and overalls of a beautiful brown—their walk and general carriage sprightly, yet majestically grave, and their affability in conversation banished every idea of superstition or sly deceit." Malcham invited some of the revival preachers including Richard and Barton Stone to his log house to meet the strangers. Within five days, he himself formally accepted their message.

It took Richard somewhat longer, although he was decidedly impressed by the speed with which his friend had succumbed to their persuasions. Richard was open-minded, but even though he and his people were branded as Schismatics, he was still minister of what had been the largest and most influential Presbyterian church in Ohio, with the possible exception of Cincinnati, and he wanted to be sure before he committed himself to this revolutionary doctrine. He talked with Issachar and the others, listened to their arguments, asked questions, weighed his doubts against their certainties. Then one day the Shakers cured one of Richard's children of a malady he had had since birth. Richard took this incident as the sign for which he had been waiting, and he too accepted the Shaker teachings. With characteristic energy he set about spreading the good news, both among his own congregation at Turtle Creek and as far afield as could be arranged.

The Shakers were received gladly in the homes of the Schismatics who rejoiced that the long-awaited opening of the way to salvation had come. "We thank thee, O God," said Samuel Rollins, "that thou hast sent a chariot of fire from the East, drawn by three white horses, to bring the everlasting gospel to this land." The Shakers—especially Issachar—were in such demand as speakers that they were kept busy going from place to place, sometimes alone, sometimes in company with others. On both sides of the Ohio River, people came from long distances to hear them. Occasionally the meetings were interrupted by boors and ruffians; even by unfriendly ministers such as Barton Stone and John Thompson, who denounced the Shakers as false prophets and liars; but on the whole they were kindly received.

The work grew so fast that in July New Lebanon sent three more men, including David Darrow, who became the head of the growing community at Turtle Creek and assumed leadership of the Believers in Kentucky and Ohio. And in September, the untiring Issachar Bates walked back to New Lebanon to raise funds for the purchase of land at Turtle Creek, Warren County, Ohio, the future site of Union Village. It took Issachar twenty-one days to cover the intervening 776 miles. After a stay of several weeks in New Lebanon he returned with "the money, $1640, and a good treasure of gospel love." Next season, in 1806, the Believers built a two-story framed house, thirty by forty feet in size, and moved into it. In June 1806, two more men and seven women came down from New Lebanon.

For the next few years the increase among the Believers was rapid. Issachar made numerous journeys through Ohio, Kentucky, Indiana, and even Illinois, sometimes alone, sometimes in company with Richard McNemar, Benjamin Youngs, Malcham Worley, Matthew Houston, or others. Between 1801, the time of Issachar's joining the Shakers, and 1811, when the Ohio and Kentucky societies were gathered into gospel order, he travelled—mostly on foot—38,000 miles, much of it through uncleared, trackless forest and river country. There were two principal Kentucky centers of Shaker influence: Logan County down near the Tennessee line, and Mercer and Bourbon Counties in the central part not far from Lexington. The Ohio magnets were Adams County on the Ohio River, Warren County northeast of Cincinnati, and Montgomery County which contains Dayton. There were scattered groups of Believers in other regions, as there were in New England at the time of Mother Ann's sojourn in and about Harvard; but on the whole the Shakers tended to congregate in places where there had been strong Schismatic preachers such as John Dunlavy of Eagle Creek in Adams County, Ohio, Matthew Houston at Caneridge in Bourbon County, Kentucky, and Richard McNemar and Malcham Worley of Turtle Creek in Warren County, Ohio.

Carrying the gospel into Indiana was a more difficult undertaking. Kentucky was settled country compared with Indiana. Even so, groups of Believers had been formed in the neighborhood of Vincennes near the Wabash. Some of Issachar's most difficult journeys were made in connection with the little nucleus of Shakers living at "Busro," a name that has long since disappeared from the maps of Knox County, Indiana, although there is a creek called Bosseran which flows into the Wabash a few miles north of Vincennes.

It was here that this most ill-fated of the Shaker offshoots was planted. Started in 1807 or 1808 by a devoted few, "gathered" in 1810, living its short life in constant danger of malaria germs and Indian attack, pillaged by groups of soldiers at the beginning of the War of 1812, moved bodily to Kentucky and Ohio for the duration of the war and then moved back again in 1814—a three hundred mile trip that took over a month to make each time—and finally closed forever in 1827 on account of the climate and its members transferred to the two Kentucky communities of South Union and Pleasant Hill—the story of Busro (West Union) is a dramatic chapter of Shaker history, a concentrate of all the hopes and struggles and hardships the Southwestern Shakers were called upon to endure.

On one of Issachar's early journeys into Indiana he took the precaution to call on General Harrison, then governor of the territory, to find out how much help the Believers in Busro could expect from the officers of the law in case of persecution. "We want to know," said Issachar, "if there are any laws in this territory to protect the people." "The same law," said the governor, "that there is in any of the United States. You have a right to preach your faith and anyone has

71

a right to embrace it. So you need not fear; I will protect you."

On a second visit to Busro, Issachar and the Believers were threatened by a mob. Issachar managed to stave it off until he had time to appeal for the promised protection. When the mob leaders returned Saturday night as they had threatened, a magistrate and officer were on hand to prevent trouble and protect the Shakers in the exercise of their rights. Even the governor, however, was powerless to help them very much against depredations by the Indians and wandering bands of soldiers. He did, to be sure, offer them land and safe escort in 1812 if they would move to Vincennes which was safer and healthier in climate; but the Shakers preferred to remain on their own land in Busro as long as they could, and then to take refuge with their fellow religionists in Ohio and Kentucky.

The larger parent community at Union Village (Turtle Creek) kept a watchful eye on Busro, sending visitors from time to time to encourage and aid them. On January 18, 1809, Issachar Bates, Richard McNemar and Benjamin Youngs, each with a knapsack containing a blanket and five days food supply, started to walk from Union Village to Busro. It was 235 miles, across the southern part of Indiana, which was then heavily forested and without roads or settlements. This trackless wilderness was full of rivers and creeks that had to be crossed and recrossed without benefit of bridges. January ice could usually be counted on to make a good substitute for bridges; but this January was increasingly mild. On account of floods which filled the creeks with floating ice the five days were used up before the travellers reached the Indiana line.

In pouring rain they waded through the mud of marshy Ohio flats and river bottoms. The same conditions obtained in Indiana—rivers risen over their normal banks, floating ice cakes, flooded lowlands. They had to camp for a time beside one stream that had grown to be six miles wide, waiting for the ice to freeze strong enough to hold them. They improvised beds out of split tree trunks and branches, piled high enough to keep them off the wet ground. Many times they waded through water three feet deep, drying their wet clothes as best they could by camp fires, before trying to get a little sleep. Once they had to take time out to build themselves a raft. They came near starvation, for the floods had driven away the wild animals. One half-eaten turkey they found, left by foxes, provided them with the nearest approach to a solid meal they had had since leaving home.

At the east fork of the White River they were lucky enough to find a man who took them across in his canoe and also provided them with food. The west fork, however, had spread out to a width of two and a half miles over the river bottom. By this time the three travellers were unable to get their shoes onto their swollen feet, so they waded barefoot through the broken ice and snow. From Indians on the other side they got moccasins which made the remaining thirty miles of the trip comparatively comfortable. Half starved and half frozen, but undaunted, they reached their friends in Busro, where as Benjamin Youngs wrote, "Elder Issachar and Richard had their frozen feet poulticed and every provision was made for our comfort, and every kindness in their power proferred that they could bestow, but our greatest pleasure was to find these dear souls steadfast in their faith to the gospel work."

The following year, in 1810, the society at Busro was gathered, having been increased by the addition of part of John Dunlavy's congregation which voted to sell its land in Eagle Creek and divide its members between Union Village and the Indiana and Kentucky groups. John Dunlavy went to Busro to take charge of that community; he made it his home till his death from malaria in 1826. Meantime the societies in Ohio and Kentucky were being gathered into society order. Union Village, formerly Turtle Creek, became the parent organization of these Shaker colonies in the Southwest. David Darrow, ably assisted by Richard McNemar, initiated and administered the rules of living, both spiritual and temporal, subject, of course, to the guidance and approval of the church at New Lebanon, New York. Watervliet, Ohio (formerly Beaver Creek), in Montgomery County, was the second Ohio society to be gathered. Its organization followed shortly after that of Union Village. In Kentucky the two communities of South Union in Logan County near the southern line, and Pleasant Hill in Mercer County near Lexington, were likewise settling down to an ordered existence. Benjamin Youngs was made the leading elder of the South Union ministry.

Issachar Bates, meanwhile, continued in his work of liaison officer between the scattered groups. Much of his time was spent at Busro, where even he was unable to escape the dread malaria fever. It was he who superintended the moving of the Busro society during the War of 1812. It was he who went back to Busro in 1813 to help the six brethren who had been left in charge of the ravaged buildings. And again it was he who moved the Believers back again to Busro after the war was ended and helped them restore order to their damaged property.

For the next few years all the newly gathered Shaker communities busied themselves in the same way as the Busro brethren and sisters, clearing land, planting and harvesting crops for their food supply, erecting substantial buildings for churches, living quarters, and workshops, and "keeping a

74

good measure of faith and gospel order within their premises." They bore uncomplainingly the necessary hard work and privations that go inevitably with pioneer ventures. And the results of their toil and their thrift began to be noticeable in the gradually increasing prosperity of their communities.

The Shakers had more than climate and nature and bodily fatigue to contend with, however, in these early years. They soon found themselves suspect in the Southwest territory in the same way and for the same reasons as Mother Ann and her followers in New England. The earliest persecutions, sad to relate, were instigated by Richard McNemar's old friends and fellow Schismatics. These were the same ardent New-Lights who had, with Richard, John Dunlavy, Malcham Worley, and Matthew Houston, withdrawn from the Presbyterian church and signed the document that established the independent Presbytery of Springfield.

When Richard, John, Malcham and Matthew adopted Shakerism, Barton Stone, John Thompson and Robert Marshall, who had joined forces with the Campbells to found the Church of the Disciples (somewhat arrogantly called the Christian Church), began immediately to discredit, accuse and persecute the Shakers. Barton Stone wrote in a letter to Campbell, "You have heard no doubt before this time, of the lamentable departure of two of our preachers and a few of their hearers from the true gospel into wild enthusiasm, or *Shakerism*. They have made shipwreck of faith and turned aside to an old woman's fables, who broached them in New England about twenty-five years ago. These wolves in sheep's clothing, have smelt us from afar, and have come to tear, rend and devour."

The "few hearers" mentioned above included Richard's whole Turtle Creek congregation which had followed him almost as one man into Shakerism. But his former friends

75

and associates, who had themselves been called heretics for worshipping according to the new light they had received, now united to accuse the Shakers of heresy and to refuse them an opportunity of speaking for themselves. When Benjamin Youngs went to Concord, Kentucky, by invitation, and was there forbidden to speak by R. Marshall and Barton Stone, the only answer he made to them was, "I am sorry to see you abusing your own light."

The persecutions went farther than denial of free speech, however. Stories began to circulate about the Shakers, first in whispers that "Mr. Such-a-one heard a man say that he saw a woman, who had it from a very respectable man, who saw the person, etc." Soon it began to be repeated openly that the Shakers had been sent down with the deliberate intention of destroying the Revival, "that their scheme was to get people's land and property by parting man and wife, ruining and breaking up families." Before long it was authoritatively stated that "the Shakers castrated all their males and consequently exposed their necks to the gallows; or divested of all modesty, stripped and danced naked in their night meetings, blew out the candles, and went into a promiscuous debauch. And what was still more shocking— the fruits of their unlawful embraces they concealed by the horrid crime of murder."

Individuals were prosecuted on such vague and unproved charges that the foreman of a grand jury reprimanded the presenter of such a bill. Public opinion, however, began to crystallize into action against the Shakers. Acts of vandalism began to be perpetrated. Unknown persons assaulted the Shakers with stones and clubs, injured their property under cover of the darkness, breaking windows, setting fires, destroying fences, ruining crops and fruit trees, abusing Shaker horses, etc. They went out of their way to interrupt the

Shaker worship, not only by jeers and mockery, but even by entering the churches and laying brutal hands on the worshippers. It was the same story of mob violence that Mother Ann and the Elders had known in Massachusetts.

Yet the story was not quite the same, for these Shakers of the Southwest were all Americans. Many of them, like Issachar Bates and Richard McNemar were men of the world, used to handling people in or out of crowds. They knew, too, what they could expect from the courts in the way of protection. When they were attacked on August 27, 1810, by a mob estimated to contain two thousand men, they had the moral support of many of the sober citizens of the region, and what was doubtless even more effective, the open backing of Judge Francis Dunlavy. They chose, however, to handle the attack in their own way so far as possible.

The mob was led by a body of armed men under the command of Colonel James Smith, an ex-soldier of the Revolution, an ex-Presbyterian, an ex-New-Light preacher, and an ex-Shaker. Smith had a personal grudge against the Shakers for family and property reasons. His son was a member of the Shaker Society. The mob's announced purpose was the tarring and feathering of Richard McNemar and the driving out of the Shakers who had come to Ohio from New York state. The Believers—less than a tenth the size of the mob in numbers—met their assailants calmly, listened to their demands, and answered with moderation that this was a free country, that they were upon their own land which they had bought and paid for, and that they intended to stay there. Thereupon they invited the leaders of the mob to enter and inspect their premises, to see for themselves whether they were holding anyone against his or her will, whether they were abusing children, whether the place looked like the scene of wild orgies and disorderly living, etc. The leaders

77

were obliged to admit that the Believers gave the impression of happy, busy, normal human beings, and that their buildings and grounds showed evidences of orderly care. The mob finally dispersed.

As time went on people began to see how peaceable and well-meaning the Shakers really were. This closer knowledge of them, together with the results of various inquiries and personal examinations by the courts, gradually won for the Believers the respect of the communities in which they lived. "For there are but few, in the present day," says the *Summary View* published by the Shakers in 1823, "who are willing to persecute an honest people for their religion, when once their real sentiments are well known; and, unhappily, those few are generally found among the most bigoted professors of some false religion; *for true religion never produced any persecutors.*"

With the Shaker communities scattered throughout New England, New York, and the new Southwest of Kentucky, Ohio and Indiana, intercommunity visiting became a necessary and pleasant way of establishing and keeping up personal contacts. To the Shakers, fellowship with their own meant more than a foregathering with congenial souls and old friends. Even after the "world's people" surrounding the little oases of Shakerdom became tolerant and friendly, they were never wholly understanding. If they had been, if they could have comprehended the passionate quest for perfection that made the Believers give up natural human relationships and instincts for a spiritual conception of love and of family, they, too, would perhaps have been Shakers. As it was, an invisible wall stood between them and these strangers in their midst.

So it was a happy day for the Shakers, whether of New York, New England or the frontier Southwest, when a company of Believers arrived on horseback from one of the other communities. In New England, even, most of the groups were separated by many miles of hard travel. Alfred and New Gloucester, Maine, were about fifty miles apart, and they are both some hundred miles or more from Harvard, Massachusetts. Canterbury, standing about equidistant between Enfield, New Hampshire, and Alfred, Maine, was over a hundred and fifty miles from Hancock and New Lebanon. The roads were so poor that horseback was at first the only practical way of travel, and even when they had been improved enough to permit the use of carriages, the Canterbury Shakers took five weeks for a journey to Hancock or New Lebanon, stopping doubtless to visit other groups on the way.

In the Southwest, the distances were greater and the roads worse, if not nonexistent. South Union, Kentucky, was 130 miles from the other Kentucky Shaker settlement at Pleasant Hill, and 275 miles from Union Village, Ohio. And Union Village, which became more and more the center of Shaker authority in the Southwest, was 776 miles from New Lebanon, the parent of them all.

Many problems arose as the scattered groups grew in numbers and resources, which had to be referred to the New Lebanon ministry for settlement. The simplest and easiest was for the leading elders and eldresses of the puzzled group to go in a body—two men and two women—to the source of all authority, New Lebanon, there to consult with Mother Lucy Wright who was the official head of the church from the death of Joseph Meacham in 1796 till her own death in 1821.

The parent society was much excited about the progress in the Southwest, as may well be imagined. The fact that Mother Ann had prophesied it before her death, the favorable state of mind found in the Revivalists toward the Shaker doctrine, and above all, the presence on the field of influential men like Richard McNemar, John Dunlavy, Malcham Worley and Matthew Houston all filled the souls of the Shakers back home with renewed courage and enthusiasm. The immediate result for the northern communities was a kind of sympathetic Revival (probably superinduced) that spread through the New York and New England Shaker societies in 1807.

Mother Lucy at New Lebanon felt that the northern Believers had grown cold in their professions of faith compared with the early Believers and with these new converts in the Southwest, and she sent word by messenger to Harvard and the other New England settlements that a "gift" of livelier worship and keener soul-searching had been sent by God. Thereupon the "lively dance" of past days and many of the old emotional songs were revived, and the Shaker meetings again took on some of the fervor of the early beginnings. New dances were arranged to honor the "gift," and new songs written. The spiritual reverberations of the Kentucky Revival thus echoed through northern Shakerdom.

Mother Lucy was unable to undertake the long, hard journey into the Southwest herself, but she followed closely the progress there through letters and through personal reports from the untiring Issachar and others. What she most desired, however, since she could not go there to see it with her own eyes, was a first-hand report from one of the leading converts. So when Richard McNemar rode up to the door of the Trustees' building in New Lebanon in 1811—the year after the successful repulse from Union Village of Colonel

James Smith's mob—he was instantly accorded an interview with Mother Lucy.

Richard was an impressive figure, even without his record of bringing a whole congregation into the Shaker fold. It is told of him that such were his powers of oratory that at one time thirty thousand persons assembled to listen to him. He is described by one who knew him as "tall and gaunt but commanding in appearance, with piercing, restless eyes, ever in motion, and an expressive countenance." He was, moreover, schooled in the classics—able to read Latin, Greek and Hebrew with ease. He was skilful too with his hands, being a chair and cabinet maker who loved his tools. He even wrote poetry. And "his mind was ever open for more light." Shakerism had already attracted a few men of learning, such as Joseph Meacham and Benjamin Youngs, but Richard wore his scholarship debonairly as befitted a man of many other accomplishments.

Mother Lucy asked him many questions about the Revival, the forming of the new communities, the nature of the people in that frontier territory, and the territory itself. He answered them. They were traveller's tales of a strange country to her—the low flooded river land, the rough log cabins. New Lebanon and the other eastern societies were already a generation beyond frontier conditions. Richard understated his own part in what he told. He was never given to bragging of his exploits. He was too active and busy planning the next steps ever to dwell much on the past. But Mother Lucy could read between the lines. She was well pleased with his report of the Southwest and with him. When he took his leave she told him that since everything he had done had been right, she wished to change his name to Eleazar Right. And Richard, accepting the suggestion with a gesture reminiscent of Raleigh and Queen Elizabeth, asked that he might be allowed to add one extra letter to the last name, making it Wright, like hers. From that time on, Richard signed his name Eleazar. Being given to writing verse, he recorded the incident in a neat stanza.

> The world hates the name of the old McNemar,
> And threatens to coat him with feathers and tar.
> But his name and his nature may go to the ditch,
> I'll cleave to my Mother and call myself rich.

There were yet to be three new Shaker communities established within the next ten or fifteen years, but the formation period was about over. A generation after Mother Ann's death had seen the pushing out of the Shaker gospel into the Southwest; another generation marked the close of the era of expansion. North Union, Ohio (in what is now part of East Cleveland), was gathered in 1826; Groveland, New York, was gathered in 1826 at Sodus Point whence it was later removed to the neighborhood of Sonyea; Whitewater, Ohio, near Cincinnati, was gathered in 1824, largely through the efforts of Issachar Bates who liked to think of himself as its founder. There were no new colonies formed after 1826, though two or three unsuccessful attempts were made at starting others.

Converts increased, however, to swell the numbers of the already established communities. The Believers gradually withdrew more and more from "the world," spending their energies in fighting spiritual foes instead of mobs, in strengthening their system of government, in building up their thrifty, successful units of communal life. If they seemed to have cooled in their ardor as time went on, it was simply because enthusiasm cannot be kept at white heat forever. The adventurer has to build himself a little haven of security somewhere, even if only as a springboard for fresh adventures.

The *Summary View of the Millennial Church*, published in 1823, uses the following simile to explain the Shaker evolution. "The first leaders of the Society may be compared to people going into a new country and settling in the wilderness, where the first object is to cut and clear the land and burn the rubbish before the ground can be suitably prepared for cultivation. In this operation, the axe and the fire are used with no sparing hand; and the falling of trees and the crackling of burning brush and useless rubbish occasion much noise and bustle and great confusion, especially among the wild beasts and noxious vermin that infest the land.

"These are now obliged to flee for their lives, into some other part of the wilderness or the fire will consume them. But when the land is sufficiently cleared, and the rubbish consumed, and the wild vermin have all retreated, and the careful husbandman has securely fenced his field, he can then go on to prepare and cultivate his ground in peace; and if he is faithful to manage his business as he ought, he will continue to improve his premises from year to year; so that in a few years this once dreary wilderness will be seen to 'blossom as the rose.' Such has been the progress of the United Society, and such is the nature of the changes which it has passed through."

PART TWO
THE ADVENTURE AT ITS PEAK

V. THE WORLD LEFT BEHIND

IN the early days while Mother Ann was still alive, no need was felt for a formal covenant between Believers. The instinct of the Shakers to avoid anything resembling a creed was sound, since they had suffered so often from the intolerance that creeds develop. Their simple belief in the mother and father element of God, in the perfectibility of human nature and in the imminence of the millennium, made their three-fold way of life so inevitable and so practical that they were wholly satisfied with it. If they confessed their sins honestly, if they lived thenceforth a pure life—and purity meant more to them than celibacy alone, implying also abstinence from all worldly desire for power, fame, riches—and if they withdrew from all contact with the world so that they could be free to pool their resources and strive together for that perfection which they craved, it seemed obvious that the God they loved and served would help them to gain the goal they were seeking.

A creed would only limit and hamper them, since they believed God's revelation was a growing thing, not a neatly labelled parcel of finished truths handed out once for all in some distant past. They were always looking confidently for more revelations to be given them in accordance with their changing needs. Besides, a creed implied the shutting out of all who would not subscribe to it. The Shakers never shut out anyone. They never asked new members to sign articles of faith. They assumed that only such as believed in their three cardinal principles would want to join them. And they respected individual variations of belief, subject to conscience, within that inclusion.

Most of the "world's people" also, for that matter, would have been willing to grant freedom of *belief* to the Shakers, if that were all. A man's thoughts and feelings were his own in America if he kept them to himself. Communal ownership of goods, however, was something else. Property rights concerned a whole town or county. They had to be stated and defined. The "world's people" felt they had a right to know the policy and attitude of these fanatics in their midst toward ownership of land, and to check up on their financial responsibility. How were rights to family property to be handled when part of a family joined the Shakers? How far were the Shakers as a body liable for debts contracted by individual members? Would they stand back of business ventures undertaken by members? New converts themselves did not always understand clearly what their rights and obligations were. A formal statement became necessary—a covenant which all members might sign in order to make clear both to themselves and to outsiders their intentions and their position in these matters.

The covenant was drawn in 1788. At first it was verbal only. In 1795, after seven years of practical testing, it was put in writing, "for the security of their just and natural rights, on account of those who were envious without; and for the more perfect information of all whom it might hereafter concern." In 1801, and again in 1805, 1822, 1829, and

1832, it was renewed with revisions to meet growing needs. The authorized form of the covenant emanated from New Lebanon and was made available to all the societies. Sometimes the different communities made slight variations in it, but in the main they used the wording of the original covenant as follows.

"In the year of our Lord one thousand seven hundred and eighty-eight, the year in which most of the members of the Church were gathered, the following order and Covenant was then, and from time to time after, made known and understood, received, and entered into by us, members of the Church, agreeably to our understanding of the order and Covenant of the Church in gospel order.

"It then was, and still is our faith, being confirmed by our experience, that there can be no Church in complete order according to the law of Christ, without a joint-interest and union, in which all the members have an equal right and privilege according to their calling and needs, in things spiritual and temporal.

"And in this, we have a greater privilege and opportunity of doing good to each other, as well as to the rest of mankind, and of receiving according to our needs, jointly and equally, one with another, agreeably to the following articles of Covenant.

"*First.* All, or as many of us as were of age to act for ourselves, who offered ourselves as members of the Church, were to do it freely and voluntarily as a religious duty, and according to our own faith and desire.

"*Second.* Youth and children, being under age, were not to be received as members or as being under the immediate care and government of the Church, except by the request or free consent, of both their parents, if living; but if they were left by one of their parents to the care of the other, then by the request or free consent of that parent; but if the child had no parents, then by the request or free consent of such person or persons as had just and lawful right in the care of the child, together with the child's own desire.

"*Third*. All who were received as members, being of age, who had any substance or property and were free from debt or any just demand from those that were without, such as creditors or heirs, were allowed to bring in their substance as their natural and lawful right; and to give it as a part of the joint-interest of the Church, according to their own faith and desire; to be under the order and government of the Deacons or overseers of the temporal interest of the Church, for the use and support of the Church, or for any other use that the gospel might require, according to the understanding and discretion of those members with whom it was intrusted, and who were appointed to that office and care.

"*Fourth*. All the members who were received into the Church were to possess one joint-interest as a religious right; that is, all were to have just and equal rights and privileges according to their needs in the use of all things in the church—without any difference being made, on account of what any of us brought in, so long as we remained in obedience to the order and government of the Church, and were holden in relation as members. All the members were, likewise, equally holden, according to their abilities, to maintain and support one joint-interest in union and conformity to the order and government of the Church.

"*Fifth*. As it was not the duty nor purpose of the Church in uniting into Church-order to gather and lay up an interest of this world's goods, but what we became possessed of by honest industry, more than for our own support, was to be devoted to charitable uses, for the relief of the poor and such other uses as the gospel might require. Therefore, it was and still is our faith never to bring debt or blame against the Church or each other for any interest or services which we have bestowed to the joint-interest of the Church, but freely to give our time and talents, as Brethren and Sisters, for the mutual good one of another and other charitable uses, according to the order of the Church."

In 1801, when the growing prosperity of the northern Shaker communities demanded new provisions for the business management of the Shaker property, the two following paragraphs were added.

"And we do, by these presents, solemnly covenant with each other for ourselves and assigns, never hereafter to bring debt or demand against the said Deacons, nor their successors, nor against any member of the Church or community, jointly or severally, on account of any of our services or property thus devoted and consecrated to the aforesaid sacred and charitable uses.

"And we also covenant with each other to subject ourselves in union, as Brethren and Sisters, who are called to follow Christ in Regeneration, in obedience to the order, rules and government of the Church. And this covenant shall be a sufficient witness for us before all men and in all cases relating to the possession, order, and use of the joint-interest of the Church. In testimony whereof, we have, both Brethren and Sisters, hereunto subscribed our names, in the presence of each other, this twenty-fourth day of June, in the year of our Lord, one thousand eight hundred and one."

For further clarity in the matter of property rights, the Shakers stated both orally and in print their policy toward new converts who had not yet completed the process of separation from the world. Sometimes these probationary

Shakers were held back by an unbelieving husband or wife; sometimes they had minor children who must be provided for; sometimes they had not as yet fully satisfied the Shaker elders as to their fitness for the Shaker life; sometimes they had not wholly made up their own minds to take the final step of renouncing the world. The same formula prevailed for all such cases as these. These tentative Shakers were required to make a careful inventory of such property as they brought with them into the Shaker community.

During their connection with the community, they were allowed to donate the free use of this property and of their services to the communal estate. If, however, they wished to leave the fellowship of the Believers at any time, they were free to withdraw not only themselves, but also the property which they had brought in with them. It was understood and stated, however, that no claim should be made by them or their heirs to interest on the said property, nor to wages for hours of labor during the period when the property, with its owner, had been dedicated to the Shaker interests.

As a further safeguard against lawsuits by the "world's people," all donations of property, even by accepted Believers, were carefully scrutinized. Nobody was permitted to join in gospel order until all debts and obligations incurred while "in the world" were paid. A husband with an unbelieving wife was expected to make provision for the wife's support before devoting himself and the rest of his estate to the common interests of the group. The same applied to fathers of minor children. Shaker integrity required that converts should come with a clean slate, so far as financial obligations were concerned. The obligatory confession of sins took care of the previous moral delinquencies.

The practical wisdom of the original covenant and of its revisions resulted partly from the honesty and tolerance inherent in the Shaker mentality, and partly from the hard knocks of experience with the "world's people." Many of those who were attracted by the Shaker teachings to attempt to enter the Shaker way of life found themselves unwilling —or unable—in the end, to go the whole way. When it came to giving up "the world" with its human instincts and relationships, its ambitions, and its tempting rewards, for a life that seemed to offer little else than self-denial, many of them backed away from the prospect. The Shakers let them go in sorrow rather than bitterness. They grieved for them as for weaker brethren and sisters who had seen the promised land from afar and had been too easily discouraged by the obstacles between it and them.

If they felt bitterness for any, it was for the apostates: those who had started on that hard trail, knowing all its hardships, had promised to follow it to the end, and then had changed their minds. It was by these apostates that most of the attacks against the Shakers were made after the organization of the different societies. Colonel James Smith of Ohio, for instance, who had apostasized after joining the Shakers, leaving his son in the Union Village society, wrote a violent and venomous book about them. Mary Dyer of New Hampshire, after taking her husband and children into Shakerism with her, left the Shakers and spent the rest of her life in bitter attacks upon them. John Woods of Kentucky, after several years of life with the Shakers, went "to the world" and wrote a book against the Believers. In all these cases the property element entered in—the motive of recovering from the Shakers property which, relatives felt, should have stayed with the family.

Hence the insistence by the Shakers in the Shaker covenant and other Shaker rulings, on the need of a clear understanding on both sides.

The Shakers were consistent at every point in their attitude toward property. Never, even in their most prosperious days, did they allow themselves to be influenced by the profit motive. True, there were cases of individual lapses from this ideal, but remarkably few. The wealth the Shakers acquired through their thrift and hard work was truly common wealth, gladly shared, just as the early days of privation had been communal poverty, cheerfully borne. All of the Shakers, even the elders who composed the "Ministry," had their trades at which they worked. They were chair makers, farmers, horticulturalists, weavers, bookbinders, etc., and they were expected to do their share of the kind of work for which they had been trained.

No Shaker officials ever received money for their services. When they said "Such as are entrusted with the greatest care are the greatest servants," they really meant it. The "world's people" made the mistake of not taking the Shaker covenant at its face value. The Shakers never pretended. They were so simply honest that the sceptical worldly mind looked for craft and deception behind that too guileless front, just as they suspected florid immorality beneath the disguise of an impossibly austere purity. It was years before the "world's people" began to understand that the Shakers were hiding nothing, that they meant exactly what they said.

Purity and unity were the two essential tenets of the church: purity the aim and unity the means. The Believers cultivated unity in faith and practice—unity in government, unity in interest and "in the mutual and equal enjoyment of all things both spiritual and temporal." This unity of purpose and interest is stressed again and again in the covenant. It was in order to achieve unity that the Shakers completed their withdrawal from the world. It was because of their success in achieving it that they were able to stand successfully against attacks from without. So long as they held together in this unity of "all things both spiritual and temporal," they were inspired and safe, knowing both adventure and security. The ardor of their quest for purity—for perfection—provided the adventure; their covenant ensured to them security during that arduous quest. And their belief in the millennium was an ever comforting promise of spiritual security throughout eternity, when the earthly adventure should have been ended.

With the signing of the covenant, the Shakers found themselves banded together in separate societies which were also parts of a united church. A form of government had to be devised to foster the unity they so much desired. The Shaker government was never democratic in the sense that all of the members had a voice in choosing their leaders. Rather it was an aristocracy of ability on the practical side, a self-government under a Divine Theocracy on the spiritual. The Ministry, which was the highest authority, was self-perpetuating. Beginning with Mother Ann, who herself appointed her successor, James Whittaker, and after him, Joseph Meacham, authority was handed on from Ministry to Ministry, to be held during life, or *good behavior*.

The only charge on which any elder or eldress could be removed from office was that of unseemly behavior. The elders were responsible to the members morally, but *no other way*. The mere fact of their having been chosen for administrative posts proved their ability. And since each group of leaders had derived its appointive power from the previous group straight back to Mother Ann, their authority was invested with a sort of divine sanction. Both men and women were represented equally in the governing bodies.

As early as the covenant was formulated, the New Lebanon Ministry was regarded as the superior governing body of the whole sect. It was found practical to have at least three—and usually four—elders to head the church. The leading elder and eldress of these three or four were usually addressed as Father and Mother. "Father Joseph Meacham, Mother Lucy Wright." These, with the aid and approval of their associates in the Ministry, had the choosing of the leaders of all the other societies, who were, of course, directly responsible to them in matters of policy, although some latitude was allowed in the settlement of purely local problems.

The four "leading characters" thus chosen, whether at Harvard, at Canterbury, or at Union Village, were likewise called the Ministry, and were charged with the spiritual leadership of their respective groups. They did the preaching, both to the Believers at home and elsewhere, and to "the world," whenever missionary work was undertaken. They met and talked with all sincere inquirers who came seeking to know the truth about the Shakers. They received and instructed applicants for admission, and had the final decision in this matter. Sometimes two or three Societies were united under one Ministry in a "Bishoprick," as Enfield and Canterbury, New Hampshire, under Job Bishop and his associates, or the Societies in the Southwest under David Darrow.

As the societies grew in numbers and were divided into two, three or more families, it became necessary to appoint elders for each family. The duty of these elders (usually two men and two women) was similar to that of the Ministry. All the spiritual concerns of their respective families were in their hands: the calling and the conduct of meetings, hearing confession of sins, the handling of any moral problem that presented itself, all necessary intercourse with "the world," etc. Their decisions were final, subject, of course, to the approval of the Ministry of their area, and through them, to that at New Lebanon.

They also determined matters of policy in the temporal affairs of their particular group, but for the management of such practical matters as food, clothing, industries, farm work, etc., they appointed deacons and deaconesses. These were responsible for the material welfare of their charges: for housekeeping, farm management, workshops, social regulations, care of children and young people, care of the sick, etc. When the communities began to prosper to such an extent that trade with "the world" became important enough to require time and business experience, the elders created another group of officers called trustees, or "office deacons." These men and women were empowered to act as agents for the Shakers in all business transactions with "the world," arranging for the sale of the Shaker products, the investment of funds, the handling of any legal questions that might arise, etc.

It was impressed upon them always that they were never to incur any debts. In some of the communities they were required to make annual reports; in others, no regular business statement was demanded of them, since all their acts were subject to scrutiny from the elders and the Ministry. There are cases on record where inexperience, overenthusiasm, or personal ambition got the trustees and their families into financial difficulties, but as a rule the trustees were not only scrupulously honest and conscientious, but shrewd business men as well.

On the whole, this scheme of government worked well. It required subordination and obedience from all the members to make it work, but in most cases these were rendered willingly. After all, there was no other incentive to leadership than a desire for prominence and power, and such a desire was among the sins that the Shakers had supposedly left behind in "the world." The elders and the deacons had no perquisites that were denied to the members at large. They were not paid anything for the extra work of management performed by them, and they were required to do their share of manual work in their respective trade or craft along with the lay members. They were sometimes excused temporarily from these tasks when the Ministry needed their services for preaching, writing, or such work, as for instance James Whittaker, or Richard McNemar while engaged in the revision of *The Testimony of Christ's Second Appearing*; but they were never permanently relieved of manual work. James went back later to his weaving, Richard to his bookbinding and cabinet-making. Actually those in the Ministry, and those entrusted with the business management, worked twice as hard as the purely "hand-minded" Believers.

There were, of course, from time to time, grumblings of dissatisfaction at the Shaker regimen. Aim as the Shakers did for perfection, there were always some members who fell far short of it. Mistakes were made in the members admitted, even with the care exercised by the Ministry in their examination and their testing of the applicants. It was impossible to prevent or to stamp out all feelings of jealousy and envy—particularly when a member happened to have a disgruntled wife or husband or brother or sister among the "world's people," waiting for an opportunity to stir up and encourage such feelings. Many of the early converts were emotionally unstable; the majority of them were simple people, easily influenced by those about them.

The wonder is not that a few of them were moved to rebel against the strict Shaker rules and to turn back to "the world," but rather that so many were content to accept this straightened way of life and to conform to it. Added to the disciplines of a uniform communal life was a technique the Ministry used for the testing of members. Those slated for possible promotion were often deliberately humiliated by demotion to unpleasant tasks or by slighting treatment. Believers who accepted this discipline as a "gift" of the Holy Spirit used it as a voluntary self-abasement, but those who saw nothing in it but an attempt of the Ministry to humiliate them, were angered and embittered by it, and reported it to their friends outside, who straightway used it as another argument against the highhandedness of the Shakers.

There was a time in the early years of the nineteenth century when the New Lebanon Ministry decreed a "gift" of self-abasement for everyone, feeling, doubtless, that human pride had better be crucified once and for all. It had the result of sifting the wheat from the chaff and sending lukewarm Shakers back to "the world." A number of anti-Shaker publications appeared, written and usually published at their own expense by these apostates who took it upon themselves to expose the Shaker life and faith. Reading between the lines of John Woods's *Shakerism Unmasked*, for instance, which was printed in Paris, Kentucky, in 1826, one sees a plodding religious zealot who has lost his shining vision in a haze of daily duties and restrictions. Once he begins to question the worth of the faith for which he has forsaken his wife and family, he begins to eye with suspicion every move of the elders, to doubt their motives, to be irritated by their rulings, to rebel against their demands.

Undoubtedly some of the elders in the various Ministries were inclined to be autocratic, but it seems highly probable that the Believers who went back to "the world" and fell immediately to writing virulent attacks on their former friends and associates may have been natural malcontents. The fact that these attacks were comparatively few in number, that they were always associated with attempts to recover property rights that had been voluntarily relinquished, that they were unrestrained in tone and extreme in the epithets they applied to the Shakers, and above all, that the Shakers (who after all were only small, isolated groups living in larger communities of the "world's people"), went on peacefully prospering and increasing, makes it impossible to accept them at their face value. Besides, there were plenty of ex-Shakers from time to time who remained friendly with their former coreligionists, and reported only good of their stay among the Believers.

It was only with the "gathering" that the need of governmental rules and regulations was felt. Up to that time, the Shakers had lived mostly in scattered households throughout their communities and would have been unable to arrange a systematized plan of life even if they had wanted to do so. The early Believers had on the whole a religious life of extreme emotional excitement, worshipping when and where they could, and in the individually inspired and unorganized manner to which they were moved. With the gathering into gospel order it became possible and desirable to plan a mode of life.

Mother Ann had been forced to carry on her teachings under the most difficult conditions of physical hardship: in households disorganized by persecutions, complicated by sudden influxes of unexpected guests, and hampered by poverty; and among the emotional excesses that characterize the beginnings of any revolutionary form of religion. But through it all, she managed to instill into her followers a yearning for stability, a passion for order. When the Shakers came to have homes and lands of their own, they took great satisfaction in putting into practice the rules of everyday life and conduct Mother Ann had formulated for them. "Be faithful to keep the gospel; be neat and industrious. Put your hands to work and your hearts to God." Order, industry, subordination of the individual to the good of the whole—these were the aims of Shaker government. Its efficiency was attested by its success in attaining these aims.

VI. THE LOG OF THE SHAKER
ADVENTURE

THE beginnings of Shakerism in this country were without contemporary recordings. The Shakers saw in this circumstance another parallel between the ministry of Jesus and that of Ann Lee. It was some time after Jesus' death before the first written accounts of his life came into existence. It was sixteen years after Mother Ann's death when the first authorized statement was printed about the Shakers in America.

The Shakers gave three reasons for this deliberate silence. First, they wanted to test themselves by walking in Christ's footsteps without regard to the persecutions or the accusations of the "world's people," believing with Christ that "Blessed are ye when men shall revile you, and persecute you, and shall say all manner of evil against you falsely for my sake." Second, they wished to prove their faith by their works in the eyes of the world before they talked about it.

And third, they believed that "no testament is of force while the testator liveth," quoting Christ's charge to his disciples to "tell no man that he was the Christ." "It is also evident," they wrote in the preface to *The Testimony of Christ's Second Appearing*, "that the testimony of the apostles was verbal for many years, and nothing was written for the information of those who were unacquainted with the work of Christ, or at a distance from where the first scene was transacted, until the work of that day was fully established, and even then, their writings and sayings were far from being common, but were kept close, and spread no farther than the operation of the spirit of God had prepared the way for them to be received by faith. Therefore it need not seem strange if the circumstances preceding the public opening of *Christ's second appearing* should be similar to those of his *first appearing*."

A small unsigned pamphlet printed at Bennington, Vermont, in 1790 was the first Shaker publication. It was entitled *A Concise Statement of the Principles of the Only True Church of Christ*, and was written by Joseph Meacham, then head of the Church. A letter from James Whittaker was also included in the pamphlet. *The Kentucky Revival*, written by Richard McNemar at Union Village in 1807, and printed in Cincinnati, was the first bound Shaker work.

The following year saw the appearance of the so-called "Shaker Bible," *The Testimony of Christ's Second Appearing*, which is the most important of all the Shaker books. This was published on December 1, 1808, in Lebanon, Ohio. The preface is signed by David Darrow, John Meacham and Benjamin S. Youngs, but the actual writing of the book was done by Youngs with the probable help of Richard McNemar, Matthew Houston and Malcham Worley, all scholars of some repute. Like most of the early Shaker works, it was unsigned, since the Shakers felt that labor of any kind should be anonymous, done for the sake of the cause rather than for personal glory. The signing of the preface was done to give the book standing with the outside world as an authorized statement of Shaker faith.

The aim of the Shakers in putting their history and theology into print was threefold. First, they had begun to realize that they now had a past, and therefore a history which ought to be recorded before those connected with the earliest beginnings had gone to join Mother Ann, William Lee, James Whittaker and John Hocknell. Second, they deemed it their duty to inform the world of their beliefs, their way of life, and their glorious vision of the millennium, thus giving the "world's people" an opportunity to know and perhaps share the millennial prospects. And third, they decided the moment had arrived for answering the many scurrilous attacks which had been made on their beloved Mother Ann and other revered leaders.

They came reluctantly to this last decision, since turning the other cheek was more consistent with their faith and practice. In some quarters, however, dignified silence was being mistaken for guilt or cowardice. Also, the Shaker leaders felt that their period of probation was over, and that they had sufficiently tested their powers of silent endurance, that they had proved the value of their faith by its works. "An evil tree cannot put forth good fruit." And now that the early leaders were gone, it was time to gather up the records of their deeds and words and lay these before the still doubting world. This could not be done without a refutal of the charges that had been made against them. The Believers broke silence and published *The Testimony of Christ's Second Appearing*, a volume of over six hundred pages presenting completely, once for all, the history, philosophy and theology of the Shakers.

The Testimony of Christ's Second Appearing covers a much larger area of human history than merely that occupied by the Shakers. It is a book of great dignity and fine sense of proportion. In it the Shakers proved the sincerity of their desire for the submergence of the individual in the group, for they deliberately subordinated the personal human factors of Shaker history to its spiritual aim and meaning. Out of six hundred and fifty pages, less than fifty are devoted to a factual recording of Shaker personalities and communal happenings. The rest of the book concerns itself with world history as reflected in organized religions, with the etching in of a background for the evolution of Shaker theology, with a logical array of facts arranged to show the inevitability of the Shaker belief as forecast in prophecy.

The book shows a grasp of Bible and European history that implies years of intensive study. The writing of it was done in Warren County, Ohio, which contained at the time only four post offices and was situated in what was practically a wilderness. Its author, Benjamin Youngs, had no libraries to consult, except such private collections of books as might be available in the simple homes of pioneer ministers like Richard McNemar, Matthew Houston, John Dunlavy, or Malcham Worley.

Yet this book, begun on July 7, 1806, and completed on Sunday, April 10, 1808, was declared by Thomas Jefferson to be the best ecclesiastical history that had been written. It outlines medieval European history with masterly simplicity and clearness, quoting unimpeachable authorities for its startlingly convincing charges against the established Christian Church, handles the age-old problem of the origin of evil with skill and logic, and builds up a very good case for Shakerism. When Thomas Jefferson acknowledged the copy that was sent him on publication, he stated that he "had read it carefully three times three," and "that if the principles contained in that book were maintained and carried out it would over throw all false religions."

The small first edition of *The Testimony of Christ's Second Appearing*, at the completion of which its author is said to have weighed only ninety-eight pounds, was soon followed, in 1810, by a second edition of from two to three thousand copies, printed in Albany. A third edition, revised and corrected by Benjamin Youngs and Richard McNemar, working together at Union Village, was printed there in 1823. Richard gave his whole time to the project, working early and late in order that the book might be finished during the lifetime of the now aged leader David Darrow.

The foreword, "To the Reader," concludes with the following statement: "Seeing the work never was intended as a standard of orthodoxy to bind the faith or conscience of any, we have simply improved the common privilege of correcting and improving it, according to the faith and travel of the church, leaving the door still open for a further increase." And in the preface, which was written in 1808 and is the same for all three editions, are these words: "We are far from expecting, or even wishing any of our writings to supersede the necessity of a living testimony, or in any way to prevent a further increase of light and understanding in the things of God. As far as the builder is superior to the thing which he buildeth, so far the living subjects of the knowledge of God stand forever superior to any thing that they can possibly comprise in letters. The living testimony of God is not of the letter, but of the spirit; for the letter killeth, but the spirit giveth life.

"And as it is certain that the work of the latter day, spoken of by all the prophets, hath verily commenced; therefore we are fully persuaded that the true knowledge of God will increase, from one degree to another, until the full manifestation of his glory. And for this purpose God will continue to raise up chosen witnesses, to give the knowledge of salvation to those who sit in darkness, until the whole of his work be accomplished."

Other books followed, mostly doctrinal, of which perhaps the most important were John Dunlavy's *The Mani-*

festo, written at Pleasant Hill, Kentucky, in 1818, and *A Summary View*, published at Albany with the sanction of the Ministry on May 12, 1823. In 1827, the Ministry sponsored the issuing of a work of entirely different type: the *Testimonies Concerning the Character and Ministry of Mother Ann Lee*. This was a collection of individual experiences of early Shakers in New York and New England, gathered together by Seth Y. Wells of New Lebanon for the purpose of clearing the names of Mother Ann and the Elders of the many false charges that had been brought against them. All the contributors to this book had been personally acquainted with Mother Ann and the English group. They were now growing old.

The foreword to the reader vouches for the truth of their testimonies as follows: "A part of these testimonies have been written by the persons whose signatures they bear, but as a number of the witnesses, either from age and infirmity or want of practice in writing, were unable to draft their own testimonies, they communicated the substance to some of their brethren or sisters who were able to write it for them, and the manuscripts have either been examined by them or carefully read to them, and wherever any thing occurred that was not stated exactly according to the sense and understanding of the witness who gave it, it was altered or amended agreeable to his or her feelings; so that nothing should be published or put on record but what should meet the sense and feelings of the subscribing witness. Great care and pains have been taken in this respect by those concerned in writing these testimonies, as well as by the subscriber in preparing them for the press. And as the witnesses are still living, they are ready and willing to bear testimony to the truth of what they have stated, and to give all necessary information to any candid and honest enquirer who may desire it."

The importance of this book is that it stresses the human rather than the doctrinal side of early Shakerism. It paints Mother Ann and the Elders as warm, simple, and kindly, making real and credible their spiritual parenthood toward their followers. Among those whose names appear in it are John Farrington of New Lebanon, Aaron Wood of Watervliet, Elijah Wilds of Shirley, Massachusetts, Benjamin Whitcher and Job Bishop of Canterbury, New Hampshire, Ezekial Morrill of Enfield, New Hampshire, Abijah Worster of Harvard, Massachusetts, who was a fellow sufferer with Mother Ann when the Harvard mob attacked the Believers in 1783, and Eliphalet Comstock of Enfield, Connecticut, where James Whittaker passed his last days.

Since the two favorite charges against Mother Ann and the Elders were those of drunkenness and immorality, most of the testimonies go into detail on these points, asserting with a passionate loyalty that burns through the words that such charges were false in every particular. Zipporah Cory says, "In all the opportunities and privileges I have had with Mother and the Elders, I can truly testify that I never saw the least imperfection in them. They taught me to live a life of purity and godliness, and I always found an example of it in them. . . . As to the charges of intemperance, I never saw the least thing of the kind in them, but always considered them very temperate in all things; and they always taught us temperance. . . . Even the very smell of rum has ever been nauseous and disgusting to me from my earliest infancy, and no person ever appeared so odious in my sight as a drunken person, whether male or female. But I never saw any ardent spirits where Mother Ann was, nor did I ever smell any there, and I am confident I should have smelt it if any had been there. And had Mother or the Elders been given to intoxication, I should most certainly have discovered it, and should have quit them at once."

Thankful Barce corroborates this testimony in these words: "When she [Mother Ann] was at Nathan Goodrich's in Hancock, I was there, and prepared victuals for her and for the elders, and took care of her room, and saw and knew everything she had in the room, and had a fair opportunity to know that she had nothing to support drunkenness or any kind of intemperance."

Daniel Moseley of New Lebanon testified: "As to temperance, regularity and good order in the management of their affairs, these people exceeded all that I had ever seen. I was brought up in New England among good farmers, but such neatness and good economy as was here displayed in the wilderness [at Watervliet] I never saw before. . . . I visited Mother and the Elders three times while they were at Harvard. I also visited them at Ashfield, Richmond and Hancock, and always found in them the same spirit of meekness, temperance, kindness and charity. . . . I had sufficient opportunity to find out the characters of Mother and the Elders, not only from my own personal knowledge and observation, but from the constant intercourse kept up with them by great numbers of my friends and acquaintance for more than four years; yet I have no knowledge that any appearance of intoxication or intemperance, or any other kind of evil was ever discovered in them, or even suspected, by any honest Believer from first to last. . . . They may as well try to persuade me that the saints in Heaven live in drunkenness and whoredom, as to make me believe that Mother and the Elders lived in these things."

The testimonies leave no doubt in the reader's mind of the sincerity of these early Believers. On the contrary, they

accuse plainly, through understatement and through infer-
ence, the type of mind that vilified and persecuted the
Shakers. Job Bishop says, "Had she been a lewd woman as
they said, they would never have persecuted her as they did.
It was the purity and innocence of her life, and the pointed
plainness of her testimony against the sins and abominations
in which they lived, that excited their enmity against her,
and caused them to revile and persecute her." And again,
"Had she been guilty of the base things charged against her
by her enemies, they would have had no occasion to continue
their accusations down to this day; for both she and the Society which she planted would have been sunk in oblivion
many years ago."

With the publishing of these early records, Shakerism announced its coming of age. The unthinking trust of childhood, the natural exuberance of youth now gave place to the
considered caution and the restrained purposefulness of the
maturity that experience had brought them. Henceforth
they were guarded in their intercourse with the world. They
knew they could trust their own, so they withdrew more and
more unto themselves. They had proved the value and the
workability of their chosen faith and way of life. The Ministry had made authoritative announcement of it to the world;
the earliest American converts had testified that it was of the
stuff of daily bread.

The Believers were a united people, an established church
with its own early saints and martyrs, its own printed word
of God. They had fought their good fight with the powers of
evil in their own souls and were on their way to victory. If
the "world's people" would have none of them, let the
"world's people" go their own blind path. "The smallness
of the work is no discouragement to us, nor any disparage-
ment to its first founders. It is indeed a work of too much

purity to find a rapid increase among the inhabitants of a sinful world who are so far lost and sunk in their carnal corruptions. . . . As the work of salvation advances, the light becomes more clear, and truth appears more plain; and while those who receive and obey it find increasing peace and justification; so those who see and reject it, will find their condemnation to increase with the increasing light of truth."

Just what was the Shaker Bible? How could the simple teachings of Mother Ann be expanded to fill a whole book? If her followers truly put their "hands to work and their hearts to God," what more needed to be said on the subject?

It seems to be true of every teacher of a new religion that his original statements are strikingly simple. The truer and clearer they are, the simpler. Christ's teachings were summed up in the words: "Love the Lord thy God with all thy heart and with all thy soul and with all thy strength and with all thy mind; and thy neighbor as thyself." But the simpler the basic statement of any belief or rule of conduct, the more complex the meanings that are attributed to it, the interpretations that are drawn from it. A countless number of books of ingenious interpretations and fantastic explanations have stemmed from the simplicities of the four gospels —some of them so far from early Christianity as to seem utterly alien to it. And even the gospels themselves are undoubtedly less simple than Christ's actual words.

The Shakers, believing that Christ and Mother Ann stood side by side as the two manifestations of the spirit of God in man—the father and mother elements of the deity—felt a compulsion to interpret Ann's work to the "world's people" in the way they believed she would have approved. They wanted to do it themselves, while some of them could still remember her in the flesh. And they wanted to leave nothing unsaid that would make for an understanding of her teachings. They were looking forward confidently to a continuing increase in numbers until the whole world would be preparing with them for the coming millennium. This book would point the way to it. And if its author, or authors, overelaborated the simple teachings upon which their faith was based, they did so with the sanction of a united church.

The Shaker theology was startlingly radical, even for the end of the eighteenth century. It repudiated all the fundamental tenets of orthodox Protestantism: predestination to sin and damnation, infallibility of the Bible, the Trinity, man's salvation through the atonement of Christ, the resurrection of the body and a static heaven after death. The first to go was man's essentially sinful nature, imposed upon him by Adam's original sin in the Garden of Eden. With the Universalists, the Believers held that God was too just and good to condemn all men to everlasting damnation because of a sin committed by one man. They further agreed with the Unitarians that man was too good, in his potentialities for perfection, to be thus condemned. The Bible they accepted as the word of God as far as it went. But they did not believe it was God's final revelation to man. "God was never beholden to letters," they said, "as the only means of revealing his will, but he that formed the soul of man can also form, in that soul, a conviction of his will. And nothing but the ridiculous doctrine that God actually died, could ever have given occasion to the blind error of the Antichristian world, that the Bible was his Last Will and Testament, and the priests his executors and administrators."

The doctrine of the Trinity seemed an absurdity to the Shakers. Who ever heard, they said, of such an anomaly as a three-fold male God in a universe where male and female were the order of nature! Their own conception of the father and mother elements of God were much more in keeping with the logic of the universe. The immaculate conception, likewise, had no place in their creed. If Christ were God how could his example help mere man? The fact of his humanity was what made his example an inspiration and a help. Besides, what justice in making one suffer and struggle alone to atone for the many? No, said the Shakers: every man has to fight his own fight against the powers of evil within him, and win the victory for himself with the help of God and God's spirit as exemplified in Christ and in Mother Ann.

The resurrection of the physical body they also dismissed as an unpleasant and impossible thought. The body was of the earth; only the spirit was able to survive beyond the span of earthly life. Christ and Mother Ann had pointed the way for mankind to crucify the flesh and to live the life of the spirit. Nothing else mattered. The physical life of the body on this earth was elementary, temporary, only a preparation for the life of the spirit which was to be eternal. And even this eternal life of the spirit was to be a progression toward something always beyond: there would ever be new truths, new light to break forth from God's word. The millennium for which they were preparing would be no static, finished heaven, but a further opportunity for spiritual adventuring.

The Testimony of Christ's Second Appearing divided the history of the world into four parts, beginning with man's temptation and fall in the Garden of Eden. The first part deals with man in his fallen state up to the time of Noah and the Flood. The second ends with the coming of Christ and the founding of the primitive Christian Church. The third records the beginnings of the apostolic church interrupted by the rise of "antichrist" about the year 313 A.D., when Constantine was converted to Christianity and began immediately to organize and purge the church.

The reign of antichrist, which comprises not only the heyday of the papacy, but the birth and growth of Protestantism as well, lasted till about the end of the seventeenth century, when the rise of the Quakers, strengthened by the edict of William of Orange establishing liberty of conscience in England, marked the beginning of a new epoch in which freedom of thought and belief were increasingly stressed. It was about this time that the Camisards—the "French Prophets" who were the forerunners of the Shakers—became active on the continent. And it was shortly after this that Ann Lee was born and the Society of James and Jane Wardley started. Ann's birth, or rather her association with the Wardleys in forming the first Shaker Society, marked the beginning of the fourth era of world history, the final dispensation which was to end in the coming of the millennium.

Man's disobedience of God in the Garden of Eden, the sin by which, according to the Shakers, all evil came into the world, was the sex act. To be sure, God had commanded all created things to be fruitful and multiply, but with this limitation: "in the times and seasons appointed by the Creator and established in the law of nature." Only man disregarded the terms of this command. Only man was guilty of lust and the sins it entailed. And woman, who fell first and then tempted man, was more guilty than he and was therefore placed in subjection to man until both should have travelled out of sin by conquering the physical nature. This was the reason that the first, and male manifestation of God's spirit in Jesus Christ preceded the second, and female, in Ann Lee. The human race had to struggle through two long eras before the first Messiah came, and then through hundreds of years more before the beginning of the second dispensation. With the coming of Ann Lee, men and women stood equal in God's sight.

The celibate life, then, was the logical way to begin to conquer man's physical nature. The Shakers did not condemn marriage as a sin among the "world's people," but they considered those who practised it to be on a lower spiritual plane than themselves. The first era of human history, according to *The Testimony*, was one of unbridled passion and indulgence. That was why it ended in the flood. The second period saw the enacting of laws to regulate and restrain sex relations. The Mosaic law was explicit in these matters: witness circumcision, and the barring of women from the temple for a fixed interval before and after childbirth. The third period saw the increase of celibacy both among religious leaders in the established church and in the many small groups of so-called heretics. (The shockingly immoral lives of many of the clergy in medieval Europe were due to antichrist.)

The fourth era ushered in the United Society of Believers which taught that in order to attain the perfection of which mankind was capable, the flesh must be wholly conquered. "Those who are willing to yield obedience to a superior principle, and to deny themselves and take up their crosses against the propensities of that nature which they have received from their parents, are justly entitled to eat of the tree of life and live forever."

The division of *The Testimony* which concerns itself with the third era of human history is primarily a chronicle of the orthodox Christian Church from the founding of the papacy down through the story of the Reformation to the coming of the Quakers, the Camisards and the Shakers. Actually it is an arraignment of ecclesiasticism from the standpoint of the *failure* of "so-called" Christianity. "If ecclesiastics had never created a virtue called orthodoxy," said the Shakers

115

(quoting from Robinson's *Ecclesiastical Researches*), "the world would never have heard of a crime called heresy."

The book then goes on to prove that the small groups of so-called heretics who sprang up again and again during the Middle Ages (the Marcionites, Manicheans, Priscillianists, Albigenses, Waldenses, etc.), were far nearer the early apostolic church and the teachings of Jesus than the orthodox clergy who persecuted them. The Shakers thought of themselves as being in the line of these small persecuted sects: "a people who taught the principles of virtue and practised what they taught; who took no oaths, bore no arms, and held the reins of spiritual government in the strictness of their morals." They saw the line of righteousness reaching back from them through the ages even to Jesus and his disciples.

It is an interesting speculation whether these small groups of gentle nonconformists would have become intolerant persecutors of other smaller groups if they had grown in size and power. It seems to be the history of all sects which have developed into influential churches that as they gain numbers and power, they lose the tolerance which characterized their beginnings and begin to oppress those who differ from them. The Shakers were marked throughout their history by their tolerance of other religious bodies. Inflexible ·as they were toward their own conduct in the practice of their faith, they accorded the same right to others. If they had become numerous and powerful, would they in turn have become intolerant? Or was it the other way around? Did their tolerance, perhaps, keep them from gaining numbers and power in the world? It is one of those questions that can never be answered.

It is evident all through *The Testimony* that the Shakers were appreciative of the liberty they enjoyed in America. For this liberty they gave no credit, however, to the leaders of established churches of religion. They pointed out that it was not "in a general council of Christian bishops, but of noble advocates for civil and religious liberty that the wise and generous Washington established the rights of conscience by a just and equitable Constitution. And truly, if the rights of conscience are still respected under the present administration, we are not indebted to ecclesiastical tyrants for the privilege; for such never will respect nor promote an establishment which has a tendency to diminish the current of their unrighteous gain, by allowing every one to think and act for themselves in matters of religion." The Shakers looked about them at the world as it was, and could find no grounds for believing that the orthodox church had in any way improved it.

Many chapters of *The Testimony* are taken up with proving that the Biblical prophecies in Revelation and parts of the Old Testament were fulfilled in the coming of Mother Ann and the Shakers. References are made to the repeated use of the word "shake" in many of these passages. "Thus saith the Lord of hosts, *Yet once, it is a little while, and I will shake the heavens, and the earth, and the sea, and the dry land. And I will shake all nations, etc.*" For the Shakers had adopted the epithet once given them in derision and had turned it to their own uses.

It is in these sections of the book that the logical arguments of the historian begin to shade off into the mystical symbolism which characterized much of Shakerism. For the Shakers were thorough in whatever they did. As historians, they were logical analysts; as farmers and artisans they were practical workmen; and as spiritual adventurers, they followed the gleam far beyond the confines of what the world called the probable and reasonable. The same mind that appraised the medieval Christian Church with logic and keenness, saw nothing fantastic in the kind of arithmetic required to make the prophecies of the Old Testament tally with the dates significant to Shaker history.

A small part of the fourth section of *The Testimony* contains accounts of some dozen or so of Shaker miracles. For Ann Lee, like Jesus, had performed many miraculous cures in her short ministry. These cures are attested by affidavits out of deference to the scepticism of the world. The Shakers explained this departure from their usual custom as follows: "Among ourselves, a plain and simple statement of the truth is sufficient without the formal ceremony of an affidavit to enforce it. But the world of mankind have become so faithless towards each other, that they cannot believe nor be believed without something like legal attestation." The writer then goes on to deprecate the necessity even of mentioning the miracles at all, since the Believers themselves considered these cures of bodily ills in no way extraordinary, and indeed far less miraculous than the operation of the spirit of God in the mind of man. The truly miraculous thing was that this body of Believers had their own church, their own home, in a land where they were free to follow the call of their adventure as far as they chose.

The book ends on the exalted note of "A few thoughts addressed to Young Believers," urging upon these fortunate ones a realization of the opportunity that was theirs. "What millions from sequestered vallies and desolate mountains, from lonely cottages, and silent groves, from torture-rooms, and racks, and devouring flames, have looked, and wept, and prayed, towards this latter day of liberty and peace! How have they talked of the rights of man, and laboured to describe in words what your eyes behold and your souls daily enjoy, namely, the blessings of peace and salvation in a land sacred to freedom! . . . Unshackled by superstition, unbiassed by the terrors of tyranny, and redeemed from false systems and the reigning power of iniquity, by which your souls were held in bondage, you stand free to judge between truth and error, light and darkness, good and evil, and to chuse that which you, as a free and chosen people, deliberately judge to be productive of the greatest present and eternal good."

The Shaker theology might well be summed up in these two beliefs: the perfectibility of human nature through the life of the spirit and the moral responsibility of each individual man and woman. This is a robust creed. The Shaker never whined and complained against the universe; he never blamed God for his temptations or his misfortunes; he did not try to excuse his shortcomings and failures either by heredity or environment. How could he, when he claimed divine paternity for his spiritual nature, and when he deliberately chose and made his own physical environment? The Shaker way was a hard way, but the Shaker walked in it with integrity and dignity. And in time, when the early haze of suspicion and fear had been cleared away by more exact knowledge and better understanding, the "world's people" came to respect that dignity and that integrity which the Believers wore as a garment.

VII. A HOME OF THEIR OWN

FROM the time the Shakers came into possession of the "wilderness tract" at Niskayuna (Indian name for good maize land), they set about making themselves self-supporting and self-sufficient. At Niskayuna in 1776, and again at Busro, Indiana, in 1811, they went through all the struggles of pioneers in a new country where nature is the first foe to be subdued. They cut down trees, drained swamp lands, built themselves temporary dwellings of logs until such time as they were able to start sawmills to saw the logs into boards; they arranged for a water supply, and they planted seeds in their newly cleared fields in order to raise the crops necessary to provide them with food during the coming winter.

The New England societies were spared this preliminary task of clearing all their land, since many of the early converts in Massachusetts, New Hampshire and Maine brought already cultivated fields and houses already built into the joint ownership. Land was the first common possession of the Believers; ownership of land was the mooring to which they tied the questing bark of the spirit. All through their existence they have remained faithful to the land—an agricultural people, living by necessity and preference in country districts. These industrial workers from the city of Manchester, England, founded a society of farmers and orchardists and horticulturists and breeders of fine cattle in the new land of their hopes. Their one desire, whenever they were obliged to go on business to "great and wicked cities," was to get back as soon as possible to their homes in the country.

Except for two or three cases of bad judgment—notably at Niskayuna where even today the lower lands show traces of the swamp from which they were reclaimed during the war of Independence, and at Busro, Indiana, which had to be abandoned after fifteen years of struggling with the malarial climate—the Shakers seem to have been good pickers of land. New Lebanon, home of the central ministry, just over the New York line from Massachusetts, on the fringes of the Berkshires and Catskills, has as beautiful a situation as one could find anywhere: a side hill with a view out over a wide fertile valley to low pleasant hills beyond. On either side of the country road that runs over this long shelf on the western slope of the hill lie the buildings of four of the Shaker families which composed the New Lebanon society. The other four that brought the total to eight when the society was most prosperous, were situated nearby: two of them in the adjoining town of Canaan, New York. East of the road the wooded hill rises steeply enough to ensure a good water supply; on the west the sunny farm lands slope away down to the broad valley below.

The two Maine communities and that at Enfield, New Hampshire, lie near bodies of water. The Shaker settlement at New Gloucester, Maine, is on the side of a little hill that slopes down to a lake, the whole surrounded by other higher hills. As a visiting brother from North Union, Ohio, remarked, "Take a large wooden bowl and invert a smaller one inside it, and you will get some idea of the situation." In Enfield, New Hampshire, the North family, the Church family and the South family border the Fourth New Hampshire turnpike, once the route of stagecoaches from Boston to Montpelier, but for many years just a pleasant country road through the narrow fertile valley between Montcalm Mountain and Mascoma Lake.

Pleasant Hill, Kentucky, is situated in the famous blue-grass region, near the picturesque Kentucky River. The Shakers of Harvard, Massachusetts, had their home in another river valley: the valley of the Nashua, which flows between long ridges of higher land through one of the loveliest parts of Massachusetts. Union Village, Ohio, was in the rich lands of the Miami bottom. Tyringham, Massachusetts, chose the "Fernside" of a long narrow valley, ranging its buildings on so steep a slope that two stories on the upper side became four on the lower, and the farm and pasture lands lay far below. All the Shaker holdings were chosen with an eye to practical facilities for living: water rights, drainage, fertile fields, etc., combined with a sufficient degree of remoteness from towns to ensure the isolation their owners desired. The Believers liked to be able to lift their eyes to the hills, but as practical farmers they preferred foot-hills to mountains.

After the sites of the various communities had been acquired, and the preliminary work of clearing land, raising buildings, developing water supply rights and determining the crops most suitable for cultivation had been done, the Shakers set about improving and systematizing their farming. If human life were perfectible, so were the lower orders of animal and plant life. Men and women who had turned their eyes toward the goal of spiritual perfection could do no less than their best in the physical and material tasks that lay before them on earth. Those appointed as "farm deacons" farmed in the service of God.

If the earth could be made to produce larger crops, and if the quality of the plants grown could be improved from year to year, theirs was the responsibility for this improvement and this increase. They had an advantage over individual farmers in that they were able in times of stress to get as much temporary help as they needed from brethren usually employed at something else. At mowing time in Enfield, New Hampshire, it is recorded that forty Shaker men were called from their divers duties to swing scythes together in rhythmic rows up and down the long fields that lay between the mountain and the lake. The first crops to be raised by the Believers, besides hay for their livestock, were wheat, oats, rye, barley, corn, flax and potatoes. Orchards and small fruits were also established early.

The Shaker love of order was found on the farm, as else- where. All tools and implements had to be put back in their proper places each night, if practicable, but in any case, on Saturday night. If gates into a field were opened, they must be closed; if bars were let down, they must be replaced be- fore leaving. Any break in fence or wall had to be mended or reported to the person in charge of mending it. Nothing was allowed to get out of repair. The stitch in time was always taken. Even on the Sabbath, work was permitted if emer- gencies arose such as a broken fence through which grazing cattle might invade the garden, or a threatened rain that might ruin the mown hay. The Shaker fields came to wear a prosperous look that drew envious glances and comments from less thrifty neighbors. Yet the Shakers were not over- worked. Farming, as they did it, was healthy exercise. Peter Ayers, for instance, who joined the New Lebanon Shakers in 1787 and went in 1792 with Job Bishop to Canterbury, mowed his last "swarth" the season he was ninety.

Out of the Shaker preoccupation with soil and crops came an inevitable interest in seeds. In 1790, Joseph Turner who was supervising the two-acre family garden at Watervliet, New York, began to offer a few surplus seeds for sale. It was the first time anyone in that part of the country had mar- keted seeds. Turner's successor, Ebenezer Alden, invented a "printing box" for hand-printing the seed bags instead of marking them in longhand. In 1811, when David Osborne went from New Lebanon to become trustee at Watervliet, the Watervliet Shakers were raising $300 worth of seeds a year. During the next thirty years, Morrel Baker experimented with improving the stock from which the seeds were taken and increased the business to thousands of dollars per year.

The care and the integrity that went into building up the Shaker seed industry are reflected in a pact signed at New Lebanon on April 13, 1819, by Morrel Baker and three other Watervliet gardeners, six deacons from Hancock and two trustees. "We, the undersigned, having for sometime past felt a concern lest there should come loss upon the joint interest and dishonor upon the gospel by purchasing seeds of the world and mixing them with ours for sale, and having duly considered the matter, we are confident that it is best to leave off the practice, and we do hereby covenant and agree that we will not, hereafter, put up, or sell, any seeds to the world which are not raised among believers."

The Shakers not only sought to improve and guarantee the quality of the seeds they sold, but they also tried to improve methods of handling and distributing them. This industry again illustrates the flexibility of the Shaker organization. Sisters whose usual work might be spinning or sewing, were impressed temporarily into making and marking seed bags and putting the seeds into them when the seed business went into its rush season. The methods of distribution developed and changed with the growth of the industry. In the beginning, farmers in the locality simply went to the Shakers for the seeds they wanted. As the business enlarged, the Shakers tried different ways of reaching their expanding market. They had their own seed wagons in which they sent out brethren at certain seasons to travel over routes apportioned between adjoining communities.

Henry Daily of Pleasant Hill, Kentucky, was a well-known figure in the vicinity of Lexington, driving out with his great wagon laden not only with seeds but other Shaker products as well. Simeon Atherton of Harvard, Massachusetts, and Benjamin Bailey of Alfred, Maine, were familiar sights in their respective regions, with their horse-drawn pedlar's carts carrying Shaker wares. The Shakers also sold their seeds through agents in cities. The first big markets to be used by the New York Shakers (New Lebanon and Watervliet) were Albany, Poughkeepsie, Hudson and later New York City and Brooklyn. Enfield and Canterbury, New Hampshire, used Boston as a distributing center. Some of the northern New England Shaker societies claimed priority over Watervliet in the actual marketing of garden seeds, but the uniformity of the Shaker mind, combined with the standardization of the habits of life in the various communities and the Shaker custom of intercommunity visiting, made it easily possible for two or more societies to start and develop the same project simultaneously.

It was a short step from marketing seeds to the packaging and selling of herbs. The Shakers were among the first in this country to practise a systematic and more or less scientific gathering and classifying of herbs for medicinal uses. Many of these herbs were put up in dried form; others were converted into extracts and oils which were either sold as such or made into ointments and medicines. Some of the herbs were cultivated; but a large number of them were found growing wild and were sought and gathered in the woods and fields—a task often assigned to the Shaker children. Thomas Corbett of Canterbury, New Hampshire, made the much advertised Corbett's Shaker Syrup of Sarsaparilla, buying many of the ingredients from the New Lebanon Shakers.

The Shaker herbs had so good and so far-flung a reputation that they were frequently ordered from such distant points as England and parts of Europe. New Lebanon, Harvard, Massachusetts, Canterbury, Sabbathday Lake—to mention a few only—developed the herb industry to such an extent that they had to build large herb houses to handle it. Under the head of herb products were listed rose water, attar of roses, and violet blossoms which they also put up for sale. One of the buildings at Union Village, Ohio, was stacked in season with wagonloads of rose bloom, from rose bushes cultivated for this purpose. Roses and other flowers were cherished for their usefulness, not their beauty. Lest a weak sister might be tempted to adorn herself with a flower, it was ordered that all flowers should be plucked without stems. The essence of a flower was like the spirit of man—better freed from the physical body!

One of the earliest Shaker industries, closely connected with agriculture, was broom making. This, also, seems to have been started at Watervliet, where broom corn was introduced along with other kinds of corn in 1791, and cultivated separately in 1798. Brooms soon became one of the major Shaker products. They were made and sold by all the societies from the earliest days almost up to the present. It was eminently fitting that this should be so, for the Shakers practised cleanliness thoroughly and consistently in every department of their lives. They were exceptionally well-qualified to be judges and makers of brooms. That they used the ones they made was no idle recommendation. All the housewives who were fortunate enough to live within buying radius of a Shaker community did likewise. Even as far away as Boston it was possible to buy Shaker brooms and brushes made in Canterbury and Enfield, New Hampshire, from 1805 on till well toward the end of the nineteenth century.

Other Shaker activities that had their origin in cultivation of the land were the raising and marketing of fruit. The Shakers were able orchardists. They even originated certain species of apples such as the quince apple, the Shaker pippin, the Shaker greening and several fine sweet apples for drying. Not only was their fruit the best obtainable, but their young trees were in great demand by farmers. In the fall, such of the ripe fruit as was not sold immediately or taken for family use, was preserved in one way or another for winter needs. Cider was made, of course, and there was a special Shaker applesauce made from boiled cider and dried apples that was in great demand. Shirley, Massachusetts, turned out great quantities of this annually for sale to the "world." Apple drying was done on a large scale both for community use and for sale to outsiders. The drying of corn also was an important part of the Shaker economy from the very earliest days. In 1828 it became one of the major industries of the New Lebanon community. Many of the northern societies made maple sugar to use and to sell. In one particularly good season, the Enfield, New Hampshire, society made nine hundred gallons of syrup, part of which they sold to a Mr. Shepherd of Cambridge, Massachusetts, for eighty cents a gallon. In 1874 Canterbury's output was between three and four thousand pounds of sugar.

Other Shaker industries which stemmed less directly from the cultivation of the land, but which were a necessary part of the agricultural scheme, were the dairy products: milk, butter, cheese, poultry and eggs, and the raising of stock. Livestock was an essential part of the Shaker economy from that day during the Revolution when young David Darrow was seized along with the flock of sheep he was driving to

Niskayuna, and accused of being in the pay of the British commissariat. Country people could not go out and buy their meat and milk, eggs and butter in those early days; they had to raise the animals to produce it.

The ownership of hens and pigs and sheep and cattle was a very necessary concomitant of the ownership of land. Cattle played an increasingly large part on the Shaker farms, since not only were cows needed for milk, butter and cheese, but oxen for draught purposes. Sheep were also raised extensively. In 1843, Enfield, New Hampshire, owned between twelve and fifteen hundred sheep, of mostly Saxon and Merino strain, which afforded wool for their own wear and for the renowned Shaker flannels which they sold to the world. The Shakers with their usual painstaking experimentation, improved the quality of their livestock from generation to generation, till farmers began to turn to them "when they wished to tone up their stock or change the strain of blood."

About the middle of the nineteenth century, Union Village, Ohio, was exporting stock to Europe. In 1853 they sold $8,420 worth of blooded Durham cattle. The barn at Tyringham, Massachusetts, held forty yoke of oxen. Canterbury had a barn that housed one hundred cows. Groveland, New York, also raised stock extensively. For some strange reason the Shakers never bred horses, although they sometimes allowed their stallions to be used for that purpose by others. Also, they never used mules on their farms. It is ironic to think of the celibate Shakers developing superior seeds and fruits and running stock farms on the most approved eugenic principles of stock-breeding. Possibly if they had applied those principles to themselves, as the Oneida community did, they might have "toned up" the human stock. It is an interesting speculation, but one of which the Shakers would have strongly disapproved. The physical regeneration of the human race never seemed important to them. Man's spiritual nature held the possibility of so much higher development than his physical that the Believers thought all their efforts should be turned in the direction of perfecting the spiritual. Their real adventure was always in the realm of the spirit.

The Shaker system of communal life seems almost to have sprung full-grown into existence. It was so many-sided and it developed in so many different directions at once, that the recording of it in any kind of chronological order is difficult. The land, of course, came first, then the crops. But while the crops were being raised there had to be buildings for the farmers to live in; there had to be livestock to help with the farming and barns to shelter the livestock and store the crops. Harness for the draught animals was an early important item; smithies for repair work on tools, wagons, etc. were indispensable; one need led to another, and all of them had to be filled.

Before long the simple, yet complex, machinery of Shaker communism had been set in motion and perfected to such an extent that it ran of its own momentum years after the needs and the energy that started it had dwindled away. Side by side with the development of the seed business, the broom business, the herb business, the raising and selling of fruits and livestock, came machine shop work, tanning, cooper's wear, weaving and many other small industries that not only supplied the needs of all the brethren and sisters, but furnished articles of commerce with "the world." And each new industry presented new problems of building construction, power, adaptations or inventions of machinery, etc.

One of the basic needs of every Shaker community was an adequate water supply. This had to be more than sufficient for drinking, bathing and other household purposes, because water for a long time furnished the only kind of power available for running machinery. This meant the acquirement of riparian rights; access to some stream or lake which could be made to supply a fall of water of sufficient volume and speed to turn a water wheel. The float or "flutter" wheel was the earliest used, being the simplest since it could be set up in the bed of a shallow brook and turned by a comparatively small volume of water running against the paddles which projected transversely from its broad rim. But the flow of water had to be steady—dependable; and brooks are seldom dependable all seasons—especially in hilly country like New England and eastern New York.

Mill ponds became necessary—the artificial damming up of a stream in order to store water and hold it for future use, when it could be released gradually through a gate, as needed, to run into a narrow sluiceway. This flume, or penstock, led to a water-wheel which was pushed into motion by the weight of the water against the little paddles or vanes in its rim, and which was connected by means of a shaft with other wheels and machinery in the mill. The three kinds of water-wheels in commonest early use were the undershot (a variation of the float wheel), the breast wheel which received the force of the water on a level with the hub and the overshot wheel where the weight of the water, coming from the top, augmented the force of the current.

By one means or another, all of the Shaker societies acquired valuable water rights. That of Alfred, Maine, got its mill privilege by an exchange of the lands which the Shaker Eliphaz Ring owned at Poland Springs for those owned by Jabez Ricker at Alfred. Jabez Ricker started the famous

Poland Springs house, and the Shakers acquired a mill privilege and rich lands between lakes Massabesic and Bungaunt, and both were happy in the exchange. The Rickers, incidentally, always remained staunch friends of the Shakers in Maine.

The Enfield, New Hampshire, Shaker lands were well placed between a small mountain and a lake. At the top of the mountain was a little pond set in a bowl of white granite and fed by springs. A stream flowed out of it down the mountain side and across the Shaker lands into Lake Mascoma. By damming this pond, the Shakers increased its capacity and also their control of the brook's volume. They placed one of their first mills by this dam and added others at different levels below it. Because the stream had a rapid fall they were able to use their water power over and over again. The first overshot wheel was thirty feet in diameter, with buckets six feet long. After three saw mills of varying types had been constructed, a grist mill was put up, then a threshing mill, a tan house, a fulling mill, a spin mill, etc., not to mention a laundry and a churn operated by water power. The water system was further elaborated by the building of a reservoir lower on the mountainside and the laying of canals to hold aqueducts for carrying water to various points in the village below.

This pattern of industrial beginnings was approximately the same in all the Shaker societies. At Canterbury and at North Union, Ohio, the Shaker lands lay on high plateaus. Canterbury built a series of eight ponds or reservoirs in a row, with mills on all of them, and carried the water used for household purposes one mile by aqueduct. North Union developed what were later known as the Shaker Lakes from small swampy pools on Doan Brook which ran through their land. Pleasant Hill, Kentucky, opened a spring at the foot of the hill behind Center House, built a large cistern to hold the water, and pumped the water to the various houses in the village by wooden force pumps driven by horses in a treadmill. The fact that all the Shaker villages were remarkably free from epidemics of any kind attests the care and thoroughness that attended the building of their water systems.

Wood was plentiful on the Shaker property. Most of the northern communities were fortunate in owning large areas of old growth pine—some as thick as five feet in diameter and over a hundred and fifty feet tall. In the New Hampshire Shaker buildings put up before 1845 are found the extremely wide boards that were cut by the early Shaker sawmills from these trees. After that date, when the railroad was pushed through north from Concord, the best trees were sold to be carried away for masts.

Although wood was commonest in the Shaker buildings, brick and stone were also much used. The bricks were made by the Shakers and the stone quarried on their own lands. New Hampshire used granite; North Union, Ohio, sandstone. Union Village, Ohio, burned brick not only for its own needs, but to sell at two dollars per thousand to "the world." A machine shop built in Enfield, New Hampshire, in the middle eighteen hundreds had outside walls of granite which were faced on the inside with bricks covered in turn by wood sheathing and plaster. All the Shaker buildings were constructed with equal care, once the Shakers had their source of supplies and their machinery under control. The communal life, both domestic and industrial, was soon operating at full force.

The Shaker regard for good and careful work was their heritage from their English founders. The Manchester immigrants may have had small experience with farming when they first came to America (though they lost no time in acquiring it), but they were certainly skilled artisans, all trained in the apprentice system of the time. James Whittaker had been a weaver, Ann Lee a cotton worker, her brother William Lee, a blacksmith. They all had the habit of manual work and the mastery of a trade. It was told of William that when travelling on one of his missionary journeys through New England his horse lost a shoe and he stopped at a blacksmith shop to get a new one. The blacksmith was busy, so William went to the anvil, made the shoe himself and fitted it on the horse's hoof. Before he had finished, the blacksmith was standing at his elbow watching the operation intently. When William asked him what he owed him for the material and the use of his tools, the blacksmith replied, "Nothing. I am more than repaid by the privilege of watching so skilled a workman."

Over and over again Mother Ann had repeated to her followers, "Put your hands to work and your hearts to God." Every Shaker was expected to have his or her trade in the exercise of which the utmost integrity was demanded. It was no more possible for a true Believer to put his hands to shoddy or dishonest work than it was to put his heart insincerely to God. With this standard of workmanship and the combined resources of a united brotherhood to back all efforts toward continuous improvement, it was no wonder that articles bearing the Shaker stamp were increasingly in demand. No article was ever permitted to be offered for sale until it had been passed as perfect by the trustees.

A list of the Shaker products is a list of all the things most used in early nineteenth century rural America. Hayforks and other farm implements, pails and tubs, dry measures, sieves, spinning wheels, leather goods including shoes, & yarn, cloth, chairs, stools, baskets, hats, buttons, etc., were all made by the Believers in their own shops. As late as the eighteen-eighties, townspeople of Enfield, New Hampshire, were going to the Shakers for ladders and ladder rungs, knowing from experience that any wooden article the Shakers made was from wood properly seasoned. Shaker leather tanned a hundred years ago is still strong. The seasoning of wood and the tanning of leather take time when properly done, but the results justify the time spent.

Besides using the best and most thorough work methods known, the Shakers were responsible for creating new methods and for inventing new machines. Since most of these inventions were unpatented, they were borrowed freely by the world's people. The Enfield, New Hampshire, Shakers claim to have invented the brimstone match. The Watervliet, New York, Shakers invented the needle with an eye in the middle for use in sewing brooms, later to be adapted to the sewing machine. Pleasant Hill, Kentucky, made a four-wheeled dumpcart. Enfield, Connecticut, is credited with the first one-horse buggy in the country. A washing machine was invented at New Lebanon and was later improved and patented at Canterbury whence it was sold widely to hotels.

The first circular saw is claimed by three different societies: Alfred, Maine, Enfield, New Hampshire, and Harvard, Massachusetts. It is probable that the invention may have happened spontaneously in all three places. Sarah Babbitt, the Harvard sister who conceived it, also suggested the cutting of nails from a sheet of metal instead of forging them singly. In many cases no individual credit is given to the inventor, only to the society of which he or she was a member. Probably some of the inventions were joint affairs. In other cases many inventions are credited to the same man. Hewitt Chandler of Sabbathday Lake, Maine, invented a mowing machine and also a method of bending staves without set-

134

ting them up in casks. Daniel Baird of North Union was the most prolific of all the Shaker inventors. Some of the inventions credited to him were the rotary or revolving harrow, the automatic spring and Babbitt metal.

The general efficiency of the Shaker industrial system was due, of course, to Shaker unity and Shaker thoroughness. The central ministry had perfected a dependable and controllable organization. Not only could ruling elders be shifted from one community to another as seemed wise, but inventions and improvements that worked successfully in one village could be introduced into all the others with no lost time or waste motions. Or if one place had better facilities than another for the manufacture of certain articles, it could easily turn them out in sufficient quantity to supply the united brotherhood. New Lebanon, for instance, became the manufacturing center of the famed Shaker chairs. Canterbury specialized in the washing machines, also in the small Shaker wood stoves. It became, furthermore, the publishing center for the northern societies, as Watervliet, Ohio, was at one time, for the southern.

South Union, Kentucky, raised its own silk from its own silk worms on its own mulberry trees, and furnished the beautiful yard-square silk kerchiefs for the sisters' wear to all the northern communities. When Union Village, Ohio, was found to excel in palm leaf bonnet making, sisters from other societies went to Union Village to learn the art. On the other hand, brethren from Union Village visited the Whitewater community near Cincinnati to "obtain insight into bookbinding." All of these borrowings of ideas and visiting back and forth had the further result of preserving the unity of the Shaker church. It was a circle of efficiency, closed to "the world," but revolving constantly and successfully in its own orbit.

VIII. ORDER AND SECURITY
ACHIEVED

THE Shaker period of expansion began almost immediately after the gathering into society order and continued till about the middle of the nineteenth century. The peak of prosperity and influence was reached at slightly different times in different societies, but roughly speaking the epoch of largest numbers and completest activity came between 1825 and 1860. The decade from 1820 to 1830 saw the abandonment of one established society and the formation of three new ones. The only Indiana settlement, at Busro, was given up in 1827 and its members distributed between the Union Village, Ohio, and the Pleasant Hill, Kentucky, communities whence some of them had originally been drawn. Sodus Point, New York, later to be removed to Mt. Morris, New York and known under the two names of Groveland and Sonyea, was gathered in 1826 by Richard Pelham of Ohio.

Whitewater, Ohio, which had been started at Darby Plains in 1820 by Richard McNemar and Calvin Morrill, was "gathered" at Whitewater by Issachar Bates early in 1824. North Union, Ohio, founded at Warrensville (just outside Cleveland) by Ralph Russell in 1822, was gathered under Richard McNemar's watchful eye in 1826. No new societies were added after 1830. The Believers had come to realize by this time that the "world's people" were for the most part deaf and blind to the message and the shining vision the Shakers had tried to share with them; so they turned their energies toward building up their own small domain both spiritual and material. While they were never wholly independent of the world in which they dwelt apart, they were as near self-sufficient and self-sustaining as it is possible for a group of human beings dwelling in the midst of a civilized nation of other human beings to be. They minded their own business and gradually gained the respect of "the world" for this preoccupation with their own affairs.

"The world" also found other reasons for respecting this group of religious communists in their midst when they began to have business dealings with the Shaker trustees. Not only did the integrity of these representatives of the Millennial Church become a byword, but also, and perhaps more surprisingly, their business acumen as well. The Shaker trustees—those "office deacons" who managed all business transactions for the Shakers within and without the circle of community life—became familiar figures in commercial districts of the "great and wicked cities" which they visited frequently on buying and selling missions for their respective societies. They were often better known among the "world's people" than were the elders to whose judgment and final decisions they owed obedience. If "the world" found it difficult to accept or even to judge the spiritual values of the Shaker way of life, they had no trouble in recognizing the business efficiency that had developed out of that communal economic system.

The trustees were governed in all their acts by specific rulings. They were truly trustees in the original meaning of the word of the Shaker property entrusted to their care. Honesty and dependability were prerequisites. Individual initiative was not demanded, nor even encouraged, though a good deal of leeway was allowed to some of the trustees in the use of their own judgment. On no account, however, must they involve the society whose agents they were in debt or in any commitment which might work to its disadvantage. In all sales or purchases cash payments were required. The Shakers believed in a pay-as-you-go policy, whether they stood in the position of sellers or buyers. The trustees were the middle-men in all business dealings both with "the world" and with other Shaker communities. So long as they acted in accordance with the wishes and instructions of the elders, they knew they could rely on the backing of the whole society.

In the few recorded instances where trustees disregarded these wishes or exceeded these instructions, the results were so disastrous to the families involved as to prove the wisdom of the ruling. For such was the honesty of the Shakers that even in cases where they might have disavowed responsibility for the act of a disobedient trustee, they voluntarily assumed it rather than bring dishonor upon the Shaker name. On the whole, however, the record of the Shaker trustees was a clean one. In honesty and competence they averaged far higher than men holding similar positions of trust in "the world." Though more than half of the eighteen Shaker societies suffered money losses at one time or another during their hundred years of existence, the losses were due mostly to overenthusiasm. The rare cases of actual dishonesty were a sad tragedy to the families in which they happened.

The first duties of the trustees had to do largely with real estate transactions, since such of the Shaker lands as were not donated by converts had to be acquired by purchase. The early records of Union Village, Ohio, for instance, contain memoranda of such acquisitions in the names of Peter Pease and David Meacham.

"Dec. 5, 1806. Peter Pease, Issachar Bates and Malcham Worley went and surveyed Abram Larew's farm, paid for it and took a deed conveyanced to David Meacham, Trustee.

"May 21, 1807. N.E. Quarter of Section No. 24 purchased and conveyanced to David Meacham.
"Sept. 22, 1807. 100 acres purchased of Isaac Morris; deed made out to Peter Pease, Trustee."

It was not, however, until Shaker products began to have a wide sale among non-Shakers that the trustees attained the full measure of their power. As the various communities grew and enlarged their activities, the trustees came to occupy positions almost as important as those held by the Elders. They had even more prestige in the eyes of the "world's people" because the material prosperity the Shakers were achieving was far more impressive to "the world" than any spiritual attainments. To the Shakers, of course, the spirit was still preëminent, yet the recognition won by the excellence of their material products and manufactures could hardly help bringing some satisfaction to them.

There was a danger here that the trustees, being more exposed to the contaminating influences of "the world" than were the rest of the Shakers, might acquire worldly attitudes toward wealth and ambition. To offset this, they were required to travel always in threes when they went to the "great and wicked cities" to trade, and they were not allowed to remain away more than four weeks at a time. While absent from home they were not to engage in unnecessary conversation with the "world's people," and they were expected on their return to report all conversations and actions to the elders. Sometimes written cash accounts were kept; sometimes only verbal reports were demanded.

Another duty performed by the trustees was the managing of the family household expenditures. These included upkeep, clothing, food, materials and tools for the workshops and the farm, the handling of charity funds, etc. Each Shaker society and each separate family within the society handled its money affairs separately and dealt scrupulously with all the other families or societies. A large amount of intercommunity business was transacted, as well as that carried on with the outside world. Although the whole amount of money raised by any family became theoretically subject to disposal by the elders of that family and the ministry of the community to which the family belonged, actually those who had had most to do with the raising of it were often allowed some voice as to the use made of it.

At New Lebanon in 1836, the female trustees or "deaconesses at the office" were permitted by the ministry to keep their own accounts of money earned by the special labors of the Shaker sisters, and to "make purchases of such articles as they need, exclusive of the general purchases made for the use of the family." As a rule, however, everything went into the common pool. And any Shaker who desired any necessary article such as shoes or clothing had only to ask for it and feel reasonably certain that his desire would be promptly granted. He did his allotted work and he had no economic worries. The trustees looked after everything for him. This was indeed security.

If the elders found it necessary to guard the trustees against temptations when they went abroad, they became aware that there were also temptations lurking at home. Many of the humbler "hand-minded" Believers found the practical trustees more understandable and more admirable than the spiritually, and sometimes pontifically, aloof elders and eldresses. Occasionally a trustee became puffed up with his own importance and was seized with a desire to shine even more brightly in the eyes of his fellow-Shakers. In such cases he was likely (if lucky and of outstanding ability) to find himself transferred to another community at some distance away; if his talents were too small to be of much value, or if his fall into temptation had been too great, he was simply demoted from his post of trustee back to the ranks of the "hand-minded."

Even the elders themselves were tempted at times to encroach on the field of the trustees and venture into the realm of finance. They were dealt with in the same way as the trustees. Such was the case with Elder Augustus Grosvenor of Harvard, Massachusetts, who let his ambition and enthusiasm run away with him when he built the forty-room Rural Home at Harvard and saddled the Believers there with a $25,000 debt. The Shaker conscience was tender; the consciousness of sin and disgrace so overwhelmed Augustus when he found himself stripped of his title and reduced to tending the swine, that he soon died of a broken heart. The expression is used literally here; for it is recorded that an autopsy revealed a cleft of full three inches in that organ.

On the other hand, there were many trustees who administered the business affairs of their societies so successfully that they not only increased the property value of the Shaker holdings, but won the respect and admiration of all who knew them. David Parker of New Hampshire and Richard McNemar of Ohio are outstanding examples. David Parker, who entered the Shaker society of Canterbury as a child of ten in 1817, was appointed trustee when only nineteen and soon became well known as one of the most active and honorable business men of New Hampshire. It was under his general oversight that the two New Hampshire societies of Canterbury and Enfield reached the peak of their material prosperity.

An interesting picture of him is given in the "Boston Journal" of 1862. "Everybody knows David Parker, one of the chief managers at Shaker Village, New Hampshire [Canterbury]. . . . Mr. Parker is an upright man. Nobody except some poor specimen of humanity who may, perchance, have undertaken the difficult task of outwitting him in a bargain, ever pretended anything to the contrary. . . . He is a man of business. Now I see him at half-past eight o'clock in the evening, after the arrival of the last train from Boston, ready for a hasty supper at the Eagle Hotel [Concord, New Hampshire], and then a drive of twelve miles to Canterbury to sleep. Now you will find him looking over Shaker wood lots in the wilds of New York. Again you will meet him in Washington, Buffalo, Philadelphia or New York, always with an eye to business, whether he happens to make a call on the President or the proprietor of a wholesale drug store."

Besides Parker's duties toward woodlots in western New York, city outlets for Shaker herbs and other products, and intervention at Washington anent Shaker pacifist attitudes toward the war, he was obliged at times to turn his hand to defending the Shakers before the New Hampshire legislature against certain false charges of improper and immoral conduct that were brought against them. He handled such a case in 1848 and came off victorious, with his prestige and that of the Shakers much strengthened throughout the state. Since most of the attacks on the Shakers, whenever and wherever made, were prompted by the property motive, it is interesting and illuminating to read a statement made by Parker in regard to the amount of money passing through Shaker hands at Canterbury in the twenty years from 1826 to 1840. The statement covers the expenditures of one family only—the Church family.

Amount of property received into the Church family in 20 yrs. [This means property donated.] $961.62

Amount paid out in clothes	$3268.68
" " " " cloth and tools	$ 362.70
" " " " cash	$1373.56
Charities.	
To Insane Hospital	$500.00
To the Irish Famine	$109.38
To sundry	$803.85
To other Shaker Societies	$5469.67
To North family at Canterbury	$2000.00

This totals $13,887.84, or about $694.39 per year, hardly a large enough budget to make the Shakers the financial menace that some of their enemies accused them of being.

Nevertheless, enough lawsuits were brought against the Shakers from time to time to make the handling of these suits an important part of the trustees' duties. As early as 1811 the Ohio legislature passed an act providing that the property of married men who joined the Shakers should be given to the wife or children in part *or in whole, according to the discretion of the court.* There was a further provision for the fining of the Shakers for "enticing" any married man or woman to join them. The "world's people" were constantly irritated at the thought of property being diverted to the Shakers, and they kept thinking up new ways of getting it back.

Many lawsuits were brought by individuals who either fancied they had a real grievance against the Believers, or else thought they saw a good way of making some profit out of such litigation. For a time the Shakers were looked upon as "legal prey" by some of their more unscrupulous neighbors. They were driven into defending themselves at law—a course which was repugnant to them and which was entered only as a last resort. After being haled constantly into court and fleeced out of several thousands of dollars by crooked lawyers and hostile judges they decided to revise their covenant again and make it legally airtight.

The new covenant differed very little in intent from the original one. The phraseology, however, was more exactly legal, and the duties and responsibilities of the trustees were more carefully defined. This revised covenant had, of course, to be signed by all the members of all the families. Some of the Believers, especially in the southern communities which were less tractable from the start than the older northern groups, balked at signing the new instrument. It required a man of tact and experience to handle the matter. Richard McNemar, who had been in the forefront of all the struggles and who knew that region as few others of the Shakers knew it, was chosen to be the man. The final revision of the covenant was made in 1829. As it was not till four or five years later that all the Believers in the Southwest were induced to sign it, Richard's task was not an easy one. Nevertheless, he accomplished it, and henceforth the legal rights of the Shakers in regard to the holding of property were clearly established.

Richard McNemar became, in fact, the official "trouble shooter" for the whole Southwestern region. This made him in some ways a more influential man than David Darrow who had been sent down from New Lebanon to be leading elder of Union Village and head of the southern church. David depended on Richard in all things, and Richard never failed him. Whenever there was conflict or confusion, whether among the Believers themselves or between them and "the world," there Richard was sent to soothe, straighten out, or defend. When Calvin Morrell was "scrouged out" (in his own hurt words) of the leadership at Whitewater on account of old age, Richard had to pacify Calvin and smooth the way for Archibald Meacham, his successor. The speech Robert Wickliffe made before the Kentucky senate in defense of the Pleasant Hill, Kentucky, Shakers was written by Richard. And when the ill-fated Shaker community of Busro was left leaderless by the death of John Dunlavy, it was Richard who took the long, hard trip across Indiana again to assume charge and to make the final decision of removal from that unhealthy site.

The most spectacular incident of Richard's services as representative of the Society of Believers was a case in which the Shakers hit back successfully in an unanswerable technique of their own against the many harassing attacks from the "world's people." The "Western Star" of Lebanon, Ohio—a newspaper which had been consistently hostile to the Shakers—had grown more and more vindictive, supporting, and even instigating many unfounded charges of cruelty, immorality, etc., against them. These charges had actually resulted in mob attacks and in lawsuits. The people of Dayton, on the contrary, had always been friendly to the Believers. In 1817, just after the Shakers had won a lawsuit for which the "Western Star" was responsible, David Darrow received a command from heaven to put a curse on Lebanon and a blessing on Dayton. He chose Richard McNemar and Francis Bedle to administer this command. Richard and Francis demurred a bit at carrying out this order. After all, these were their home towns, so to speak, while David was an importation from New York. Nevertheless, they were morally obligated to obey the ruling elder.

On the morning of the day appointed, they went on horseback to Lebanon and rode up and down the principal

street waving their hats and pronouncing the Shaker curse
on the town. In the afternoon, they appeared on the main
street of Dayton, where they again waved their broad-
brimmed Shaker hats as they rode up and down blessing
Dayton in the name of the Shakers. Richard being the
orator and man of action that he was, undoubtedly put his
usual gusto into the ceremony. At any rate, he and Francis
did such a thorough job of administering both curse and
blessing that from that day Lebanon dwindled and Dayton
grew. Dayton's prosperity may in a sense be attributed to
the Shakers.

There were other lawsuits against the Shakers besides
those brought on charges of immoral conduct or for recovery
of property. There was the matter of military service, poll
taxes, alienation of the affections of husbands whose wives
charged that the estrangement had been caused by Shaker
proselyting. In Ohio, in New York and in New Hampshire,
to mention three, the Shakers had to appear before the
state legislatures to explain their position in regard to military service, etc. If they really were American citizens why
wouldn't they fight for their country and why didn't they
vote? In some cases the Shakers found good friends among
the lawyers and lawmakers. John Bretherton of Kentucky
and Durbin Ward of New Hampshire, for instance, pled
their cause with both ability and fervor and helped establish the principle that these Believers had the right to act
as their consciences dictated.

Even the sensational charges brought against the Shakers
by such emotionally unstable people as the woman, Mary
Dyer, of New Hampshire or Eunice Chapman of New
York, who both claimed that the Shakers had taken their
children away from them, were discredited as time passed
and the Shakers became known and understood for the

moral and industrious, though eccentric, people they were. And it was mainly through the trustees that this understanding was brought about. The "world's people" could understand the business side of Shakerism, the practical results that came out of that strange belief. They could appreciate and even envy the security achieved in the Shaker communities, even while still looking askance at the spiritual adventure on which the material prosperity was based.

Contradictory as it may seem, family life was emphasized and cherished by the Shakers. The word family had, of course, a larger meaning for them than the usually accepted sense. The world's use of the term seemed narrow and selfish to the Believers. To be brothers and sisters in a consecrated communion of the spirit was to be joined not only in human comradeship with one another, but also in a spiritual relationship with Mother Ann and all Believers living and dead—a mystical fellowship that reached back to the beginning of man's yearning toward God, and forward into Eternity. It was part of the mission of the Millennial Church to make the Shaker communal life a practical demonstration of the earthly Utopia they preached. And since the family was a natural grouping of the human race, they continued in their growing communities the family divisions with which many of them had begun.

New Lebanon, largest of all the Shaker societies, numbered eight families at one time, calling some of these by the names of the originators: Rufus Clark's family; John Bishop's family; the Walker or West family. The average number of families in a society was three, and was likely to include a *Church* or *Center* family with the others designated by the direction in which they lay from the *Church*. Enfield, New Hampshire had a *Church* family, a *North* family and a *South* family. Each single family contained anywhere from thirty to ninety persons. The church family was usually the home of the Ministry, that is, of the ruling elders and eldresses. Of the other families, one was the Novitiate Order where applicants for admission resided until they had proved to their own satisfaction and that of the elders that they were ready and fit for the Church Order. Each family was like a tiny village, self-contained and separate in most of its week-day activities.

As the Shaker communities grew in membership and possessions and activities, the communal life fell into ordered patterns of everyday existence. The earliest dwelling houses were built in divided fashion with separate doors, stairways and apartments for the brothers and the sisters, the men using the left side, the women the right. It was the same with the churches; the left entrance was for the men and the right for the women. At mealtime, the two sexes ate in the same dining room, but at separate tables. All relations between the brethren and the sisters were carefully regulated and formalized. Even the elders and eldresses were required to conform to the rule that a third party "of over ten years" must be present at any meeting between two members of opposite sexes. If elders and eldresses travelled together to visit other Shaker communities there were always at least two of each sex in the party.

In the beginning, when husbands and wives and sometimes whole families consecrated themselves together to Shakerism, these rules were not needed—at least so far as the Shakers themselves were concerned. The fanatical devotion of the early converts to their chosen life of asceticism was in itself a safeguard against any deviation from that path. But the increasing number of applicants during the early and middle eighteen-hundreds included some who were looking for economic security rather than spiritual adventure. These could not be wholly depended upon without some regulations for conduct. And besides, the very enforcing of such rules at all times was a safeguard against criticism by "the world." It was found expedient to require of the elders the same conformity as was demanded from the rank and file.

The Shaker day started at four-thirty a.m. in the summer and an hour later during the winter months. When the sound of the rising bell was heard through the dwelling houses where from four to eight of the Believers slept in rooms like small dormitories, each brother in the left half of the house and each sister in the right half, got out of bed, knelt for a moment in silent prayer, then set two chairs back to back, laid the pillows on the seats of the chairs, stripped the bed, folded the bed clothing neatly, and laid it piece by piece across the chair backs to air. Fifteen minutes was allowed for dressing. After all had left their rooms, the sisters in charge of the chamber work came in to sweep the room and make the beds. The sweeping was quickly done since the slatted chairs could be hung out of the way on the wall pegs that encircled the room, and the beds, being provided with large wooden rollers, were easily movable as were also the woven or braided mats that lay on the smooth wooden floor. Other sisters on kitchen duty were busy getting breakfast, while the brothers tended to the heavier chores such as bringing in wood, making fires, feeding the stock, milking, etc. Since breakfast time was an hour and a half later than rising time, all household chores were finished by the time the breakfast bell called the brothers and sisters to table.

Some of the Shaker dining rooms had two doors on the left for the brothers and two on the right for the sisters. After

149

the Believers had taken their stand by the long trestle table, they knelt by their chairs for a moment of silent prayer. The tables were set so that each four people were served as a unit, thus avoiding the need of passing or reaching. There was no conversation at all during mealtime. When all had finished, they rose, knelt once again in silent thanks for what they had received, and went out as they had come in, each to go to his or her morning's work.

The sisters attended to the housework in turn, each serving a month at a time in cooking, washing, ironing, etc. Aside from these and other household tasks such as preserving, butter and cheese making, and mending both for themselves and for the brethren, the women had charge of the spinning, education of children, tailoring, bonnet and hat making, basket making, etc. The men went to their work in the shops, the mills, on the farm or in the orchard. Even the elders were not excused from manual work. James Whittaker had been a weaver; Job Bishop, head of the church in New Hampshire, was a chairmaker; John Vance of Alfred, Maine, was a tailor; James S. Prescott of North Union was a mason; Richard McNemar was a bookbinder as well as a cabinetmaker.

At ten minutes before twelve, the bell again summoned the Believers to leave their various tasks and present themselves for the twelve o'clock dinner. The afternoons were usually spent like the mornings, except when special religious services were held. Supper was at six, and bedtime at nine or nine-thirty. The evenings were given over to planned "diversions" of a wholesome—often religious—nature, the same evening or evenings each week being set apart for the same special kinds of meetings. On Monday, for instance, there might be a general meeting at which selected articles from the newspapers were read—general news of world politics, scientific reports, information of a social or economic nature. Many of the later Shaker leaders were deeply interested in theories of sociology, economics, government, etc.

On Tuesday they might meet in the assembly hall for singing and marching; on Wednesday in small "union meetings" for conversation; on Thursday all together for a "laboring meeting," which was a regular religious service when the Believers "labored to get good" through song and dance; on Friday, for learning new songs and hymns; on Saturday, for worship. On Sunday evening, which was considered not to be a part of Sunday since Sunday theoretically ended at sundown, they had another union meeting, visiting in each others' rooms. Three or more sisters called on the same number of brethren who were waiting in their rooms to receive them. The two sexes sat facing each other in parallel rows, five feet apart, their hands folded on clean white handkerchiefs which they had spread on their laps. They conversed and they sang together, and the conversation was as near to small talk as they ever came in their serious-minded lives.

Sunday was a day apart: *the* day of the week. The sober and industrious craftsmen and farmers and houseworkers of the working week were changed on Sunday to a band of excited adventurers. They laid aside their weekday reserve along with its duties and regulations to join in an emotional outburst of prayer and praise. They savored to the full the "gifts" that were brought them from the spirit world by those blessed ones who were chosen to receive them. Gifts of singing and movement were the most general, though there were also gifts of tongues, when the inspired ones spoke or sang in unknown languages, and sometimes there were gifts of imaginary baskets of fruits and flowers. The ritual varied from week to week, sometimes according to instructions from the Ministry at New Lebanon, sometimes through spontaneous leading from the spirit world, but it always included music and the march or the dance.

Most of the Sabbath day was spent in worship, whether by families in the separate family assembly halls or all together in the meeting house that belonged to the whole society. No work at all was done on Sunday except what was absolutely necessary. Even the food had to be prepared the day before, though it might be heated before being eaten. Such necessary chores as the feeding and care of the livestock and such emergencies as the gathering of a crop that might otherwise be ruined by rain, were also permitted. But Sunday was definitely a consecrated day, the holy day that was likewise a holiday on which the souls of the Believers went adventuring into spiritual realms far removed from the practical domain of their daily physical lives.

In the matter of food the Shakers practised frugality and restraint. Mother Ann always deplored waste; her followers laid down rules to prevent it. Nothing was to be left on the plate when a Shaker had finished his meal. He could help himself to however much he wanted, but he must eat it all after he had taken it. Even strangers who dined with the Shakers were expected to conform in this matter. Lest there be any misunderstanding about it, a set of printed rules was posted in the dining room. The Shaker fare was plain, but wholesome and plentiful. It tended more and more toward vegetarianism. In some communities there were separate tables laid for the meat eaters and for those who did without it. Pork was forbidden throughout Shakerdom after the early years. A Shaker health authority stated that after discontinuing the use of pork, there was a marked decrease in deaths from cancer. Always on a Shaker table was found plenty of fruit. Dairy products—milk, butter, cheese—were much used and plenty of eggs. In the early days, wines and other alcoholic drinks were used sparingly at table or for medicinal purposes; later this practice was given up, as was also to a great extent, the use of tobacco. In many communities neither tea nor coffee were served.

The Shaker costume went through many changes from the earliest days when the Believers wore what they had and were thankful for that, to present-day dress which conforms in a general way to the style of the age. Its most characteristic period, however, was during the middle part of the nineteenth century, the era of greatest prosperity and uniformity when the Believers were not only prescribing the details of dress for all their members but also manufacturing the various articles of apparel themselves. In this period, which lasted from about 1830 till well on toward the end of the century, the costumes of both men and women bore a marked resemblance to the costumes of Breton peasants.

The men wore broad, stiff-brimmed hats of white or grey felt in winter, and straw in summer. Their shirts were buttoned neatly at the throat and worn usually without neckties. A long, rather light-blue coat with many buttons and buttonholes was used for formal wear. The women wore gowns of various soft colors: grey, blue, brown or plum-color with close-fitting bodices and many-pleated ankle-length skirts over which long narrow aprons were worn. Around their shoulders was either a folded and pleated kerchief or a short round cape added for the obvious purpose of concealing the shape of the bust.

A long, hooded Shaker cape was worn outdoors in cold weather. In the house a close-fitting net cap covered the hair completely, and over this a deep sunbonnet, sometimes called a "Shaker bonnet," was used for out-of-door wear. This bonnet was made of woven straw or palm leaf with ties in front and a little silk cape behind of some soft, bright color such as pink, lavender or light blue. Contrary to general belief, the Shakers were very fond of color. For winter use, the bonnet was made of cloth, padded. The high shoes worn by the early Shaker women were high-heeled; after 1853 a low-heeled type came into general use. In some communities and on certain occasions, white dresses were prescribed for the women to wear in church. The "world's people," however, were most accustomed to seeing them in the costume described above.

The Shaker practice of visiting about from community to community was partly responsible for the uniformity in dress, food and habits of life. It was a custom encouraged by the New Lebanon Ministry, for, besides giving opportunity for mutual inspiration and strengthening union through fellowship, it provided a legitimate form of variety and excitement in a life of unrelieved daily routine. It was a great moment for younger brothers and sisters when they were allowed to go visiting with the elders. In the beginning this was done on horseback; later, high, three-seated carriages were used. These had doors very much like automobile doors with pockets on them and tops, but no sides, to keep out the weather. The carriage would be driven up to the stone mounting-platform by a Shaker brother, and six other Shakers would step into it—three to sit on the broad back seat which was entered by folding back one of the two hinged middle seats, two in the middle and one with the driver.

It was a good twelve-hour trip to go the forty miles between Canterbury and Enfield, New Hampshire, in this carriage drawn by two horses—a journey through foreign territory to another Shaker outpost where the travellers were welcomed by their own. Aurelia Mace, writing of a later visit, by train, from Sabbathday Lake to Alfred, Maine, says, "a week to rest from the cares and burdens incident to home life that, during the past season, from the rush of business, was almost overpowering. Instead of caring for others, all are striving to care for you." A peaceful and ordered routine of daily work broken each week by the emotional release of worship, and varied on rare occasions by the excitement of a journey to other societies of fellow Believers, then the quiet happiness of the return to their own beloved homes—this was the pattern of Shaker life.

The Shaker stress on habits conducive to good health sounds slightly inconsistent with their belief that the body was of slight worth compared with the spirit. But the Shakers were always a strange combination of the practical and the mystical. Even though they believed they were living in the beginning of the millennium, that the second coming of Christ to which people had so long looked forward had already taken place, and that they would soon leave behind forever this world of the flesh to be united with him and with the other Believers who had gone before, they never used that belief as an excuse for neglecting the material and physical aspects of their earthly life as did the Millerites and the Second Adventists. Mother Ann had said, "Do all your work as though you had a thousand years to live, and as you would if you knew you must die tomorrow." The Shaker lands and buildings bore evidence that this precept had been obeyed; it behooved the Believers to take equal care of the bodies that were allotted them during their earthly sojourn. The thought given to health among the Shakers was a logical result.

Cleanliness, order and simple habits of life were the foundation on which the traditional good health and longevity of the Shakers were built. Their cleanliness was a byword in any region where they lived. Their houses were so constructed and so furnished that whatever dirt might collect was plainly visible to the most casual glance and could not be overlooked. There were no elaborate moldings in the rooms, no pictures on the walls, no ornamentation on the furniture. The handmade rugs on the floors were removable and washable, the windows were uncurtained. Around the walls of every room, at about five or five and a half feet from the floor, were one or more flat narrow boards in which were set rows of wooden pegs to hold chairs when the floors were cleared for sweeping, or racks for tools, or garments. Each outside door had its footscraper fastened to one end of the top step for cleaning the shoes of the entrants. Each stove had its dustpan and brush beside it. One of the first Shaker industries to be developed was the broom industry. There was neither reason nor excuse for dirt.

The word orderliness was coupled with that of cleanliness in speaking of the Shakers. Their buildings were planned for orderly communal living. Most of the rooms had built-in cabinets and drawers, designed to hold the tools or the supplies required for the use to which the room was put. There were drawers of all sizes and shapes: drawers for seeds and seed bags in the seed sorting room, drawers for herbs in the nurse room or the herb shop, drawers in the retiring rooms. The cobblers' shops had racks on the walls to hold lasts of shoes, for each Shaker brother or sister had his or her own last. Although the Believers never tried to make life easy for themselves on the spiritual plane, they spared no pains to provide the best facilities for work whether of shop or household. The kitchen at Canterbury contains an oven with a revolving rack that made baking easy and safe. It was the same with the buildings that housed the stock.

The best barns in the country were the Shaker barns, which were fully as clean as the houses and were often equipped with the latest improvements. Nearly all the Shaker barns were built with entrances on two or more levels, so that the hay could be thrown down instead of pitched up when it was unloaded into the mows. Elijah Wilds of Shirley, Massachusetts, caused the water which ran to the drinking trough of the cattle to be warmed in winter, believing it was better for them thus. At Canterbury, the big cow barn that housed a hundred cows was wood-ceiled and sheathed. The milking machines with which it was at one time equipped, were later taken out after the Shakers decided they were bad for the cows. This barn aroused the recent admiration of a visitor from Montana (a state which might be supposed to know something about the care of stock!) for the individual trapdoors in the floor behind the stalls to facilitate cleaning them.

Cleanliness and order were a good beginning for the attainment and preservation of bodily health, which was further maintained by regular and simple living habits. Plain, wholesome food eaten in moderation when hungry was a preventative against indigestion. The taboo on pork was partly for religious, partly for health reasons; the use of meat generally was considered less beneficial than a diet of dairy products and especially fruits and vegetables. Elder Frederick Evans looked forward to a day when all would be vegetarians. The Shaker *Manifesto* contained many articles about diet and especially diet in relation to health.

Certain ones among the Shakers seemed to have a special power of healing. Many of them knew a good deal about the properties of herbs and were versed in the use of commonsense remedies for the curing of colds or digestive upsets. They had theories about the care of the eyes; they invented an electrical machine for the treatment of rheumatism. Occasionally a medical student was found among their converts. They had no scruples against calling in a doctor from among the "world's people" when they really needed one; but as a rule they were quite competent to handle the few cases of illness that appeared among them. Simple food, regular hours, bodily activity, order, cleanliness—the human machine ran smoothly under this régime. As Elder Frederick Evans said, "I hold that no man who lives as we do has a right to be ill before he is sixty; if he suffers from disease before that, he is in fault."

Always there were some children among the Shakers. In the early days the converts frequently brought their entire families in with them. Other children were added from time to time either in the same way or by temporary adoption at the request of parents or guardians who were unwilling or unable to care for them. According to the Shaker covenant, all such children had the right on coming of age to decide whether or not they wished to remain with the Shakers. Many of them chose to go back to the world. Nevertheless, while they were there they were in the Shakers' care, and they had to be given some kind of education. What should that education be?

The Shakers for the most part mistrusted a too great development of the intellect. Mother Ann had said "hands to work and hearts to God"; she had made no mention of the mind. The teaching of the Shaker children was thus turned mainly into two channels: religious training and the learning of a trade. The Shakers were not wholly oblivious, however, to the need for some book-learning. Even if they had been, American democracy was founded partly on a belief in the right of all children to an education and the Shakers were quite willing to conform to this American ideal. In some ways their early schools were more efficient than many of the town schools. They used the Lancastrian system which was much in vogue in the first part of the nineteenth century, and according to which some of the teaching was done by the older pupils, thus giving more individual attention to the learners. Recitation in unison was also much used. Some of the Shaker teachers were even placed on the town salary list and taught the children of the "world's people" along with the little Shaker children. From the beginning, Shaker schools were under inspection by district officials and were scrupulous in their conformity to the school laws of the county and state.

The New Lebanon, New York, Shaker community gave some teaching to its children almost from the start. In 1808 they supplemented this with voluntary evening schools for adult members, and in 1817 a public school for all the children was formed with a four-month summer term for the girls and a winter term of the same length for the boys. Reading, writing, spelling, grammar, geography and arithmetic were the subjects taught; later on, music, algebra, astronomy and agricultural chemistry were added to the early curriculum. New Lebanon built its first school house in 1839; Canterbury, N.H., had already done so in 1823; other societies followed suit. This was at a period when public schools as we know them were just beginning to be established in the larger cities of this country.

As a rule, the Shaker sisters taught the girls, and the brothers, the boys. The use of any kind of physical force for discipline was frowned upon, although now and then there were cases where punishment had to be administered. Usually, however, the Shakers refused to take or to keep such children as were too refractory to respond to gentle and reasonable treatment. Here, again, were often found easy grounds for complaint against the Shakers. It was all too easy for "the world" to choose to believe the stories of some incorrigible boy or girl whom the Shakers had found it necessary to send back to parents or guardians. John Woods of Ohio and Kentucky, who wrote *Shakerism Unmasked* in 1826, stated as one of his reasons for complaint against the Shakers that they would not let him use corporal punishment in handling some of the boys in his care while he was a member of the Society, while accusing them at the same time of various kinds of cruelty.

On the whole, the "world's people" and the Shakers found it possible to coöperate rather closely in matters of education of children. This state of harmony existed in Enfield, New Hampshire, where Elder William Wilson was made a member of the school committee, and also in Harvard, Massachusetts, where Elder Elijah Myrick served in a similar capacity. Nevertheless, the Shakers erred on the side of under- rather than over-education, believing that the "hand-minded," who were always in the majority, were better off in a craft they could understand and manage than floundering in intellectual waters which were manifestly too deep for them. They might be willing for their leaders to be men of learning, but they doubted the advantage of too much mental training for most of the followers. Even in the leaders, sometimes, they distrusted braininess. Too much mental stimulation seemed like a dangerously close approach to the excitements and temptations of "the world." Perhaps the thing they were subconsciously fearing was what is currently termed rationalization. Only simple faith and a single mind could keep the Shakers untroubled in the straight and narrow path they had chosen to follow. Black was black and white was white; the grey of doubts that often assail the adolescent mind faced with a suddenly broadened intellectual horizon would have led the Believers far astray into a morass from which there might have been no returning to the trail that pointed toward Ann Lee's Utopia.

IX. SHAKERS AS CITIZENS

ALTHOUGH the Shakers consistently remained apart and aloof from the neighboring farmers and townspeople by whom they were surrounded, they were never uncoöperative in the matters of taxes, poor relief or local improvements. Since they believed that their interest in the things of the spirit might be diverted to worldly channels if they became involved in political issues, they chose not to vote. They were content to follow Christ's admonition, "Render unto Caesar the things that are Caesar's and unto God the things that are God's," for they paid their taxes promptly and cheerfully, and then assumed that they were free to turn away from the temporal government of the country to that spiritual régime which seemed always most real to them. Since they neither voted nor sought to hold office, since they supported their own poor and contributed to the support of the town poor and since they performed their share of the town work on roads and bridges, they felt that they had a right to devote themselves, their services and the rest of their property to the Lord in the way they saw fit.

In 1872, the Canterbury society, with an assessed valuation of $31,000, was paying taxes in four towns. Its total tax for that year, including state, county, town and school taxes, was $1,103.58. Although the society was diminishing in numbers, it continued uncomplainingly to meet its annual tax bills, until its decrease both in members and in property value forced it to ask for amelioration. In 1939, on petition from the Shakers, their taxes were finally wholly remitted by the town. Nevertheless, the Shakers still make a voluntary payment of as much as they can afford.

The relations between the Canterbury Shakers and the townspeople have always been friendly. Except for the two matters of military service and the refusal of the town during several years to let them become a school district by themselves, there is no record of conflict between them.

During Caleb Dyer's trusteeship at Enfield, New Hampshire, from 1838 to 1863, the Shakers were at the height of their prosperity and success. They owned thirty or forty milch cows, six or eight yoke of oxen and as many more steers, and, before 1849, a fancy herd of swine. They were able to pay as much as $1,100 for a merino buck and two ewes in order to develop a fine strain of sheep of which at one time they owned three thousand. Their fields were the best kept in town, their crops were abundant, their houses and workshops were furnished with the latest labor-saving devices.

Their membership at the peak was over three hundred persons. During a period of twenty years they took in and cared for one hundred and seven of the town's children. They coöperated with the town in the matter of education, care of the poor, work on the roads, etc. They paid one-fifth of all the town taxes. They were prosperous and influential. In fact, their influence was great enough to enable them to change the industrial development of the town by dictating the route the railroad should take when it was continued north from Concord to Enfield and White River Junction in 1847. And their wealth enabled them to undertake and accomplish the building of a half-mile bridge across the middle of Lake Mascoma to make the railroad station easily accessible to them.

The logical route for the railroad, and the one that many of the townspeople felt (and still feel) it should have taken, was along the Fourth New Hampshire turnpike through the center of the Shaker property. Although this would have benefited the Shakers commercially, since it came at the time of their greatest expansion, it would have destroyed the tranquillity of their site. The Shakers consistently placed spiritual advantages ahead of material, so they persuaded the railroad to lay its tracks on the opposite side of Lake Mascoma. Being practical people, they implemented their plea with the gift of a strip of land on the northeast margin of their property across the lake from their village. The grateful railroad named one of its first four engines *The Shaker*, gave Caleb Dyer a lifetime pass and promised him that all trains would always stop at Enfield. This promise was kept till long after the Shakers left Enfield, and is still potent in assuring Enfield better service than other nearby towns of like size and importance. The railroad, however, changed the commerce of the town to such an extent that the south part of it—formerly active and thriving —has now changed places with the north side where the railroad is. And some of the south-enders still hold this against Caleb Dyer. North Enfield, however, felt only gratitude toward the Shakers.

If, however, the Shakers were to profit at all themselves from the coming of the railroad, it was necessary for them to have better access to it than that provided by ten or twelve miles of poor country roads. It would have been in vain for the Shakers to expect the town to build them a bridge, since more than half of the townspeople were annoyed (to put it mildly) with the Shakers for inducing the railroad to enter the north end of Enfield instead of proceeding along the Fourth New Hampshire turnpike over which the stagecoaches from Boston had always run. So the Believers undertook the difficult engineering project of building what was to be known for nearly a hundred years as Shaker Bridge. How difficult the task was to be they did not realize when they started it in the winter of 1847.

The lake is about half a mile wide at the point chosen, nearly midway of its six-mile length. A trestle bridge was first planned in consultation with a Boston engineer, John Clarke. "Boston John," as he was called, was one of the best and most experienced bridge builders available, for the Shakers, being perfectionists themselves, always demanded the best and were willing and able to pay for it. It soon became apparent, however, that John's first plan was impracticable, since beneath the thirty-foot depth of water lay thirty or forty feet more of mud. The Shakers were used to meeting problems and so was Boston John. Two rows of sixty-foot piles taken from the stand of old growth pines on the montainside were driven thirty feet apart into the soft mud at the bottom of the lake to mark the line of the bridge. When winter came and the lake was frozen over other logs were laid crosswise between these piles, spiked together, and spiked also to other longer logs laid at right angles to them outside the driven piles. Stones and gravel were carted onto the ice by oxen and piled on top of these rough rafts which sank with their loads to the bottom when the ice which held them was cut or melted in the spring. This process was repeated till at last a comparatively solid roadbed reached from the west to the east shore.

The bridge was finished in the summer of 1849 and offered to the town which, at a late summer town meeting, voted to accept it and pay the Shakers $5,000 for it. The Shakers agreed to this figure and promised furthermore to keep up the bridge for ten years in place of paying a highway tax. The upkeep of it constituted a real problem and expense, because owing to the nature of the lake bottom, the bridge subsided from time to time in one place or another and had to be counterbalanced on the opposite side. Divers who saw it from below shook their heads and said no one would drive over it who could see the underside. Yet the bridge stood for ninety years until the hurricane of 1938 broke it in two. In the summer of 1939 a new bridge was started by W.P.A. labor to take its place, and when the old logs were removed to make room for the new H beams, they looked to be in perfect state of preservation with the original spikes made in the Shaker workshops still in them. Many of these old logs were used again and are now helping support the New Shaker Bridge.

The two Maine Shaker societies at Alfred and New Gloucester have always enjoyed harmonious relations with the two towns in which they are respectively situated. From the beginning, when the Shakers and the Rickers swapped land, and Father James Whittaker was made welcome by the best people of the town, the attitude of the "world's people" was friendly. Perhaps Maine, being a state of individualists, has a natural respect for eccentrics. In any case, it has a record of having treated the Shakers well.

They were always welcome visitors at the Poland Spring House, whither, in 1895 they were specially invited guests of the Rickers on the occasion of the dedication of the Maine State Building (from the Columbian exposition at Chicago) which was reerected near the Poland Spring House. There were senators and members of congress present beside the governor. One of the speakers, Senator Eugene Hale, said in apostrophizing the building, "My young friend, if you are wise and sensible stay right where you are and thank the Lord you are out of Chicago. You ought to feel like a man who has just emerged from an election riot in the lower streets of New York City, and has launched himself into the placidity of a Shaker meeting here in the state of Maine."

The Sabbathday Lake society at New Gloucester allowed people of all Cumberland County to make use of its mill privilege for sawing, grinding, planing, etc. In 1891, when a sensational attack on the Alfred Shakers appeared in the pages of the "Boston Herald" on the basis of the statement of an incorrigible girl who had been cared for by them, the best citizens of Alfred rose in a body to protest and to bear witness to the good character of the Shakers.

It was the same in other Shaker communities as time passed by and the "world's people" grew used to seeing the Shaker brothers and sisters go quietly about their business, paying their taxes unprotestingly, helping wherever they could, asking only to be left unmolested. The townspeople came so completely to accept this experiment in practical communism which was being tried before their eyes that they took it as a matter of course. They would have been startled—many of them—at hearing the Shakers called by the terrifying name of communists. To the "world's people" the Believers were only a group of eccentric but practical and efficient farmers who chose to believe in some queer kind of religion.

The Shakers met the demands of state and national government in the same spirit manifested by them toward town and local authority. They declined steadfastly to vote. In some states this meant refusal to pay a poll tax. It also brought up the question of liability for military service. It was not till the Civil War that the legal status of the Believers as conscientious objectors was established. Before this, envious neighbors were never slow to argue that these non-conformists in their midst could not be real patriots or they would not refuse to do their twin civic duties of voting and bearing arms. If they were not patriots it was obvious that they must be disloyal to the state.

The Shakers found themselves involved from time to time in lawsuits to define their status as citizens. The three periods when their loyalty was most in question were during and just after the Revolution (when the leaders were definitely *not* American by birth), in the era before and after the War of 1812, and at the time of the Civil War. In each case, the popular state of mind was sufficiently troubled to foster suspicion of any group of eccentrics, and if further motive were needed, there was always (after the earliest days) the property motive. These people were wealthy, or so their neighbors said, surveying the prosperous lands and buildings; what did they do with their money that they refused to pay a poll tax? And what right had they to the protection of the American government and army if they would not do their part toward furnishing men for purposes of defense?

A pamphlet called *Shakerism Detected* was published in 1811 by James Smith of Ohio—an apostate from Shakerism. It is interesting for two reasons: first, as an instance of the kind of accusation that was being made against the Believers in the early nineteenth century, and, second, as a typical example of the charges that fear-ridden and hysterical accusers always make in any age against any form of economic or religious belief that they dislike. It might have been written today. "The Shakers are a hidden people; they say they are not of this world, and all others they call *the world*, and have no connection with them only to buy and sell what they can, so as to make gain and bring money into their treasury. I believe their leaders live in ease and luxury and conceal their principal views from the lower class, who are slaves. . . . They condemn all religion except their own as anti-Christian; they also condemn all government both civil and ecclesiastical except their own. Let Shakerism predominate and it will extirpate Christianity, destroy marriage and also our present free government, and finally depopulate America. . . . It may be thought the enlightened state of America is a sufficient security, but from the progress of Shakerism for a few years past [there were at the time about three hundred members at Union Village] I think it is time for the friends of liberty and of mankind to bestir themselves. Tories have also increased in subtlety and artifice. I believe if all the despots on earth, and all the infernal spirits had united to destroy Christianity and enslave mankind, Shakerism could not have been exceeded. . . . Can we not touch a treacherous nest which is hatching and breeding among us? . . . Can it be supposed that they have no design in forming such a wonderful money-making machine, without some way to lay it out, or to make use of it? . . . Can it be supposed that their money is designed only for the support of their riding ministers, who deceitfully live low when they are travelling about making proselytes? If the leading Shakers do not intend to live sumptuously on their money they must have something worse in view: that is, to collect a fund in order to raise and pay an army of tories whenever an opportunity offers. I believe they have both these ends in view, and that the leading Shakers live in luxury and wine and women as far as their plan of secrecy will admit of."

From 1817 to 1818, the Shakers were very unpopular in New York, New Hampshire, and also in Ohio and Kentucky. They had been always consistent and insistent pacifists. From the very beginning, when they turned the other cheek to the Harvard mobs, they steadfastly refused to sanction the use of violence of any kind in their dealings with others. The New Hampshire legislature of 1808, perhaps following the lead of the Massachusetts legislature of a year or so earlier, had passed measures exempting the Shakers from military duty and "from all equivalents on that account." The New York, Connecticut and Kentucky legislatures had followed their example a little later.

But in 1816, a clause was offered in the New Hampshire legislature subjecting every able-bodied Quaker or Shaker of from eighteen to forty-five years to the payment of $2.00 per annum and the compulsory draft. The hearing was postponed to 1818, when the Shakers sent a "Memorial" to the legislature protesting against the clause. This Memorial is an able and convincing presentation of the Shaker views on the subject: a strikingly logical statement of the futility of war.

The opening paragraphs present the right of all men to be judges of what their respective consciences dictate; the Memorial then goes on to analyse the experience of history with regard to the value of wars. "The Jews said that if they should let Christ alone, the Romans would come and take away both their place and nation; and the Roman writers objected to the Christians that if the whole empire should be of their opinion, they should be overrun by the Barbarians. Yet notwithstanding all the caution of both Jews and Romans, with all their warlike exertions, neither of these evils was prevented; and there is little doubt that the persecutions which they raised in order to prevent these dreadful evils were the very causes which brought the evils upon them."

The Memorial offers five reasons why the Shakers had the right to claim exemption from military service.

"1st. We abstain from all politics of the world, and from all posts of honor, trust and profit; and also from all commercial and other speculations from which wars generally originate.

"2nd. We support our own poor and contribute to support of the poor of the town.

"3rd. We give donations to distressed humanity in other places.

"4th. Our work on roads and bridges amounts to $3000. yearly.

"5th. Our missionaries are supported by us and do not seek subscriptions elsewhere."

They further pointed out that they had already suffered many losses from war, notably at Busro, Indiana, at the time of General Harrison's campaign against the Indians. And they concluded with the statement: "It must be granted that one man has as good a right to devote himself and service to the Lord as another. He has also as good a right to devote his property as his service. . . . And a whole society must have as good a right as an individual to do the same. . . . Nor do any people more readily pay their civil taxes than we."

For the time being the Shakers again won their right to act according to the dictates of their consciences. But once more the question arose in 1862, when George Ingels, a Shaker of North Union, Ohio, was drafted into the United States army. Benjamin Gates, one of the New Lebanon trustees, visited Lincoln in Washington and got a reprieve for Ingels. Frederick Evans also had an interview on the subject with Lincoln. Acting on the suggestion of the President and the War Department, he sent duly certified petitions to the proper authorities at Washington asking exemption for all the Shakers. So convincing, apparently, were his arguments, that these petitions were granted, to apply to all Shaker conscientious objectors.

An entry in a Shaker diary from Pleasant Hill, Kentucky, has the following comment. "It is now thoroughly understood at Washington that Shakers are not going to serve in any capacity in the military department; it is also understood that they will not compromise their principles by paying money for substitutes or to commute for exemption from service." When one remembers how torn asunder the whole country was by the Civil War, near what debatable territory the lands of the Ohio and Kentucky Shakers lay and, most of all, how small and powerless a body the Shakers were—never numbering over six thousand even at the peak—this quiet achievement of their purpose is amazing.

The Shaker lands in Kentucky did not escape despoilment by military forces any more than any other rich farm holdings in the war area. The society at South Union, Kentucky, lost buildings, stock, etc. to the value of over a hundred thousand dollars, not to mention money in bad debts. Yet they fed hungry soldiers, dispensing at least fifty thousand meals to both sides with kindly impartiality. It is worth recalling that the Pleasant Hill Shakers, near Lexington, Kentucky, were protected by the notorious General Morgan against looting by his own troops, for Morgan had been born nearby and he knew and respected the Shakers. Before the war was ended, a few of the young Shaker men did enter the army, but they did it without coercion from the government. And afterwards, some of them went back to the Shakers and were readmitted.

There were instances where the Shakers welcomed criticism—even attack—from "the world." In 1855, when they were at the peak of their prosperity, some of their enemies, jealous of Shaker success in business and agriculture, introduced a bill into the New York state legislature to limit the amount of land they could own and the number of apprentices they could employ. The Shakers, it seemed, had for some time been questioning the advisability of owning too much land. Besides what they had in their home farms, some of the societies owned large tracts in other townships, or even in other states. Canterbury owned a farm in western New York state; New Lebanon owned thirty thousand acres in Kentucky. In the early days, ownership of land had meant security for the Shakers, freedom from molestation, a home of their own. When, however, they had acquired more land than they could care for without hiring outside labor, the leaders began to think they had indulged this desire to excess. So they welcomed the proposed bill, and let it be known that it had their moral support. Whereupon the sponsors of the bill quietly abandoned it.

Occasionally—especially after the peak had been reached and the Shaker holdings began to decline in value—the Shakers found it necessary to protest against what they considered unjust discrimination in the matter of federal taxes. In 1869 they engaged the lawyer Durbin Ward to appear as their counsel in the matter of an excessive income tax. "In their legal aspects," said their attorney, "they are charities and ought rather be exempted from all taxation than to be overtaxed. They are in no sense moneyed or money-getting institutions. Profit or the accumulation of property may become an incident, but is no specific object of these societies. . . . If left to myself, I would ask the department to remit the income tax on the Shakers totally. But they have instructed me not to do so, as they are willing to be taxed equally with their neighbors, though their income is so largely devoted to charitable uses." The Shakers won their case.

There are many records in Shaker annals of money donated for charity among the "world's people." As early as 1820, Enfield and Canterbury, New Hampshire, sent $500 to Troy, New York, to help relieve the suffering from a great fire. In 1847, when all Ireland was suffering from a serious famine, many of the Shaker societies sent help. Union Village, Ohio, gave one thousand bushels of corn; Pleasant Hill, Kentucky, gave 254 bushels of corn and ten bushels of beans. After the Civil War the South Union Shakers adopted twenty orphans from Tennessee. In 1878 the Pleasant Hill society contributed $50 for the yellow fever sufferers in New Orleans. In addition to these donations to non-Shakers, the different societies were always generous with each other when the need arose, as in the case of fire or property loss from some other cause. Pleasant Hill gave $500 to New Gloucester, Maine, in 1867 to help them meet a deficit that came from careless stewardship. But never were the Shakers known to ask or accept aid from any of the "world's people." They took care of themselves and of their own, and all they asked from the world was tolerance and fair treatment.

X. SHAKERS AND "THE WORLD"

TOLERANCE and fair treatment were not only asked and expected from others by the Shakers, but were always accorded by them to all sincere seekers for the truth. The Shakers might easily have subscribed to the creed of Voltaire in respect to freedom of thought and speech. Indeed, their leaders said many a good word for Voltaire, in spite of the fact that the organized churches looked upon him as an atheist. Tom Paine also received their approval and to a lesser degree, Robert Ingersoll. "Barring the fact that Ingersoll hurts our educated feelings by his sometimes apparently sacrilegious remarks, few men who say so much savor more of wisdom." Again and again the Shakers made it their business to protest publicly against intolerance and injustice, whether in high places or low, and to commend the courage of minorities.

This tendency toward justice and fair play showed itself somewhat surprisingly at times, as for instance in their attitude toward ex-Shakers who had gone back to "the world," or toward a group as diametrically opposed to them in practice as the Oneida Community. The Shakers were friendly with this group at a time when the "world's people" were accusing the Oneida Perfectionists of "free love" in its worst implications. Wherever the Shakers felt sincerity of purpose behind an act or a thought, they were ready with words or deeds of commendation and support, and wherever they saw injustice they took it upon themselves to raise their voices against it.

The Shakers were always opposed to race discrimination and to human slavery. Some of their early converts in the

175

south were slave owners, but before joining the Shakers they freed their slaves without hesitation and without compromise. Matthew Houston of Paint Lick, Kentucky, was such a one. At South Union, Kentucky, the Believers formed a colored "family" of forty ex-slaves. There was apparently no thought of segregation in so doing, for colored Shakers were found mixed in with white members in many societies. The Shaker attitude toward the Indian was always friendly (except in one or two instances, notably in Indiana where hostilities were forced upon them). Richard McNemar in 1807 risked the disapproval of neighbors who were still haunted by frontier fears of Indian attack, by becoming friendly with a band of Shawnee Indians encamped nearby and visiting them. The watchful outsiders, who had already suspected the Shakers of everything undesirable, saw in these moves a conspiracy forming against them between the Shakers and the Indians. Richard, however, did not change his attitude toward the Indians, though he must have known the danger he incurred of hostile public opinion building toward a mob attack which came in another two years.

The Shaker attitude toward labor was an enlightened one. Among their own members there was, of course, no such thing as wages, since all alike labored and all alike shared the results of their labor. As the Shakers acquired more land, however, and developed wider agricultural and industrial activities, it became necessary to hire outside workers. In the south they often hired slaves from their owners, having the pick of the best always, since they paid good wages and accorded their laborers the best of treatment. At one period before the Civil War, the Pleasant Hill, Kentucky, society employed as many as sixty hands (both men and women) in harvest time, paying them from seventy-five cents to two dollars a day, besides feeding them. In New York state farmers considered themselves fortunate to be employed by the New Lebanon Shakers, since they were sure of fair treatment and good pay. The same was true of industrial workers hired by the Shakers.

Out of the Shaker preoccupation with agriculture and their industrial experience—limited in extent but thorough—came the development of certain theories of economics. Or rather one might say the strengthening of such theories, for actually the Shaker economy was only a logical following out of lines laid down by Mother Ann. There were, during the middle part of the nineteenth century, certain leaders among the Believers who were consciously interested in economic theory—men of education who had read the works of the French Fourier and the English Robert Owens.

The best known of them outside of Shakerdom, was Frederick Evans of New Lebanon, although Daniel Fraser was a close second. Both were heard with respect by "the world" whenever they made their opinions public. The period in which they lived was one of peculiar social ferment in America: the age of the Transcendentalists, of the Brook Farm and other Utopian experiments. During the decade of 1840 to 1850, while there were only two experiments in France based on the theories of Fourier, there were forty-one such experiments—mostly short-lived—being tried in the United States. The Shakers, out of their sixty or more years demonstration of practical communism, felt qualified to stand somewhat in the position of an elder brother to these younger and inexperienced attempts.

Both Evans and Fraser were born in England—Evans in 1808, Fraser four years earlier. Fraser had worked in England with Michael Thomas Sadler, M.P., for laws limiting child labor there before he came to America in 1834, joined the Shakers at Canaan, New York (a family of the New Lebanon society), and later was appointed to be an elder there. He had very definite ideas about universal ownership of land and equal justice for all men. He wrote several books, besides articles for the "Shaker Manifesto" and many letters. "Land monopoly and financial iniquities are at the bottom of social troubles," he says. "The two bases of morality are access to the land and hygiene. . . . Justice is the foundation of peace. . . . Individuals and rings in the face of the law take to themselves millions of the public money," which has a startlingly familiar sound today. In 1881 he wrote a letter to John Ruskin, thanking him "for the standard of righteousness you have unfurled in the British empire" [by Ruskin's work on *Political Economy*], and enlarging on various Shaker beliefs which seem to have been in peculiar accord with Ruskin's ideas. He quotes Ruskin's statement, "To make men commodities is the sum of all villainies," and then elaborates it. "Modern civilization is that sum. From that central idea, we have pauperism, crime, standing armies, a vast network of debts, and a system of usury, in itself a sum of huge villainies, corrupting public morals with the presence of luxurious idlers, and with hungry multitudes offering themselves in the marts of labor. . . . It is poor economy 'to make men commodities,' dangerous to the public peace, enormously expensive, and as wicked as it is costly."

Frederick Evans, like Fraser, harped continually on the importance of individual ownership of land. "Land limitation is the one thing needful in these United States. . . . Landless people are the raw material of war. . . . Let men dig for bread, not walk for money," etc. He too was a reformer before he joined the Shakers, working in the 1830's for "land reform" and the rights of labor and against monopolies. First a socialist, later a Shaker after making trial of various other shorter-lived communities, he eventually became leading elder at Mt. Lebanon, and therefore head of the whole Shaker church.

He had the kind of opportunity that comes to most idealists only in dreams, of seeing his theories actually in practice, and the sight strengthened and clarified his beliefs. "Every commune, to prosper, must be founded," he said, "so far as its industry goes, on agriculture. Only the simple labors and manners of a farming people can hold a community together. Wherever we have departed from this rule to go into manufacturing we have blundered." He believed, nevertheless, that the community should be self-sufficient. "We used to have more looms than now," he told Charles Nordhoff in 1875, "but cloth is sold so cheaply that we gradually began to buy. It is a mistake; we buy more cheaply than we can make, but our homemade cloth is much better than that we can buy; and we have now to make three pairs of trousers, for instance, where before we made one. Thus our little looms would even now be more profitable—to say nothing of the independence we secure in working them." Events have proved Elder Frederick right. Most of the Shaker looms stopped weaving in 1853. The decline of Shakerism began in the same decade, although this fact was not to be apparent for many years.

The peak of Shaker prosperity and influence was reached under Elder Frederick's leadership. Contrary to earlier Shaker practice, when the Believers kept mostly to themselves, he was called upon to make many contacts with the outside world. He proved himself a good representative. When he went to Washington in 1863 to confer with President Lincoln in the matter of Shaker exemption from military service, he was able to prove to the President and to Secretary Stanton that since many of the early Shakers had been Revolutionary soldiers who did not draw their pensions, "Our members had thus omitted to draw from the government over half a million of dollars due as pensions for military service." He at one time carried on a correspondence with Tolstoi with whom he was much in sympathy. In July of 1871 he headed a company of Shakers who went to England to visit friends with whom they had been corresponding there, and to carry the gospel of Shakerism back to that country. They were received with far greater respect, at least, than the first Believers were accorded when they came from the old world to the new nearly a century before.

Even in their days of greatest prosperity and worldly recognition, the Shakers chose to range themselves on the side of the unpopular minorities, forming a kind of Civil Liberties Committee of their own to protest at various infringements of personal liberty. In 1879, one De Roligné Mortimer Bennett was arraigned by Anthony Comstock on the charge of "sending indecent literature" through the mails. Bennett had been a Shaker at New Lebanon, living there from childhood until he left to marry another ex-Shaker. He had always been a freethinker and disciple of Tom Paine. After he left the Shakers he earned his living selling patent medicine, using his knowledge of medicinal roots and herbs gained while among the Shakers.

The pamphlet which drew down Comstock's disapproval was entitled "Cupid's Yokes" and was about marriage reform. The Young Men's Christian Association was backing and aiding Comstock (who had started his activities working with and for them in 1869); while on the other side, the Freethinkers' Society took up the cudgels for Bennett, petitioning President Hayes for his acquittal. Hayes, however, refused to interfere; and Bennett was sentenced to a term of thirteen months in prison. The Shakers, despite the fact that

Bennett was no longer one of them, protested publicly against his sentence. It is unthinkable that they would have supported his case if there had been real indecency involved, and it is obvious that they, in company with the Society of Freethinkers, recognized the true reason for the attack to be the hostility of the established church toward so-called "Free-thought." The following letter from Elder Elijah Myrick of the Harvard society to the editor of the "Shaker Manifesto," is worth quoting.

Ayer, Mass. Aug. 14, 1879

DEAR BROTHER AND EDITOR:

Thoughts of the priestly invasion of America's boasted freedom gave me a restless night. We now realize that we have the inquisition restored with all the rigors that our attained civilization will permit. We have nothing better to expect of the clergy—the God-in-the-constitution advocates. They challenge a man's right to doubt, but to believe every falsehood that ever cursed the earth and man, that is a virtue though it prove a curse to both soul and body. It is not the "faithful believers" that have advanced the world. History tells us it is the doubters—the "infidels"—that the world owes the greatest debt of gratitude.

They never persecute nor kill, nor trample upon, but uplift the fallen; give sight to the blind, whose eyes are filled with the dust of tradition, and whose minds are warped, and dwarfed by creeds and professions of faith.

We had hoped something better than a subsided president bowing reverently to the dictum of church authority. So much at random. Now for what I intended to say when I took pen in hand.

Can you see Bennett and say a kind and sympathetic word to him? How do the warden and officers treat him? Influence them if possible, to treat him kindly, as a noble human being which he is. Who knows but some of us will be behind the bars?

E. MYRICK

Bennett, by the way, was sent, after his release, as a delegate to the Convention of Freethinkers at Brussels.

Another instance of Shaker support given in the face of public sentiment is their friendship with the leaders of the

Oneida Community. How much their friendship and their example meant to the Perfectionists is shown by this testimony from John Humphrey Noyes. He wrote: "It is no more than bare justice to say that we are indebted to the Shakers more than to any of all other social architects of modern times. Their success has been the solid capital that has upheld all the paper theories and counteracted the failures of the French and English schools. It is very doubtful whether Owenism or Fourierism would have ever existed, or if they had, whether they would have moved the practical American nation if the facts of Shakerism had not existed before them and gone along with them."

It was no wonder that many idealists from among the "world's people" went to visit the Shakers, hoping for a strengthening of their own aspirations toward a better world. In August 1896, a Russian writer, Nicholas Maxinoff, who had been in the United States for three years investigating various social experiments, became interested in the Shakers and made them a week's visit. His thoughts had been turning toward communism for some time, and he wrote an article on Shakerism for a periodical in Russia. Perhaps twentieth century communism in that country may have other origins besides Karl Marx.

Charles Nordhoff says in his *Communistic Societies of the United States*, published in 1875, "Communism is a mutiny against society. . . . Whether the communist shall rebel with a bludgeon and a petroleum torch, or with a plow and a church, depends upon whether he has not or has faith in God. . . . If priest-craft and tyranny have sapped his faith and debauched his moral sense, then he will attack society. . . . If, on the contrary, he believes in God . . . he will seek another way out . . . giving his own interpretation to that brief narrative of Luke . . . 'And all that believed were together, and had all things in common; and sold their possessions and goods; and parted them to all men as every man had need.' "

From the earliest days of Shakerism, much curiosity has been felt by certain ones of the "world's people" about this experiment in human living. Some of the curiosity was, of course, hostile, as evidenced by the mob attacks and by the false reports that were circulated. Much of it was open-minded, however, and when recognized as such was welcomed and satisfied in all sincerity by the Believers, who have always been responsive to kindly, well-intentioned inquirers. Except for two or three periods when "the testimony was closed to the world"—as, for instance, between 1787 and 1800 when the various northern societies were organizing, and again in 1837 when the wave of spiritualism swept over the Shaker church—the regular sabbath day meetings were open to "the world" and were attended by large numbers of interested and respectful visitors. Some of the great ones of the day even, showed a desire to learn more about these strange and earnest celibates; they pass in a worldly procession across the unworldly pages of the Shaker records.

The first of these was Lafayette, who had doubtless read of the doings of the Camisards in his own country nearly a century earlier and was doubly interested in these people who claimed to be their spiritual successors. In 1783 or 1784, while he was in the neighborhood of Albany on a mission of negotiation with the Indians, he heard about the Shakers at Niskayuna and went to see them. Mother Ann was still with them; there was great enthusiasm and emotional excitement among her followers, and a constant stream of new converts converging on this first Shaker home in the wilderness.

Lafayette sat quietly watching and listening to what was going on about him. His interest was roused by the strange manifestations of spiritual influence that he saw. He entered into conversation with Mother Ann, raising many questions about the Shaker faith. When he asked her why he himself might not become a sharer in this new way of life, Mother Ann told him that "his time had not yet come to share in this spirit." She added that a great work and much suffering lay before him in this world before he could enter the spiritual plane. In after years, when Lafayette's later history had unfolded, the Shakers remembered these words of their leader, and when he died in 1834 they received word of his death by spirit messenger many days before the news was brought by packet to America.

In 1817, while President Monroe was making his tour of New England, he called on the Shakers at Enfield, New Hampshire. Job Bishop was the leading elder in New Hampshire at the time, being called Father Job. According to the Shaker report of the visit, "The President was received by one of the Shakers at Enfield, New Hampshire, in a style of plain hospitality." The elder in all the majesty of conscious integrity approached the President and said, "I, Job Bishop, welcome James Monroe to our habitation." Monroe also visited the Shakers at South Union, Kentucky, this time in company with Andrew Jackson. "Monroe," said one of the Shakers in describing the visit, "was a stout, thickset man, plain, and with but little to say; Jackson, tall and thin, with a hickory visage."

Henry Clay was a frequent visitor in the Ohio and Kentucky societies of Believers. South Union knew him well. When the Pleasant Hill society was starting its stock farm, Clay used to include in his importation of stock an order for the Shakers. He visited Union Village, Ohio, on July 16, 1825, and again two days later with many Lebanon people. (The same Lebanon that was cursed by Richard McNemar some eight years earlier.) The diarist who recorded these visits comments as follows: "He was very familiar and affable. Thought he would make a good subject. He promised his assistance if the society became involved in difficulty, persecution or the like." When the Duke of Saxony paid Union Village a visit in the May of the following year, the diarist's comment was not so complimentary. "Duke of Saxony and company pay us a visit; but lo, he is only a man, a sinful man."

That the Shakers were not too impressed by the visits of presidents and dukes is understandable when we realize that they were quite used to receiving spirit visits from the great of all ages. "This evening Jacob of old and his twelve sons attended our meeting." Noah often came to them, as well as many of the prophets, not to mention Mother Ann and the founders. And doubtless some of these visitors from the spirit world seemed—perhaps were—quite as real to the Believers as the visitors from that other world of which most of them knew so little. The most startling record is the following from North Union, Ohio: "In the year 1843, when the Millerites were looking for Christ to come . . . he was among the Shakers spiritually. . . . He took up his abode at North Union for the space of three months."

It was during this period of spiritual exaltation among the Believers that some of the Transcendentalists became interested in the Shakers. The Brook Farm experiment was going on, though not too successfully. Another similar scheme called the Con-Sociate Family was started in 1843 at Harvard, Massachusetts, by Bronson Alcott, Charles Lane, Samuel Bowers, Joseph Palmer and others, the purchase of their domain, "Fruitlands," being financed by the one moneyed member, Charles Lane. Harvard had long been known as the home of one of the four Massachusetts Shaker societies. It was only natural that the Con-Sociates should become interested in these neighbors of theirs who were making such an outstanding success of a like experiment in Utopian communal living.

The records show that many visits to the Shakers were made by the Alcotts, Lane and others, with the result that after the failure of Fruitlands in about a year's time, Lane and his son William joined the Believers. Alcott too was obviously influenced by the Shaker way of life to such an extent that his anxious wife took decisive steps to prevent his following Lane's example. Lane, a seeker who never quite found the Holy Grail for which he was looking, wrote to Mrs. Alcott of the Shakers, "I think nowhere is the twofold purpose in human life, of being good and doing good, so fully provided for. If I but imagined a better place I would instantly explore and test it." For a time after the abandonment of Fruitlands, the property was left in Shaker care.

Many of the "world's people" visited the Sunday services of the Shakers during the early part of the nineteenth century. The Shakers encouraged them to do so, even arranging seats for them at one end of the church building, and special entrances. New Lebanon's second meetinghouse, built in 1824, was planned with this in view. When the North Union, Ohio, society built a new church in 1848, it provided raised seats at the south end of the room to accommodate five hundred people. The rhythmical and spirited dancing and singing, done with sincerity and dignity in spite of grotesque features, made it a show worth seeing if only as entertainment—which was what many of the visitors went for.

In the decade after 1837, when the spiritual revival was producing the kind of frenzied and disordered movements that called forth ridicule from unsympathetic visitors, many of the societies closed their church doors against "the world"; when they were reopened about 1847 or 1848, people came at first in even greater numbers than before. Walt Whitman visiting New Lebanon in 1853, made note of an audience of over three hundred. After the Civil War, however, when the Believers began to dwindle in numbers and the singing and dancing lost its early fervor, fewer and fewer outsiders went to the services. In time, the remaining Believers grew too few in numbers to fill the meetinghouses, which were gradually closed. The Sunday services came to be held in the assembly rooms of the family dwellings. Visitors were still made welcome at these smaller gatherings, but after a while—in the early nineteen hundreds—the Shakers again withdrew their religious rites from public gaze.

Even after religious services were closed to outsiders, the Shakers were still glad on week days to receive and talk to visitors who called on them in sincerity of friendship and purpose. Until toward the end of the nineteenth century, bountiful meals were served to visitors, and sometimes overnight accommodations were arranged for them. Many distinguished people have gone out of their way to visit the Shakers; William Dean Howells's novel, *The Undiscovered Country* is based on his contacts with the Harvard and Shirley Shakers, and Shaker guest books show numerous names of the near-great as well as the lesser known.

Of late years, when the discontinuation of most of the societies has made it evident both to "the world" and to the Believers themselves that the earthly days of the Millennial Church are numbered, they take a nostalgic pleasure in conducting sight-seeing trips through their grounds and buildings, pointing with quiet pride to the evidences of their former prosperity and success. Their voices are quiet, their manners gentle, their faces content. They have always been

187

a gallant band, hospitable to their friends, charitable to their foes, honorable to their neighbors and to all men. They were gallant in the beginning, against the odds of hostile nature and hostile mankind; they will be gallant to the end because, in spite of their repudiation of worldly pride, they are too proud spiritually ever to admit defeat at the hands of "the world."

PART THREE

THE MEANING OF THE ADVENTURE

XI. SHAKER FUNCTIONALISM

THE word esthetics had no meaning for the Shakers. According to their philosophy and religion, beauty was one of the devil's snares to catch the worldly-minded. An eye that found sensuous delight in arrangements of color or line, a mind that occupied itself with planning for symmetry in the combination of masses and materials—both these preoccupations were as much to be feared as an interest in the forbidden indulgences of the flesh. Yet craftsmanship was sought and encouraged. The Shakers even made it one of their rules that every Shaker child must learn a craft, that every Shaker man or woman must spend at least a part of his or her time working at this craft. And the work must be honest work.

The only kind of beauty tolerated was that springing unsought from what is today called functionalism. For in spite of themselves, the Shakers produced things of beauty. They never tried to do so; they would have been the first to disclaim any right to the title of artist. If their songs, their furniture, their buildings had beauty, it was a by-product not of their planning. Their aim was to make the lines right so that their buildings, their chairs, would be strong and would endure. Because they developed the ultimate rightness of line in all these things, they unwittingly achieved beauty. It is a paradox which the early Shakers would not have appreciated that their furniture is now being collected and their buildings admired as contributions to American art, while the spiritual principles on which their religion was built have already gone to join the beliefs of the Manicheans, the Waldensians and all the other small heretical sects that once put up a good fight against the engulfing current of the prevailing churches of their respective periods. The Shakers would not have minded being called heretics, but they would have minded intensely that their particular brand of heresy was becoming history rather than prophecy. Mother Ann would have been sorrowful and disappointed that the spiritual beauty the Believers tried to bring to the world by putting their hearts to God should have been perpetuated only through the material beauty they produced when they put their hands to work.

If the Shakers had no interest in theories of esthetics, they had a profound interest in practical technique. They were craftsmen with pride in their craft, or rather with pride in the contribution their handling of their craft was able to make to the common interest of the society. Technical problems challenged their ingenuity. With nothing short of perfection for the goal, technical problems assume importance. The first requisite was usefulness; everything was made for use, nothing for show. To be perfectly useful an article must be perfectly suited to the need that calls it forth. A chair had first of all to be strong; it had also to be light, since it must be easily movable and convenient for hanging on the wall pegs that bordered every Shaker room.

It had to be made from the kind of wood best fitted for supplying both strength and lightness. And the wood used had to be properly seasoned if the chair were to endure. The Shakers were never in a hurry; they could wait till the wood was seasoned. They never conserved effort; they were willing to spend themselves unsparingly in their search for the perfect chair. Any piece of furniture that is strong and light and durable must conform to laws—stated or instinctively understood—of balance and stress. Just the right amount of thickness here, a safe degree of slenderness there, a proper length of the uprights to fit the human body; and the chair, when it has attained this ideal of combined strength and lightness and suitability cannot help having beauty as well. As the Shakers said, "Every force evolves a form." This is all that functionalism means.

Some of the Shaker societies even went so far as to make chairs to fit certain individual measurements, just as they made lasts to fit the shoe needs of the different members. Whatever contributed to greater efficiency of the members or of the society as a whole was worth doing. And the comfort of the members—at work or at rest—came under this head. For this reason the Shakers were in advance of their neighbors in having and using the latest labor-saving devices. Sometimes they invented them; sometimes they availed themselves of what was already on the market. But they were always ready to try something new. This attitude was, of course, reflected in their architecture and their furniture. Sometimes their attempts were unsuccessful. Reports of such failures spread to other communities, as did accounts of successful patterns or inventions, and the other societies profited by the mistakes or successes. This is the reason for the uniformity found in almost every aspect of the Shaker life and culture. And this is the reason that much of the architecture and furniture that is considered typically "Shaker" has beauty and distinction.

Shaker culture derived immediately from colonial America. The English founders of Shakerism belonged to an artisan class very little removed from the peasant class. Most of the early American members came from the same stratum of society. English and European peasant crafts of a couple of centuries ago had many points of similarity, and this was also true of peasant costume. Shaker dress of the most characteristic period, for instance, resembles both the Breton and the Swedish costume. There is also a strange and striking likeness between Shaker furniture and "Swedish Modern."

It would seem that the influence of Swedish craftsmen among the early Believers must have been great. There were Swedes at both New Lebanon and Watervliet when those societies were gathered. The southern communities also apparently felt some affinity for the Swedes, because the Pleasant Hill, Kentucky, society paid the passage money of several Swedish immigrants to this country, thinking they would make good Shakers. The "round barn" at Hancock, Massachusetts, is also in the Swedish tradition. A particular type of wooden pitcher or stoup found with the Enfield, New Hampshire, Shakers is almost the exact counterpart of those made today in Sweden. And the Shaker chair seats of colored woolen tapes plaited in a checkerboard design are found on "Swedish Modern" chairs. This influence, whatever its source, must have been strong to color the English colonial pattern.

The best period of Shaker craftsmanship fell in the era before the Civil War; in those years when the Shaker communities were still growing, still gaining new members, putting up new buildings, writing new music, recording their theology and their rules of living. The early enthusiasm had not flagged. The original desire for simplicity and order was still warm and creative. The Shaker furniture was simple not from lack of imagination, but from a passion for the essential; their rooms were orderly not from emptiness and lack of use, but for purposeful efficiency. Their music was lively and rhythmical to fit their dance ritual; their literature logical, with a nice feeling for the right word. Nowhere was there redundancy or superfluity; no words, no lines, no tones were wasted. And yet time was plentiful for the perfecting of the work. As Dr. Andrews says in his *Shaker Furniture*, "The craftsman labored neither for master nor market demand, but for a community which he believed would be timeless." Given a passion for perfection, a demand for functionalism, and time and security in which to experiment while developing the required skills, the Shakers were able in fifty years time to produce as integrated a school of art as one developed through many centuries of national culture.

Everything the Shakers made was looked upon as a practical instrument for a spiritual end. Celibacy, separation from the world, community of goods—these modes of attaining the spiritual perfection that was their goal dictated their whole pattern of life. Their self-sustained, cooperatively-run communities made them practically independent of "the world." Their binal dwelling-houses, office buildings and churches, with separate entrances and staircases and withdrawing rooms for brethren and sisters, provided adequate safeguards for celibate living. Their love of order and of cleanliness made them lay out their villages in carefully planned rows with clean, practical, narrow flagstone paths between the buildings. Their self-imposed demand for perfection made them pioneers in business efficiency.

They antedated modern quantity production and motion-saving techniques by many years, when they used the same plans and types of construction not only for different buildings in the same family, but for similar buildings in all the other Shaker families and societies. Once they had hit upon a style of architecture that seemed best suited to the use for which the building was intended, it was logical and practical for that style to be employed throughout Shakerdom wherever such a building was needed. The details might be varied in the different societies; the general plan remained the same.

In general, Shaker craftsmen, whether builders or carpenters, were encouraged to remain anonymous. Yet occasionally a name appears in the records. Moses Johnson of Enfield, Connecticut, is said to have built several of the early Shaker churches, being "an expert in hewing timber, and skilled in framing for building purposes." In the early days, the sides of wooden buildings were framed—that is, constructed separately, flat—and then raised and fastened together at the corners. The church at Shirley was "raised" in the night, on October 31, 1792, to avoid molestation by the "world's people." Most of the Shaker churches in New England were built between 1785 and 1795 and were probably all planned if not actually built or superintended, by Moses Johnson. The church now standing at New Lebanon (opened in 1824, nearly forty years after the first Shaker meetinghouse was erected there in 1785) is much larger than the usual Shaker type, and has a "boiler" roof instead of the generally used gambrel; nevertheless, it conforms in general plan to the others. Another Shaker builder whose name is remembered is Micajah Burnett of Pleasant Hill, Kentucky. Micajah was a civil engineer and an architect of the mid-nineteenth century. He designed the Pleasant Hill office building which was famed for its spiral staircase.

The common pattern of the Shaker churches was a rectangular, hip roofed wooden building of two and a half stories. Often it was set back from the road at the end of a strip of green lawn bordered on each side by maples. The Shakers loved maple trees. They set out rows of them on either side of the roads that went through their villages. At Canterbury, when the maples in front of the church were planted by the Shaker brethren, each young tree was given into the charge of one of the young sisters who tended it and gave it her name by which it was always known. There were sixteen trees in all. In the long side of the church which faced the lawn between the maples and, beyond the lawn, the road, were two doors—the left for the men, the right for the women. Three windows stood between the doors, and another window was set at each end of the façade. Above, three dormer windows projected from the long roof. Some twelve feet or so in front of the church stood a white picket fence with its two gates exactly opposite the two doors.

Inside the church was a large assembly hall with wood paneling up to the window sills, wooden beams crossing the ceiling from the long front wall to the back and rows of wooden pegs set into two peg boards between five and six feet from the floor. The walls and ceiling were white, the woodwork, blue. At Sabbathday Lake, Maine, the original paint can still be seen—a very dark blue with greenish tones. At Canterbury, New Hampshire, the woodwork was repainted fifty or sixty years ago in a lighter shade of blue which is still clear and softly bright, unfaded by time. The church windows were right in proportion and placing, and were small-paned like all early American windows. The church building at Enfield, New Hampshire, which was of the same pattern as those of Canterbury and Sabbathday Lake, was so greatly admired for its rightness of line and proportion by the sculptor Augustus St. Gaudens, that he bought it from the Shakers about 1900, after they had given up using it on account of their shrunken numbers, and had it removed to his estate in Cornish, New Hampshire, where it now stands.

The Shaker dwelling houses were the acme of plainness, neatness and symmetry. They were usually rectangular in shape and sufficiently large to meet the needs of a growing community. There were single entrances on both ends of the building, and on each long side the two separate doors leading to the two separate staircases and separate apartments above for the men and women. Different building materials were used in different vicinities. New Lebanon used stone and wood painted white. At Watervliet, New York, many buildings were of brick or wood painted red. The New Hampshire societies used both wood and granite. The main building of the Enfield, New Hampshire, society, finished in 1837, was one hundred feet long by fifty-six feet wide and four full and two half stories high. It was constructed of smooth granite blocks, cemented and further fastened together with iron trunnels, and it was considered the finest building in New Hampshire with the single exception of the statehouse at Concord. Like most Shaker family dwellings, it was surmounted by a tower containing a bell for summoning the Believers.

Inside, as inside all Shaker buildings, were partially wainscoted walls, the inevitable rows of pegs, built-in cupboards and sets of drawers with wooden knobs—all that would make for order, convenience, durability and cleanliness. The windows were recessed in walls two or three feet thick, and had paneled inside wooden shutters that folded back neatly out of the way when not in use. The rooms were spacious and airy. This building is still standing and looks to be in as good condition as when it was made; the Catholic brothers who now own it say that when they had it wired for electricity, it was as if the Shakers had foreseen this invention and had provided for it in their construction by leaving space for the wires between the floors and walls. At Watervliet, New York, the South family dwelling house built in 1822 is still in perfect alignment; its pine and chestnut beams are held in place by the old dowel pins, its hand-forged iron nails and braces are still resisting rust. The plainness of these many-windowed boxlike structures is saved from factory starkness by their uncrowded setting in spacious landscapes and by the impression they give of tranquil, ordered living.

The smaller dwelling houses, the shops and the mills vary more in design, but they all bear the same family resemblance, whether in New England, New York or in Ohio and Kentucky. In 1843, North Union, Ohio, built a new grist-mill on the north side of Doan Brook. It was of sandstone quarried on the Shaker land, and was four stories high on the south side and three in the north, with a penstock hewn out of solid sandstone to the depth of fifty feet. A machine shop erected at Enfield, New Hampshire, at about the same time was made of granite blocks like those used in the big stone family dwelling and put together with the same care. This building—four stories high and of perfect proportions—was faced on the inside with brick to a thickness of over two feet on the first floor and about one foot on the upper floors. The brick was covered with plaster, and there was wood paneling up to the windowsills besides built-in cabinets and drawers and the usual pegboards in all the rooms. The floors of the ground floor rooms were of slate. Today, after having stood empty, unheated and unused for at least twenty-five years, the doors and the drawers still fit their frames perfectly without sticking.

A Shaker architectural feature particularly characteristic of New Lebanon and Watervliet, New York, was the slanting wooden canopy which overhangs most of the doorways, giving the effect of a porch roof without visible support. Another noticeable detail of the Shaker villages was the neat fencing. The commonest kind in New England was composed of granite posts connected by three or more iron chains or square white rails. White picket fences were also used, especially in front of the meetinghouses. Gates were a part of the picket fences, but with the rail fences, two end posts with a third set between them instead of a gate offered easy entrance to persons while effectively barring out animals.

Almost a part of the fence was the dismounting platform. This was usually astride the fence near the gateway which led to the principal building. It consisted of a large flat slab of granite supported on four granite posts about four feet high. A flight of stone or wooden steps at the end inside the Shaker grounds led up to it. The other or outer end was open to the road for easy access to the high Shaker carriages. There were simple handrails of wrought iron on the two sides and sometimes on the steps. These hand-wrought iron rails which were used also on steps leading to the doorways of the dwelling houses, were noticeable for their simple distinction at a time when American taste was running to iron dogs and fountains in the front yard.

A characteristic example of Shaker architecture was the Shaker barn. Since the Believers were primarily an agricultural people, their barns were of great importance to them. The barn at Alfred, Maine, built in 1833 is 144 by 45 feet; that at Canterbury, completed after three years work in 1858, was the same width and 200 feet long, with 25-foot abutments of solid granite at each end. The one at New Lebanon is the largest of all, being 296 feet long by 50 feet wide, and five stories high. As is usual with Shaker barns, it is built on the side of a hill so that it has easy entrance on different levels. When there was no hill handy, the Shakers either put one end of the barn against a large rock or built a graduated mound from which a bridge could be run to the second or third story of the barn, so that hayloads could be driven into a loft from which the hay was pitched down instead of up in unloading. This obvious way of simplifying the haying operation is only another instance of Shaker directness and efficiency.

The stone barn at Harvard, Massachusetts, had entrances on three levels. This barn was paid for with money from making and selling the then popular turkey feather fans, the shingles of old-growth pine for the building being a gift from the New Hampshire Shakers. One Shaker barn that should have special mention because of its individuality is the Round Barn at Hancock, built in 1826. This is a perfectly round, two-story structure of stone, surmounted by a smaller, twelve-sided wooden story, which in turn is topped by a small hexagonal bell tower. The practical feature of this barn was that a load of hay could be driven completely around the inside of the barn, unloading into the center as it went, and then out through the door again. This barn is still in use. Many of the old Shaker barns stand empty, however, empty and idle. The Canterbury barn, which is still shown to visitors, has a pleasant smell reminiscent of clean cows being milked and fragrant clover hay in the mangers. All the Shaker buildings have the clean, sweet smell that lingers in rooms lovingly cared for and used for clean living.

Clean living and loving care sound the keynote of the Shaker furniture, accounting not only for its style but for its durability. If the Believers had had a formal creed they would have made order and cleanliness a part of it. And from these respect for property follows logically. For although material things were to the Shakers little more than symbols of the spiritual, yet because their property was owned in common, it was fitting that each individual member should handle carefully that which was not wholly his. Besides this, the Shakers understood and appreciated the labor that went into the making of a barn, a house, a paneled door or a chair. Thus the Shaker woodwork could be light in color, since it would not be permitted to become soiled, and the Shaker chairs could be slender, since they would not be misused.

Much of the Shaker furniture was half architecture, since it was a permanent and unmovable part of the structure of the room. A characteristic Shaker room had white walls and woodwork of pine or maple stained or varnished a bright yellow-brown. There was either wainscoting up to the window frames (as in the meetinghouses and assembly rooms) or wide baseboards, and always there were the rows of pegs running around the walls near the tops of the windows. Built-in cabinets, cupboards or chests of drawers filled the corners or lined the walls according to the use for which the room was intended. Sometimes a single wall piece of this kind would have doors opening on shelves, large drawers near the floor and, higher up, many smaller drawers of assorted sizes and shapes. There are in the large stone building at Enfield, New Hampshire, over eight hundred such built-in drawers. When doors or drawers were above the average person's reach, small steps were provided. It would have been almost impossible to be disorderly with so many aids to system and neatness right at hand. The pegs were used not only for hats, bonnets and coats, but also for candlesticks, hanging racks of tools, pipes, towels, books and also chairs.

The usual movable wooden furniture found in Shaker buildings consisted of beds, benches, chairs, desks, tables and stools. The beds were very narrow, low and simple, being hardly more than cots with low wooden head and foot-boards. They were always painted green, as was directed by the Millennial laws, and were set upon strong wooden cast-ers so that they might be easily moved. The benches served many purposes; they were used in the meetinghouses, the assembly rooms of the dwelling houses, the kitchens, the cel-lars, the shops and work rooms. They differed in size and shape according to their use. The commonest type was a plain, heavy plank supported by two or three straight, slightly narrower pieces of planking from which rounded or Gothic-pointed segments had been cut at the base. All were simple and strong and honest in construction, with no attempt at beauty save such as might come unsought when the lines were right. Occasionally some of the benches were built into the walls, forming an integral part of the room. But they were more often movable.

The woods most used in cabinet work were pine, maple, cherry and butternut. Sometimes the grain of the wood brought a beauty that could not help delighting the eye of the artisan, Shaker or not. Many of the leading Believers of the first half of the nineteenth century were skilled craftsmen as well as efficient executives and inspired prophets. Richard McNemar of Union Village, of whom it is recorded that "he loved his tools," made 1,463 chairs in the course of his life with the Shakers, besides spinning wheels, reels, looms, etc. So sure and direct was his workmanship in whatever he un-dertook that it was said of him "Never did he balk with two strokes where one should suffice."

Job Bishop, head of the New Hampshire societies, was a cabinetmaker of note; Giles Avery, elder at New Lebanon, was a builder and a carpenter. And there were many able craftsmen who were purely "hand-minded" and took no part in Shaker government. For these last, the exercise of their craft in creating things of use, integrity and beauty was an act of religious devotion—an easement of the ache of their yearning toward spiritual perfection. To a man of many talents and many responsibilities like Richard, it was perhaps that, but it was, besides, a rest and a relief from the many problems that always beset him. To retire to his clean orderly workshop, to take up his tools that he loved so much, and to use them in an act of creation that he himself could control afforded him deep joy and refreshment.

There were also clockmakers among the Shakers. Benjamin Youngs and his nephew Isaac N. Youngs (brother of the Benjamin who was sent to Kentucky with Issachar Bates and John Meacham and who later wrote *The Testimony of Christ's Second Appearing*) were the best known. Clocks, however, were for general use like the built-in cabinets. In a sense they were more truly communal possessions than desks and tables and chairs. Desks were mainly for the use of the Ministry, and were found in the rooms set apart for the elders and eldresses. Small portable lap or table desks were more numerous than desks on legs, although the use of these, too, was forbidden to the membership at large who were not encouraged to write letters either to "the world" or to other Shakers.

The Ministry was always worried over the possibility of disaffection springing up from an exchange of real or fancied grievances among members, and they therefore set up regulations of one kind or another to prevent gatherings or exchanges of thought by less than four people. Chairs and tables, however, tended toward gregariousness. A group of sewing sisters needed not only chairs to sit on, but tables to hold their work. And since the Shaker ideal of perfection demanded the efficiency that springs from perfect working and living conditions, there were many kinds of tables required, from the long, heavy trestle table for refectory and kitchen to the small, oblong drop-leaf table on four slim, tapering legs, or the "stand" with a round or square or rectangular top set on a central stem or shaft which rested on— or rather seemed to merge into—the three curved legs that supported it. Most of these smaller tables and stands had drawers in them, often at each end, so that two sisters could use the same table.

Of chairs there were many sizes, but few really different styles. It speaks well for Shaker workmanship that although there was more uniformity of plan in the construction of chairs than in any other kind of furniture, the lines did not become stereotyped. Even when Robert Wagan's chair factory at Mt. Lebanon went into the business of selling chairs to "the world," and advertised for this trade, the Shaker chairs somehow kept their distinctive style. They were for the most part straight, ladder-back chairs with three or four thin slats across the back, two turned rungs on front and sides and one behind, and seats of woven tapes, rush or cane. The tops of the front posts were slightly rounded; the back posts had gracefully turned finials. The wood was usually stained a yellowish brown and varnished. The chairs were very light, some weighing less than six pounds, yet so perfectly built that they were strong enough to withstand a century's use.

The illustrated catalogue of Shaker chairs published by R. M. Wagan and Company in the late eighteen-seventies states: "Of all the imitations of our chairs which have come under our observation, there are none which we would be willing to accept as our workmanship, nor would we be willing to stake our reputation on their merits. . . . We have spared no expense or labor in our endeavors to produce an article that cannot be surpassed in any respect, and which combines all the advantages of durability, simplicity and lightness." It also announces: "We were awarded a Diploma and Medal at the Centennial Exhibition for combining in our chairs Strength, Sprightliness and Modest Beauty." The word "sprightliness" was doubtless used not so much in its present-day slightly frivolous sense as with a thought to its derivation from the word meaning spirit.

Other examples of Shaker crafts were baskets and boxes of various sizes. The work of the Shaker sisters seems to have been even more anonymous than that of the brethren. Whether this was a sub-conscious discrimination between the sexes, or whether it was because the sisters' time went mainly into the perishables of life such as food, clothing, etc., rather than into lasting articles like furniture, it is difficult to say. Certainly there are beautiful examples of woven and plaited baskets made by the sisters which deserve to be classed with some of the men-made products, but are, nevertheless, uncredited to any individual.

Small articles like the oval and round wooden boxes were used for so many things that they were turned out in great quantities, yet they were always carefully made, whether they were to be used for grain measures in the barns or work-boxes in the sewing rooms. There was never a dividing line between art and utility. The numberless pegs that encircled the Shaker walls, the wooden knobs on the countless drawers, even the small wooden spools with holes through the middle to fit the iron spikes that were made to hold them—all these were as carefully turned and as painstakingly polished as were the writing desks made for the use of the Ministry, or the clocks that hung on the walls to tell the time for all the sisters and brethren.

XII. WORDS, MUSIC AND DANCE

THE outstanding quality of Shaker literature is its clear, direct diction. Shaker writers handled language as they handled tools when they went to the shops to work with their hands in making something useful and durable. Any production of theirs—whether a chair, a history or a song—had to be unmistakably fit for the purpose that brought it into being. There is no ambiguity, no lazy use of hackneyed expressions, no careless writing in, for instance, Youngs's *Testimony of Christ's Second Appearing*. Benjamin Seth Youngs knew exactly what he wanted to say before he set it down on paper, and more than that, he knew how to say it to present to the reader what was in his mind. The Shakers used words to expose and clarify their thoughts, never to hide or to becloud them. They produced no consciously "fine writing," no art for art's sake.

Shaker diaries and other records of pioneer beginnings relate the building of mill ponds, the setting up of the first sawmills, the framing of the first dwellings and churches, etc., as clearly as if drafting a pattern for all frontiersmen to follow. Richard McNemar's didactic hymns and jingles, while having no claim to poetry, strike straight at the problem or condition that called them forth. The inspirational writings, such as the *Holy Roll and Book*, and some of the hymns were nicely adapted to the need they were created to fill, namely the raising of the emotions to a high pitch of religious fervor. Shaker literature, like everything the Shakers made or did, is a mixture of the utilitarian and the inspirational or mystical, and it is always able to say what it means to say.

As might be expected, the theological writers outnumbered all the others. Or to put it differently, practically all the Shaker writers produced some works of theology whatever else they wrote besides. If there were any presentation of Shaker views to be made to the United Society or to "the world," the leading elders were expected to make it. Up to the end of the nineteenth century there was always someone capable of doing so. A few Shaker theologians stand out, however, from the others: Joseph Meacham, Richard McNemar, Benjamin Seth Youngs, John Dunlavy in the early days, and Harvey L. Eads, Giles Avery, Henry C. Blinn, Fayette Mace, and, especially, Frederick W. Evans in the period of greatest Shaker prestige.

Of the early five, Meacham is important because he was the first leader after the passing of the English group, although he left only one work, A concise statement of the principles of the only true church, etc. Other words of his, as of Mother Ann and the English founders may be read as recorded by the early Believers, but they were not written down by him. Benjamin Seth Youngs was far and away the most important early writer who came out of the northern group, although his major work and most of his later life were interwoven with the history of the societies of the Southwest: Ohio, Indiana and Kentucky. The Testimony of Christ's Second Appearing, which has been previously described at some length, is considered to have been mostly his work, although he was doubtless helped in planning it by McNemar, Dunlavy, Houston, Worley and perhaps others. Nevertheless, the style is his, and it is a model of clear, logical and authoritative presentation of facts and beliefs. Richard McNemar, whose Kentucky Revival had paved the way for the first edition of it, and who collaborated with Youngs on the important third edition, was a master of doctrinal dialectics. He and John Dunlavy belonged in the Southwest having grown up with the country there. Dunlavy's contribution to the early theological works of the Shakers consisted principally of *The Manifesto, or a Declaration of the Doctrines and Practises of the church of Christ*. This was published at Pleasant Hill, Kentucky, in 1818 and is very doctrinal in tone, less interesting in style than Youngs or McNemar, but clear and forceful.

Of the latterday group of theologians, Frederick Evans was the most eminent. Like McNemar, he was extremely versatile, with a mind ever receptive to new ideas and a scholar's knowledge gained from wide reading. As ranking head of the Millennial Church during the period of its greatest expansion and influence, he was called upon to answer questions and arguments raised by inquirers from "the world" and to present the Shaker beliefs in books, magazine articles, etc. It was he whose voice spoke with authority for the official United Society.

Yet, subject as the elders of the different societies were to the authority of the Ministry at Mt. Lebanon, dissenting voices were raised here and there against what was considered the over-liberality of Elder Frederick. Elder Harvey L. Eads of South Union, Kentucky, questioned the wisdom of Evans's too venturesome ideas. Elder Henry C. Blinn of Canterbury, New Hampshire, referred to his teachings as "the gospel according to St. Frederick"; others began to murmur "deist" in speaking of him. Blinn and Eads were themselves writers of ability; it is possible that they resented a pontifical vein in Evans's pronouncements. To an outsider there is not a very wide variance in the ideas expressed by the three men. Time, however, has proved Blinn and Eads right, or so it would seem. Many Shakers have felt and feel today that Evans's intellectual approach to things of the spirit was one of the causes of the Shaker decline.

Besides works on Shaker theology, Shaker writers have left a considerable body of factual records: *The Testimonies concerning the character and ministry of Mother Ann Lee*, etc., previously mentioned, are simple, direct, moving accounts of the founders, written down many years later by some of the earliest American converts. Many of the societies had diarists who kept day by day reports of their part in the communal scheme of things. The earliest and most outstanding historian was Richard McNemar, whose *Kentucky Revival* is accepted everywhere as the most authoritative contemporary history of that still unexplained religious phenomenon of 1800 to 1805. To quote from one paragraph: "Such was the unremitted flow of that Spirit, which transmuted everything into a different appearance, that were it supposable that disembodied spirits could enter living men and women, it might be thought that every visionary, recorded either in sacred or profane history, had rendezvoused in the Schismatics and borrowed their active powers to revise their endless train of types and figures . . . as the merchant hangs out signals about his door, to direct the people where to come for merchandise, so were the prophesier, the dreamer, the visionist, the sweet singer, and fragrant dancer, hung out to the view of the world, to show where God was about to open his everlasting kingdom of righteousness, peace and joy in the Holy Ghost."

Other historians were James Sullivan Prescott of North Union, Ohio, who wrote a complete manuscript history of that society, John Rankin, who recorded the beginnings of So. Union, Ky., Henry Blinn of Canterbury and Otis Sawyer of Alfred, Maine, both of whom wrote historical sketches for "The Manifesto." Anna White of Mt. Lebanon compiled from the records of the different societies a competent general Shaker history. Then there was Hervey Elkins, who wrote *Fifteen Years in the Senior Order of Shakers*, and lesser known writers, like Henry Cumings of Enfield, New Hampshire, whose careful descriptions of various phases of Shaker life as related in newspaper articles have made them vivid to us of today. Henry Cumings was a Shaker elder who left the Shakers in 1881 to get married. Although this was so much of a blow to the Enfield Believers that their church was never again opened for public worship after he "went to the world," there seem to have been no hard feelings on either side. All of Henry's articles about the Shakers are full of affection—one might almost say yearning—for these brethren and sisters he had lost by his own choice.

A good deal of the Shaker writing was anonymous. The original Shaker intent, indeed, was to submerge the creator of any piece of craftsmanship in the mass of fellow craftsmen. This was a logical concomitant of common labor and common ownership. Many of the Shaker books are unsigned though sponsored by the ruling Ministry. This is especially true of songs and hymns. Of the few whose authorship is known, more are ascribed to McNemar than to any other single source. Richard's dynamic personality left so unmistakable a mark on whatever he did, that it was difficult not to recognize his hand. There is a gusto, an intensity, indeed a passion to be felt in all he wrote, whether in his descriptions of the soul-embattled revivalists, in his arguments for the new Shaker religion or in his spontaneous hymns and his informal verses. What more satisfying easement for a welling up of joy than a hymn to be sung in the religious services that were the climax of the week's aspirations, the rewarding spiritual adventure for which all the work of the week had been preparing!

A collection of hymns printed at Watervliet, Ohio, in 1833, contains many that are probably McNemar's. His "Covenant Hymn" moves with an abandon that almost lets one see the Believers dancing. It was written for the purpose of making all the Believers familiar with the new Covenant over the adoption of which Richard labored so long and so hard. A few of the verses are quoted.

> You have parents in the Lord, you honor and esteem,
> But your equals to regard a greater cross may seem.
>> Where the gift of God you see,
>> Can you consent that it should reign?
> Yea I can, and all that's free may jointly say—Amen.
>
> Can you part with all you've got, and give up all concern,
> And be faithful in your lot, the way of God to learn?
>> Can you sacrifice your ease
>> And take your share of toil and pain?
> Yea I can, and all that please may freely say—Amen.
>
> Can you into union flow, and have your will subdu'd?
> Let your time and talents go, to serve the gen'ral good?
>> Can you swallow such a pill—
>> To count old Adam's loss your gain?
> Yea I can, and yea I will, and all may say—Amen.

Other Shaker hymns were believed to be of supernatural origin, being ascribed sometimes to angels, sometimes to Shakers already in the spirit world. These often have a haunting poetic quality that is usually lacking in Shaker verse. The following was said to have been given "by an angel from Jehovah, and accompanied by a most beautiful tune of two airs":

> I shall march through Mount Zion,
> With my angelic band;
> I shall pass through the city
> With my fan in my hand;

> And around thee, O Jerusalem,
> My armies will encamp,
> While I search my Holy Temple
> With my bright burning lamp.

One of the loveliest Shaker songs, which was, at the same time one of the earliest to be recorded with notes (at New Lebanon in 1822), is "The Humble Heart," which is quoted below.

> Whence comes this bright celestial light, what cause produces this,
> A heaven opens to my sight, bright scenes of joy and bliss.
> O Lord Jehovah art Thou here, this light proclaims Thou art,
> I am indeed, I'm always near unto the humble heart.
>
> The proud and lofty I despise, and bless the meek and low,
> I hear the humble soul that cries and comfort I bestow.
> Of all the trees among the wood I've chose one little vine,
> The meek and low are nigh to me—the humble heart is mine.
>
> Tall cedars fall before the wind, the tempest breaks the oak,
> While slender vines will bow and bend, and rise beneath the stroke.
> I've chosen me one pleasant grove and set my lovely vine,
> Here in my vineyard I will rove, the humble heart is mine.
>
> Of all the fowls that beat the air I've chose one little dove,
> I've made her spotless white and fair the object of my love.
> Her feathers are like purest gold with glory she does shine,
> She is a beauty to behold, her humble heart is mine.
>
> Of all the kinds that range at large I've chose one little flock,
> And those I make my lovely charge, before them I will walk.
> Their constant shepherd I will be and all their ways refine,
> And they shall serve and rev'rence me, the humble heart is mine.
>
> Of all the sects that fill the land—one little band I've chose,
> And led them forth by my right hand and placed my love on those.
> The lovely object of my love, around my heart shall twine
> My flock, my vineyard and my dove, the humble heart is mine.

All the symbolism of the Shaker belief is in this poem.

213

Other fields into which Shaker writers ventured were those of education, economics, sociology and—somewhat gingerly—politics. Most of them, like all reformers, were able pamphleteers. Many had a natural flair for journalism. McNemar, besides all his other talents, was a born journalist with a Barnum-like sense of what was news. He founded the earliest Shaker journal, "The Western Review," of which he was "projector, editor, typesetter and pressman." In the north, at a later period, Evans, Lomas, Dolittle and Blinn did editorial work on "The Shaker," afterwards called "The Manifesto," which ran from 1871 to 1899.

The two fields of literature into which the Shakers did not attempt to go were drama and fiction. The latter was repugnant to all their instincts of literal truth, and the former was so well represented in their ritual of worship that any cravings they might have had in this direction were amply satisfied by the symbolic dances and the mystically emotional songs. In economics and sociology, however, the Shakers were right at home. They spoke on these subjects with authority which even "the world" had to recognize, though it profited little from what the Shakers might have taught it. Nevertheless the Believers kept on trying: "voices crying in the wilderness" of the mid-nineteenth century.

Daniel Fraser and Frederick Evans were the outstanding Shaker pamphleteers of this period. The subjects of some of their articles and addresses give a picture of their varied interests—*Atlantic Cable and Materialization; The Condition of Europe; Capital and Labor, What is in a Name? Wail of a Striker; The Conditions of Peace; Shall Standing Armies be Abolished? Elder Evans to Henry George; Land Limitation; Religious communism; A Shaker on Political and Social Reform; The World's Fair! Shall it be closed one day in the week to please a certain sect?*, etc. Frederick Evans was a very prolific writer. His theological works were many and were widely read among the Shakers; his *Autobiography of a Shaker* is perhaps his most complete and best known book (certainly among the "world's people"), but the many articles he wrote for the Shaker "Manifesto" show the universality of the man, his close touch with world affairs. He was probably better informed about what was going on in the world than the majority of "the world's people"; certainly far more so than was the usual practice among the Believers. He was much criticized for this by some of the leading elders of other societies. It is possible, nevertheless, that he may have done more to disseminate Shaker economic theories in "the world" than any other single Shaker. He was, perhaps, the Shaker apostle Paul to Richard McNemar's Peter.

McNemar and Evans were certainly the greatest of the Shaker writers. Almost equally fervent in their devotion to the Shaker church, they belonged to totally different eras, although their life spans overlapped in years. At the time of Richard's death in 1839, Frederick was just beginning his leadership at New Lebanon. Richard belonged to the pioneer period: the time of the most heartbreaking hardships and the most soul-stirring growth. Frederick's connection with the Shakers was contemporary with their fastest material expansion and their greatest apparent spiritual success. Security was achieved; the adventure was in its happiest phase; the Believers seemed about to enter the Promised Land. Richard had known the doubts and rigors and the pain of the birth struggle; Frederick came along in time to aid in the education of the vigorous young society. Both men were equally loyal, fearless, logical Shakers; each faced the issues of his time with true Shaker directness and practicality.

Aside from their preoccupation with problems that concerned the Believers alone, they both found time and sympathy for the difficulties of other minorities. Richard had made gestures of friendship to the "deists," the "New-Light" dissenters from the established churches, the Indians, etc. Evans said a good word, retrospectively, for Voltaire and Tom Paine, was tolerant of Ingersoll, advocated birth control as one of the means of preventing wars, preached pacifism, votes for women, took several shots at "the poor, bigoted irrational Moody and Sankeyites, who have closed the gates of a World's Exposition upon one of the seven Sabbath days that their own sect, who visit it have adopted," and offered advice to the voters (from a non-voter!) in the presidential campaign of 1884. "The Sovereign People should vote for Measures, not Party nor Men. . . . Make women and Indians citizens. Work toward the equalization of property, thus lessening poverty, removing the temptation to crime and putting war afar off. Do right. Let the people have nothing to fight for or fight about. . . . Give us a Republic in fact as well as in theory, and all the Governments of the earth will become Republics."

McNemar writes in his *Kentucky Revival*, "If a historian cannot be disinterested and unbiased, it is necessary that he be honest." This sounds the keynote of Shaker literature. The Shakers never claimed to be disinterested and unbiased in their attitudes or their beliefs. But they tried to be honest. More than that, they tried to be fair toward others who were also trying to be honest. And this honesty and fairness adhere to all their words.

Of paintings and sculpture the Shakers produced none. The nearest they came to art in the special sense of pictorial imitation was in the "spirit drawings" which were received as "gifts" from the denizens of the other world. These scroll-like traceries in ink or pencil bear a family resemblance to the graceful handwriting that adorned the pages of early nineteenth century penmen. Shaker handwriting at times shows the same characteristic flourishes of its period in spite of the Shaker cult of plainness. In the drawings the flourishes were more pronounced. It was permissible and indeed praiseworthy to adorn and elaborate whatever belonged to that spiritual existence toward which the whole sect yearned. The drawings were all of a piece with the mystical side of Shakerism, that half of Shaker life that was generally kept hidden from "the world."

The Shaker imagination was held in tight curb during work hours, but it was given full rein in the religious services—especially those on Sundays or other days set apart for exercises of spiritual significance to the Believers. The Shakers were most nearly in the mood of the creative artist when they were tasting the full flavor of the Shaker adventure. Its essence was known only to them, and most fully when they opened the eyes of their minds to visions of beauty from the spirit world, or listened devoutly to songs brought by "Mother Ann's little White Dove, November 5, 1843," or by "a little bird which was taken from a spiritual tree that was planted in our meeting room, March 9, 1844." These visions made up in splendor for the ascetic barrenness of their daily living. Thus the spirit drawings showed elaborations of design that were wholly absent from the pictureless walls of the family dwellings.

These drawings were made during the spiritual revival that was experienced by the Shakers in the eight or ten years after 1837 when, according to Shaker belief and testimony, visitors from the spirit world came down to dwell among them. Some of the drawings were in the form of maps of the spirit land. Many of them used objects symbolically in the design, as flowers, trees, birds, altars, stars, etc. Often the words of a song made a heart-shaped or leaf-shaped pattern of fine, ornamental writing sent by an angel or by the spirit of a departed Believer as a mark of love and appreciation to one of the then living Shakers.

Never were these spirit pictures regarded as conscious art by the Shakers; rather, they were outward manifestations of inner spiritual ecstasies, a pictorial recording of the Shaker spiritual adventure. There is a strange similarity between some of these traceries and the symbolic pictures drawn by Vachel Lindsay as illustrations for his poems. Lindsay was born too late to have been influenced by the Shakers, but he came out of the same kind of revivalist background as McNemar, for instance, and he had the same fervor, the same crusading spirit tinged with mysticism as that which characterized the Believers. The resemblance may be fortuitous, but it is interesting psychologically.

If the Shakers made no claim to be artists, they were not unwilling, latterly, to be known as musicians. Music and the dance formed a major part of their religious ritual. In the beginning, however, it could hardly be called a ritual, since it was individually spontaneous with the unconstrained emotional hysteria that revivalism always shows. At this period—that is, in the days of the late seventeen-eighties, or before Joseph Meacham brought system into confusion— neither dancing nor singing showed any ordered form. According to records of earliest meetings, anybody who had a "gift" went into his dance or song with abandon and a complete disregard for the pattern of the ensemble. The songs were nothing more than syllables or phrases repeated over and over again in whatever key the singer chose. The dances were whirlings and leapings with no regularity of rhythm and no planning for the general effect. This was the phase of Shaker worship that impressed Lafayette so deeply by its sincerity and emotional fervor. As the Believers became gathered into orderly households and societies, the religious exercises also grew orderly and began to take distinct shape.

The first songs that emerge from this welter of sound were called "solemn songs" and were chanted without words. The earliest dancing was known as "promiscuous," although this did not imply a mingling of the sexes, simply unorganized individual dancing in the sisters' and the brethren's groups. Both singing and dancing were either spontaneous, outward expressions of inner joy and exaltation—something like the uninhibited shouting and dancing of happy children—or exercises of abasement and the trampling of sin underfoot—literally a "laboring to get good."

As the Shaker families, apart from the world and owning all things in common, found increasing fellowship in all that they did, as they pooled their individual skills as craftsmen to make a distinctively Shaker product, so they brought together their combined knowledge and feeling for music and dancing to build up a religious ritual that was purely Shaker. Its original sources were many: shouts and leapings of religious enthusiasm, airs of revival hymns with which many were familiar, folksongs and old tunes brought in by Believers from different national cultures, folk dances and country dances. The result was their own blend of music and movement: songs written down as inspired from above, dances that grew from simple "gifts" of leaping and whirling to formalized patterns of motion.

The earliest songs were learned by heart. This was easy and practical when the songs and the societies were few in number. Believers of a single community or region could come together easily for the purpose. But it was a different matter when the number of songs and communities began to increase, especially where communities were widely separated as in the Southwest. If songs were to be sent from one group to another as the Ministry came more and more to think desirable, a way of recording them had to be found. Notation offered some difficulties, so during the eighteen-twenties the use of letters instead of notes for writing music was begun. Shaker songs were at first gathered and preserved in manuscript hymn books; later, after 1852, they went into printed form.

In the meantime, treatises on music were being written for the use of the Believers, as "A Short Abridgement of the Rules of Music," by Isaac N. Youngs, the New Lebanon clockmaker whose chosen craft fitted him particularly well for a discussion of the elements of musical rhythm and the practical application of these to the teaching of singing. His idea of a simple metronome formed by attaching bullets to strings of various lengths for the marking of different meters came from years of experimentation with pendulums. Then there were teachers like Abram Whitney of Shirley, who was sent out in the eighteen-twenties to give instruction in theory and practice of music to the Believers of Harvard, Canterbury and other societies. Later on Canterbury became the recognized center of musical knowledge and skill, and was called upon to send teachers into many of the other communities, even as far as that remotest outpost of Shakerdom, South Union, Kentucky. Until 1870, when the Ministry finally decided to permit the use of organs and pianos to accompany the singing, there was no part-singing, no attempt at harmonizing.

The earliest recorded Shaker song is dated from Turtle Creek (later Union Village, Ohio) May 23, 1805.

> *With him in praises we'll advance*
> *And join the virgins in the dance.*

From the beginning song and dance were closely intertwined. It was only on March 22 of that same year that the three missionaries from New Lebanon (Issachar Bates, Benjamin Youngs and John Meacham) had arrived in Turtle Creek and been received at Malcham Worley's house. Just two months later, the first regular meeting of the Shakers was held at David Hill's house "with one ordained minister, two ordained elders, two licensed exhorters, two physicians and thirty other respectable persons" present. Richard McNemar was a facile versifier; Issachar had been a fifer in the Revolution and an enthusiastic singer of popular songs and ballads. It was Issachar who led the company in song at that historic meeting. The southwestern converts showed from the first a marked talent for melody and rhythm, and began shortly to influence the singing of the New York and New England societies. Almost immediately they started sending songs up north. There is a record in 1819 of a "packet" of "scored" songs being sent from Ohio to New Lebanon, and a return "packet" going back from the parent community to her lively child in the Southwest.

As the Shaker songs gradually acquired characteristics of their own, they began to fall into certain classes. There were the hymns, the "little" songs or "extra" songs, the anthems, which were sometimes quite long and often didactic (like McNemar's Covenant Hymn), the work songs or ritual songs, the marching songs, etc. Among the inspirational songs that were written during the decade from 1837 to 1847, were many in dialect or "unknown tongues" including the Negro and Indian songs. The music of these last often showed a marked resemblance to Negro and Indian rhythms. As a rule, however, the Shakers put their own mark—the imprint of their own spiritual emotion—on their music. Whether the tune were reminiscent of Yankee Doodle, a Scottish song, a revival hymn or an old English dance, the time was distorted to conform to the requirements of the Shaker ritual. The coördination of gesture and dance, plus the need of quickening the emotion of worship that was the mainspring of the service, could not find adequate expression in a conventional musical rhythm.

The songs connected with the rites of purifying and cleansing rooms, buildings and grounds called for special meters that would meet the demands of sweeping and scrubbing, and warring on the devil and all his instruments of dirt and evil. Many of the recorded songs change their rhythm from 2/4 time to 3/4 time and back again with what seems like complete disregard of all rules. It is difficult to tell from the printed notes just how the Shaker songs sounded when sung. People who heard the Believers sing— especially those who went to their meetings in the early and middle nineteenth century and wrote down their impressions—all agreed that it was impossible to convey the effect of this music to those who had not themselves heard it.

The words, the music, the gesturing and the dancing all united to form a kind of precision ensemble that would have done credit to a trained ballet corps. Military men watched admiringly the difficult march figures which the Believers executed so competently; attentive listeners tried in vain to analyze the slightly irregular tempo of the singing; sympathetic spectators were touched and even carried away in spite of themselves, by the earnestness and sincerity of the

whole performance, bizarre though it often was by all orthodox church standards. The unexplainable element in the
Shaker rhythm was possibly akin to modern "swing." It
had to be felt, not understood; it reached out to the emotions
rather than the intellect; it stimulated the nerves while
only confusing the thought centers. Communal drama as
such the Shakers did not need; they had it already in this
strange combination of music, words and dance given unity
by a spiritual vision instead of a worldly plot. And the
meetinghouse floor, which was sometimes "wet all over with
tears after the members had retired," was all the stage they
required.

A stage show it almost became at one period when the
doors of the Shaker churches were open to the "world's
people." The Shakers went so far in hospitality as to make
provision in their building of new meetinghouses for seating
space to hold large audiences from "the world." Even the
old standardized shape of the early churches and the conventional arrangement of the doors were changed in certain
communities such as New Lebanon, Watervliet, New York,
and North Union, Ohio, to arrange easy entrance for the
spectators. The Ministry did this in the hope of making
converts. A few mystics seeking for the truth were influenced
thereby to join the Believers, but the majority went only
for a good show. They were never disappointed. Some of
them made voluntary contributions of money to the Shakers
in return for the entertainment they had received, though
the Shakers never asked for this nor even encouraged it.

In one of the Maine societies, a sympathetic neighbor
who went often to their Sunday services started the habit
of passing a contribution box which he himself brought
with him for that purpose, giving the contents afterwards
to the Shakers. Whether the spectators came seeking en-

lightenment or amusement, whether they watched in sympathy or criticism, they came away with the impression of
a unified performance rendered with skill, precision, perfect
timing and, above all, the successful presentation of a burning conviction—the externalization of the spiritual adventure which the Believers could share with "the world" in no
other way. To this extent the Ministry, at least, was
audience-conscious.

But what of the actors in this drama? Did they play up
to the audience, eager for approval, if not applause? Or
were they so absorbed in the delivery of their message that
they were unconscious of the spectators? All week long
they had been rehearsing, so to speak, for it. In their mid-
week social gatherings they had even rehearsed consciously,
practising new songs. And every hour of every day they had
been preparing themselves by a self-imposed control of
appetites and passions for the "privilege" to worship God
fittingly with song and dance "as David danced before
the Ark."

No one who harbored evil or unkind thoughts was allowed
to take part. It was a sacrament, like the Passion Play of
Oberammergau. White and blue were the Sunday colors:
white for purity, blue for virginity. The women costumed
themselves in white dresses, white kerchiefs and white caps,
with blue and white aprons and blue shoes. The men came
in their long-tailed blue coats with trousers of blue and white
stripes and white shirts. They all ranged themselves in
couples for the march, the men at the left end of the room,
the women at the right, the singers in the center. The white
walls and ceilings of the church, broken by the blue ceiling
beams, the blue door and window frames, the blue wainscoting below the windows and the two blue rows of peg-boards
above them, made the background. The peg-boards were

hung with the outdoor bonnets of the sisters and the hats and coats of the brethren.

Half circles were formed at each end of the room, with the older Shakers at one end of each arc and the children at the other. At a given signal, the singers began, rising on their toes and swinging both arms in time to the song. Then the procession started to move around and around in perfect rhythm with the singing and the gestures. If the Believers were conscious of their audience when the services started, they soon lost all awareness of these outsiders from "the world." This was their worship, their adoration of their God, their reason for living; the audience grew shadowy and unreal to them, as, indeed, did the world whence it came and whither it would return. The spirit that infused this Shaker pageant was the only reality.

The Shaker ritual was at its most colorful between about 1830 and 1860. During ten years of this period, however, it was withdrawn from the eyes of the world. The manifestations of the Spiritual Revival of 1837 were so extreme in many communities that they excited the ridicule of the onlookers and brought about the closing of the church doors against non-believers. When the doors were opened again in the late eighteen-forties, many details of the service had undergone changes, though the essentials remained the same. The Shaker zenith had been reached, however. Soon their sun was to begin setting, though few noticed for years that the afternoon had begun.

The final withdrawal of their church services from public gaze came when they realized, dimly at first, then with growing clearness that the early fervor had gone out of their meetings, that they no longer had anything to excite and hold the interest of the general public. As their spiritual adventure lost more and more of its outward symbols, as their decreasing numbers closed more and more of their churches, they retreated to an upper room in the dwelling house, where the few visitors who still cared to come could be accommodated; soon even these doors were closed in finality against the curious eyes of the "world's people." Shaker ritual, and with it the Shaker music that had been made to serve it, had gone, so far as the world was concerned, to join the dead languages that people still study with interest but do not use for speech in daily living.

XIII. FULFILLMENT AND DECLINE

I T is in the nature of all earthly life that there should be
a period of growth, a time of fulfillment and blossoming
and the inevitable fading or decline into death. It is true of
plant life and animal life alike. The only part of man that
has been able to escape this fate is the human spirit. Yet
human institutions born of man's spirit run through this
same cycle of growth, bloom and decay. Nothing seems able
to remain at the point of completest fulfillment. The Shaker
church, more manifestly a foundation on spirit than most
utopias, failed to hold its hard-won victory. The Believers
stopped advancing when they reached the summit of economic success. Whether their spiritual advance was checked
first at that same point is another matter. It is easier to
evaluate material success. Did the Believers stop because
there was nowhere else to go? And what did they see from
that peak to which they had attained?

The most gratifying thing they saw was numbers: fifty-
eight separate families gathered together in eighteen societies scattered from Maine to southwest Kentucky. In the
period between 1840 and 1860—with a little shift one way
or the other in different communities—they attained their
greatest membership. There were about six thousand of
them in all, not a large number in the total population of
the country, but a notable increase from the nine original
English founders. Mt. Lebanon, New York, as it was renamed
in 1861, and Union Village, Ohio (the Mt. Lebanon of the
Southwest), led all the other societies with six hundred
members apiece. Pleasant Hill, Kentucky, came next with
about five hundred; Watervliet, New York, South Union,

Kentucky, Enfield and Canterbury, New Hampshire, and Hancock, Massachusetts, followed after with three hundred or more each. The other societies were smaller but full and active. Mt. Lebanon had at one time eight separate families which carried on their own separate business concerns, rendering separate accounts of their various transactions to the leading elders. The average number of families was three. The novitiate order in each society was filled with would-be Shakers. The "world" was regarding the Shaker experiment with interest; large audiences were going to the Shaker meetings.

Another thing they saw from their mountaintop was land: earthly possessions. They looked out on woodlots and well tilled fields, over three thousand acres in home farms in Maine and the same in Connecticut; six thousand in New Hampshire; eight thousand or more in Massachusetts; about ten thousand apiece in New York state and Kentucky; nearly the same amount in Ohio. They saw flocks of merino sheep, herds of Durham, Jersey and Guernsey cattle, orchards, fields of grain, vegetable gardens, hives of bees; and in winter neatly stacked piles of firewood, full barns and granaries, well stocked cellars and pantries. They saw rows of solid, symmetrical buildings—family dwellings, giant barns, the best gristmills in their part of whatever state they lived in. Down in Kentucky they saw mulberry trees and a thriving silk industry; they saw woollen mills in New Hampshire, cotton mills in Massachusetts, tanneries everywhere. They saw shops in both northern and southern communities turning out brooms, grain measures, and chairs that were to be still strong and useful a hundred years later. They saw Shaker presses in Ohio and New Hampshire publishing their ideas for all to read. And they saw respect in the once hostile eyes of neighbors.

If they had looked into the world outside their own orderly domain they would have seen mainly confusion, a stirring of apparently unrelated forces, a turning away from the old order toward something new. Railroads were being built to speed up transportation and connect distant points. Manufactures were increasing; business was booming. The artisan and craftsman producing finished articles at home or in small shops and mills, were being replaced by factory workers who came together in large plants to do their small, specialized bits of a whole in which they could feel no creative pride.

During the second quarter of the nineteenth century, workingmen began to organize. One of their early demands was for better educational opportunities for their children. In 1834 the act to establish public schools was passed in Pennsylvania. In 1837 Horace Mann became chairman of the state board of education in Massachusetts. One after another, the states made provision for the schooling of their children. The level of intelligence rose, with it, wages rose gradually and living conditions improved, not much, but slightly, as new inventions eased the motions of living. In 1843 the telegraph came into use. Mexico and Oregon began to engage people's attention.

The year 1849 brought the gold rush to the Pacific coast. Interests were broadened and quickened by travel, by news of travel, by education. And growing louder all the time were the rumbles of the coming conflict between the North and the South, between wage system and slavery, between an industrial and an agrarian society. The Shakers stood outside all this; most of them were not even looking on. But they could not escape being affected by it. They had always been consistently anti-slavery; nevertheless, the defeat of the Confederacy may have been partly their defeat, for their com-

munes, like the economic structure of the South, were
founded on agrarianism and derived their success from a
close connection with the land.

In the period of most rapid Shaker growth and prosperity
all the societies were carrying on simultaneous programs of
expansion. Much building was being done; new projects
were being started, such as the making of printed hymnals
in place of the manuscript copies; new methods of doing old
things were being tried. The general manufacturing of
chairs, for instance, was discontinued in many of the societies during the eighteen-fifties to be concentrated at the New
Lebanon chair factory in a modest venture into mass production. Many of the Shaker looms stopped working in
1853, since the development of factory-woven goods in "the
world" made it cheaper for the Believers to buy the cloth
they had formerly woven themselves. Other changes were
coming too, in matters of policy; early rules were being modi-
fied, as for example the rule that the Shakers should enter
into no financial transactions with "the world." The various
societies were branching out into many new business relations with "the world." The boom period of American
railroad building and industrial expansion was affecting the
Shakers in spite of their semi-isolated lives.

The story of Caleb Dyer's trusteeship of the society at
Enfield, New Hampshire, is probably typical enough of all
the Shaker societies to be worth giving somewhat in detail.
Caleb, who as a boy of thirteen went to the Shakers with his
family in 1813, became assistant trustee in 1824 and first
trustee in 1838. It was thus under his stewardship that the
famed granite dwelling house was erected in 1837. The cost
of this building has been variously estimated by different
people as from $35,000 to $75,000, but since most of the
labor was done by the Believers themselves and most of the

materials were taken from their own property, it was hard to find out the exact figure. In any case, it was all paid for when completed. In 1841 the well known Shaker Mills for the weaving of flannel were constructed by the Church Family where the leading elders and trustees lived. These mills were built in the village of North Enfield instead of in the Shaker village. In 1844 Caleb installed a new sawmill at the Church Family.

It was the coming of the railroad, however, that stimulated the Shaker building program. The Shakers took fifty or sixty shares of railroad stock when the road was extended north from Concord in 1847. The next year Caleb built a long sawmill in the town of North Enfield (at some distance from the Shaker village, but near the Shaker Mills and the newly opened railroad station), with the object of supplying the railroad with the long timbers it needed for its two bridges across the Connecticut and White rivers at White River Junction. This was an up and down sawmill, which could handle forty-four foot logs. The following year Shaker bridge, already mentioned, was constructed. That same year, 1849, saw the erection of a granite machine shop four stories high at the Church Family. Next year the North Family office building of brick was added. A wooden aqueduct was laid—eighteen inches in diameter with twelve foot staves looped with iron—to bring water down from the mountain brook.

In 1854 the great barn at the South Family was raised, and a dam was constructed in the town of North Enfield near the long sawmill for a bedstead shop which was built the following year. A second shop just below this one was put up two years later. These two shops were rented and later sold by Dyer, who was acting for the Shakers, to a local firm. In 1856 Dyer put in a foundation nearby for a gristmill, rebuilding the end of the dam. The mill was started in 1857 and completed in 1858; it was called the best equipped gristmill in New Hampshire north of Concord. That same year Caleb built an addition to the factory known as the Shaker Mills Company, which was doing many thousand dollars of business yearly in the flannel trade in New York City.

At the time of all this activity (which was being more or less duplicated in all of the eighteen societies), the Enfield Shakers had three hundred and fifty members living in the three separate families: the North, the Church and the South. One hundred of these were children; over two hundred were between the ages of sixteen and thirty. In 1840 the property valuation for the whole town of Enfield was $339,700. The total tax raised was $2,367.71, at a tax rate of $0.85 per $100, with $0.21 of this going for highways. Of the 325 registered polls in town, 58 were non-voting Shakers. The three largest tax payers in town were the trustees for the three Shaker families: Caleb M. Dyer for the Church Family, $155.36, Samuel Barker for the South Family, $85.71, and True W. Heath for the North Family, $46.16, making a total of $287.26, or about an eighth of the whole town taxes. (One year the Shakers paid a fifth.)

Of the $38,500 out at interest in the town Dyer had furnished $7,000; of the capital of $8,875 invested in mills in Enfield, the Shakers had supplied $5,500. In fact, many of the "world's people" felt that North Enfield owed its industrial development almost wholly to Shaker initiative; some of them even went so far at one time as to try to change the town's name to Dyersville. The Shakers themselves opposed this plan.

All this branching out into worldly commerce was contrary to the early rules of the United Society; and the outcome was to prove the wisdom of those rules. The Shaker

Mills Company, where the famous Shaker flannels were woven was dissolved in 1860 to continue under the name of A. Conant and Company, a New York firm to whom Caleb had extended credit (another infringement of Shaker rules!) during the hard times following the crash of 1857. But A. Conant and Company were either incompetent or else they were playing a deep game. Caleb, as agent for the Shaker interests was obliged more and more to resume management until he became virtually head of the firm.

Some of his fellow Believers began to murmur that Caleb's interests lay more in the town of Enfield than at home. Everyone admitted he was an able business man, but time was to prove that he was a careless one. He was shot in 1863, when on his way to the office building at the Church family, by the drunken father of children the Shakers had taken in and cared for. "I am shot, but not killed," he said as he walked into the office. When his unexpected death three days later threw the burden of his trusteeship onto other shoulders, it was found that he had kept no regular accounts, relying on his memory and a notebook written in his own personal kind of shorthand. A. Conant and Company, whose worried representative had tried to see Caleb before he died and who had told the elders that his company had every intention of repaying the Shakers what they owed to Caleb, changed their tune after Caleb's death. They put in a claim against the Shakers for several thousand dollars which, as became more and more apparent to disinterested parties, they themselves had actually owed to Caleb. The Shakers decided to fight this claim through the courts. They could produce no actual proof, however. The case was handled badly, dragging on for twenty years, when it was finally settled adversely for the Shakers who lost $20,000 thereby.

233

This particular account of the mid-nineteenth century boom years in one of the eighteen Shaker communities may be taken as a fair sample of what was going on throughout Shakerdom from Maine to southern Kentucky. It was a time of economic expansion, of overtures made to worldly capitalism by a communistic religious order. It was a time of chances taken and money lost, either through carelessness and bad luck as with Caleb Dyer, incompetence as with Augustus Grosvenor of Harvard, Massachusetts, or actual dishonesty as with Nathan Sharp of Union Village, Ohio. There was an abandonment not only of early policies but also of economic practices.

Other changes came during and after the Civil War which caused the Believers many losses, whether from actual war damages as in Kentucky, or from bad debts that had to be cancelled afterwards. South Union, Kentucky, lost a sawmill and gristmill by burning and $75,000 in bonds through dishonest bank officials. Enfield, Connecticut, saw their large southern trade in garden seeds utterly ruined, with back debts outstanding. In the eighteen-seventies the membership of the whole society had dwindled from six thousand to twenty-five hundred. During the eighteen-eighties and eighteen-nineties some communities were closed. By 1900 eight whole societies and a number of families of the remaining ones had been discontinued.

The reasons for the decline on the economic side are not hard to find. In the beginning, or as soon as the Shakers got under way, they were able to offer the average man or woman greater opportunities for happiness than could be found in "the world." Security was assured, food and housing were superior, hours and conditions of work were better. When the Shakers started, the techniques of trade were those of an artisan civilization in a frontier community. The articles sold were made in homes or in small factories and the Yankee pedlar handled much of the retail business. Communities were isolated; education was limited.

The Shaker commune was built to fit these conditions. It was perfectly suited to the age of the horse-drawn carriage or pedlar's cart, the ox-drawn plow. It thrived on isolation, since it could produce almost everything it needed. It did not require a public school system for the training of its members, because its own theory of education was perfectly suited to its needs and could be applied with no argument. The Shaker houses and shops and barns, their merchandising methods and their classroom teaching, too, were even ahead of their age for a while. But as the country settled down gradually into the serious job of becoming a nation, the Shaker isolation became artificial instead of logical and necessary.

When the craftsman civilization on which it was founded began to crumble, the economic structure the Shakers had raised on it sagged and settled. This was not true of their material foundations, for even today some of those perfectly laid stones are as solid and true as they were a hundred years ago. As for their spiritual foundations, the few Believers who are left still stand firm on the faith of the founders. Their economic system, however, had become an anachronism in an ever accelerating and expanding modern world where isolation is nothing now but a word. If the Shakers or some other equally earnest group were to start a similar experiment today, they would have to key it into the tune and rhythm of this age—however that might be done! Spirit may be changeless, but institutions that house it have to be rebuilt in every age.

Even after the sun has passed the meridian a good deal of the day is left. Many of the Shaker communities gave an impression of prosperity for decades after the recession in numbers had begun. Union Village, for instance, reached its peak between 1830 and 1840, but it remained in existence till 1910. It kept moving under its own momentum long after the driving force had been withdrawn. In the eighteen-seventies most of the societies were still selling their staple articles to "the world"—garden seeds, brooms, roots, herbs and medicines, sieves and dry measures, maple sugar, dried corn and apples, as well as farm and dairy products. In 1874 Enfield, New Hampshire, was doing a business of $30,000 in seeds and $4,000 in distilled valerian; North Union, Ohio, was furnishing milk and vegetables to Cleveland; Shirley, Massachusetts, was putting up five or six tons annually of their famous applesauce. The Mt. Lebanon chair factory was kept busy turning out Shaker chairs. Sabbathday Lake in Maine was exporting quantities of oak staves (already bent for setting up in hogsheads) to the West Indies molasses trade. And Union Village, Ohio, and the two Kentucky societies were raising and selling much fine stock. The Shaker standards of quality had become a byword. Farmers still knew "where to go when they wished to tone up their stock or change the strain of blood."

The Shaker products that derived most directly from agriculture were the last to be given up as they were the first to be developed. The fields were cultivated as long as there were brothers to cultivate them, and indeed longer by employing outside labor. Stock raising and dairying were carried on till they became unprofitable—that is, until dwindling numbers and an aging membership caused the hired laborers to exceed the Shaker workers. As late as 1900, however, Canterbury was reroofing with 87,000 old growth pine shingles its two-hundred foot barn which had been struck by lightning; four years later they added a creamery to their other dairy facilities, and in 1907 they refinished the interior of the barn with a sheathing of narrow matched boards on walls and ceiling, the better to house their hundred cows, and installed milking machines. The dairy business lasted till 1920, and the Canterbury Shakers still point with pride to the pictures of their prize-winning kine that today adorn the walls of the now unused creamery.

One indication that the Shaker tide had turned was the sale or leasing of Shaker property. In 1873 the Alfred, Maine, society sold part of their timber land for $28,000. They had already leased a sawmill and a gristmill to outsiders. Union Village and Watervliet, Ohio, as well as South Union, Kentucky, had all let out parcels of their land to tenant farmers. Many of the Shaker societies were absentee landlords of farms in other sections of the state, or even in other states, Watervliet, New York, owning thirty thousand acres in Kentucky. All the societies were employing hired laborers in proportions ranging from a twentieth to a third of the membership. Most of these were used on the farms. The Shaker shops were kept running to supply whatever was needed by the membership, but they sold less and less to outsiders.

As the Shaker sisters, who always outnumbered the brethren after the early years, saw the tasks they had been wont to consider theirs diminishing in quantity (the household tasks or the educating of children), or being wholly discontinued (the weaving and dyeing of cloth), they turned more and more to the making of the well known Shaker cloaks and in 1885, to knitting sweaters for the colleges. They began making small articles like pincushions, baskets, knitware, etc., that could be sold to what is now called the tourist trade. The Shaker sisters, travelling always in twos or threes, were a familiar sight in the summer hotels of Maine and New Hampshire during the last quarter of the nineteenth

237

century and the first of the twentieth. A few of them may still be seen today from the societies of Sabbathday Lake, Maine, and Canterbury, New Hampshire.

One difficult and unpleasant feature of the Shaker decline —one hesitates to say whether it was a cause or a result—was the number of money losses incurred through carelessness, incompetence, dishonesty or bad luck. At least half the societies suffered one or more of such losses. Pleasant Hill, Kentucky, lost $10,000 "through the carelessness of an aged trustee." Both the New Hampshire societies underwent money losses. New Gloucester, Maine, had several strokes of this kind of bad luck and was helped by loans from sister communities. Groveland, New York, ran into debt. South Union lost over $100,000 from causes directly or indirectly connected with the Civil War. The societies that were so fortunate as to escape this kind of disaster often felt obliged to help their less fortunate brothers and sisters.

Another drain on the common treasury was the hazard of fire. Before the coming of the automobile and the concomitant improved roads, a fire in any rural district of America was almost certain to be a major disaster. Shaker records are full of stories of the destruction of seven or eight buildings in a single blaze. At Enfield, New Hampshire, six buildings were burned in 1849, just after the completion of Shaker bridge which brought help from North Enfield in time to save the rest of the village from going. In 1875 the Church family at Mt. Lebanon lost eight buildings in a single day. Groveland suffered from both flood and fire, with seven buildings wiped out in a night by flames.

At Pleasant Hill, Kentucky, Elhannon Scott, aged seventy-eight, "expired suddenly without uttering a word, while attempting to reach a building that was on fire. He was a Trustee in the Church family at the time of his death, and he was a very faithful man." Union Village, perhaps the most turbulent and precocious of the Shaker societies, went through a decade of disaster, beginning with a series of incendiary fires in 1831, continuing with a big flood of Turtle Creek in the spring of 1835 and climaxing with the theft by an absconding trustee in September of that same year of forty or fifty thousand dollars. Close on the heels of this tragedy followed the unjust and spectacular trial of Richard McNemar in 1837. It was said that the membership dropped from six hundred to three hundred and fifty.

Into this recital of losses and discouragements come one or two hopeful notes. About 1855 a colored woman went from Watervliet, New York, to preach Shakerism among her race in Philadelphia. Twenty years later she was the leader of a little group of twelve who worked daytimes as servants, coming home at night to the house which she kept for them. They were under the friendly supervision of the Watervliet society. Another late attempt to start a new Shaker colony was made by Mt. Lebanon in 1894, when they bought seven thousand acres of land in Narcoosee, Florida, and sent down Benjamin Gates and another brother to develop it. The Shakers stayed there three or four years, writing home dutifully enthusiastic accounts about the climate, the low taxes, the nine hundred head of cattle, the fruit trees, the rice field and the grape vines. They even put up a "Fairbanks Windmill and a 5,000 gallon tank for irrigating and also domestic purposes" in April of 1897.

Apparently they had no luck in making converts, for they wrote home somewhat wistfully in May of that year, "It is now over two years since the first two pioneer brethren came to this place"; and again in September, "Our stationary number still holds to the mystic seven." "Olive Branch," as the Shakers called this newest child of theirs, was born too late. All in all, however, the eighteen-nineties were a fairly prosperous period for the Shaker societies that had managed to survive fire, flood, financial losses, desertion and la grippe which was raging everywhere and took its toll of all the Shaker communities except Groveland.

Canterbury certainly gives the impression of a going concern in its report to "The Manifesto" of April 1896: "2592 cakes of ice 22 in. square and 16 in. thick have been secured this winter. 100,000 ft. of lumber has been hauled down some four miles, sawed into boards, shingles and lathes and is now ready for market. [We have] 2 silos of 100 tons each, 32 ft. deep, 11 by 13 ft. square. April 1 ten tons still left. Nearly one ton per day is fed to cattle." And South Union sounds a hopeful if somewhat pathetic note in its October letter to "The Manifesto" of the same year. "Brick store burned. New store finished costing $2500. Our taxes though large have all been paid. Have just purchased 10 tons of fertilizer for wheat fields at a cost of $270. Times are hard and our expenses heavy, but we are out of debt." Which was quite an achievement considering their losses from the war and the small margin on which they operated.

Another optimistic venture of the Shakers was the starting in 1871 of a Shaker magazine called first "The Shaker," then "The Manifesto." It was definitely a "house organ," but it sold some subscriptions to "the world" and it carried some advertisements of non-Shaker goods. Most of its space was devoted to articles or sermons on Shaker doctrines, with occasional reprints of earlier Shaker writings or series of sketches about different phases of Shaker history and biography. There was also a department called Society Record which contained bits of news from the different societies, a public means of communication between distant members. The magazine was discontinued in 1900.

A factor not previously stressed, yet the most important single concrete element in the decline of Shakerism was, of course, the loss of members. Although the Shakers were understandably reticent about giving this information to "the world," all the Shaker diaries contain mention of defections of individuals. Entries taken at random from record of two societies give the following.

Watervliet Society, Ohio. 1857.

"Eliza Welchammer went to the world taking her five children and Peter's child."

"Martha Parker turned off to the world."

"George Grub came back and obtained another privilege."

"Lucy Lemons was kindly invited to go to the world. She went."

From Pleasant Hill, Kentucky.

"Lydia and Mary Secrest went to the world from the center family. Silly lambs, you will wish you were in the fold when the wolves get you!"

"Feb. 1861. Tabitha Shuter, silly lamb, left the East House for the wide, cold and heartless world!"

"Apr. 24, 1864. Illinois Green absconded from the West family. What a spectacle! Nearly 40 years old and starting out in the wide world hunting flesh!"

"May 20, 1864. Illinois Green returned and was readmitted into the West family whence she had fled."

The mere fact that they were readmitted after running away is significant. In the early days backsliding was looked upon by the Believers as final. And yet it was perhaps characteristic of the Shaker tolerance that these seceders should be given a second chance. In practice the Shakers were always more generous to ex-Shakers than the wording of their covenant would indicate. Although every applicant for membership promised to make no property claim of any sort against the Shakers if he left them, actually no one was ever sent away empty-handed. At Tyringham, for instance, when, as sometimes happened, a young Shaker and Shakeress fell in love and wanted to leave and get married, if they went frankly to the elders and told them of their desire the elders put them on a kind of six-months probation to make sure that they really knew their own minds. After this period, if they still wanted to marry, the Shakers let them go with their blessing, a sack of flour, a horse and a hundred dollars; for, as they themselves said, they regarded marriage and private property "not as crimes or disorders, but as emblems of a lower order of society." If those who had tasted the pure and austere joys of Shakerism found themselves unable to breathe the rarefied air of those heights, it was better that they should go back to "the world."

To the Shakers who remained, to the Shakers who still remain, it was and is inconceivable that any Shaker should want to go back to "the world." "The world" was full of dangers, full of snares for unwary feet. There was much in it that was ugly, and whatever seemed beautiful in it was perhaps most dangerous of all. There was no peace to be found in "the world," only the unrest of feverish desire. But in the Shaker villages peace walked with everyone every day—under the rows of Shaker maples, along the neat flagstone paths, too narrow for two to walk abreast, over the grass plots between the strong, orderly brick and stone and wooden buildings that made a world apart.

Peace filled the corridors and smiled from the built-in cupboards and the many shaped drawers that never stuck however damp the weather. Peace radiated from the low rectangular Shaker stoves with the long stovepipes that could so well heat a room. Here in their own little domain the

Believers were safe. As the passing years left the early frenzy ever farther and farther behind till its outlines were blurred in a haze of memory and tradition, safety and peace came to seem even more important than adventure. Or perhaps the Shakers, always realists, were accepting with resignation the fact that their adventure was nearly over. And peace is doubly sweet after adventure.

XIV. THE ADVENTURE ENDS

As has been shown, the period of greatest prosperity and influence for the Shakers came, roughly speaking, between 1840 and 1860. Up to 1830 or 1840 the movement had been growing steadily; after the Civil War the membership fell off noticeably and continuously; somewhere in between the two dates something had happened. The summit had been reached; the descent had begun. At some point, differing in time and possibly in cause also in the different communities, the gleam of the vision had faded, imperceptibly but effectively. The adventure had begun to pall; the security achieved had become more desirable than the quest in aid of which it had been developed. The nice balance between spiritual adventure and physical security had been disturbed.

In the earliest days the adventure had weighed more heavily than the need for security; in the latter days the need and desire for security tipped the scales. The point at which the two things balanced perfectly was hardly more than a point—a year, perhaps, or a week, or even an hour. Nothing ever stays at a perfect point of balance. Perfection cannot last. If it rests one moment on its dearly won achievement it becomes sterile, dead. It was so with the Shakers. The important thing is to search for the reason.

The Shakers themselves have given reasons. Some claim that they never really expected Shakerism to last. Mother Ann is quoted as saying that the movement would decline to the point where there would not be enough of them left to bury their dead. But somewhere, she said, sometime, the impulse toward the perfect life would again be felt by some other group and Shakerism would be reborn, stronger than ever. Perhaps Mother Ann, who was wiser than most, realized the fragile nature of this perfection she was striving to grasp for her followers and for the world. The Christian Church had already been through many crises; perhaps she understood that there would have to be many more before mankind became truly civilized and Christian. She is reported to have said to one of the early brethren, "You think that you will yet subdue and overcome the nations of the earth, but you are mistaken; they will have that work to do for themselves. They will fight and devour, and dash each other to pieces, until they become so humble as to be willing to receive the Gospel. . . . They will build up, but God will pull down; they will build up, but God will pull down until they can build no more! But you will have nothing to do with it."

It would seem that she was right. It would seem, also, that she had a true foreboding of what was actually to cause the decline of her brave new religion, since in her many admonitions she stressed the very weaknesses that were later to dilute the early fervor. One day when she was looking at an apple tree in bloom she said, "How beautiful this tree looks now! But some of the apples will soon fall off; some will hold on longer; some will hold on till they are full half-grown and then fall off, and some will get ripe. So it is with souls that set out in the way of God. Many will set out very fair, and soon fall away; some will go further, and then fall off; some will go still further and then fall; and some will go through. . . . The way of God will grow straighter and straighter; so straight that if you go one hair's breadth out of the way you will be lost."

The reasons for failure that are given by some of the surviving Shakers of today fall into two classes: what might be called external reasons, and those which are internal and psychological. In the first class come losses due to outside causes over which the Shakers had no control: unfriendly acts by "the world's" people, such as the killing of Caleb Dyer at Enfield, New Hampshire; destruction of property by fire, flood or war, as in the Kentucky societies during the Civil War; lawsuits, etc. Even those instances when the Shakers were betrayed by their own members were in a sense external, since they did not necessarily affect the morale of the loyal members. When an infrequent dishonest trustee like Nathan Sharp of Union Village embezzled Shaker funds, the society grieved over his betrayal of his trust, but the loyal members were in no way injured in the fiber of their personal integrity.

When Elder Henry Cumings of Enfield, New Hampshire, eloped with a woman who later boasted that she had joined the Shakers with that very aim in view, his act had no harmful effect on the attitudes of the remaining Believers. The "winter Shakers" who sought admission after the harvest was gathered in the fall only to leave when the spring plowing began, constituted something of a problem as time went on; yet here again their too transparent reasons for joining the Shakers at a time of year when work was light and shelter desirable became a matter for tolerant contempt by the Believers rather than a temptation to them. Many of the Shaker young men who renounced their principles of pacifism and turned their backs on Shakerism to go into the army and fight at the time of the Civil War, sought readmission after the war had ended.

None of these happenings need have been fatal. None of them constitute a fundamental reason for the decline of Shakerism. They were perhaps symptoms; they were not causes. No matter how many external disasters came to the

Shakers, short of complete annihilation by the forces of nature or inhuman nature, nothing outside themselves, whether from the "world's people" or from their own unworthy members had the power to hurt them. If this had not been true, the Believers would have been stamped out in England in the seventeen-seventies, or in New England in the seventeen-eighties, or in Ohio after the turn of the century. They had nothing external to contend with in the middle of the nineteenth century as hard as the actions of those early mobs.

The inward causes were much more subtle. The seeds of decay and death had been sown in the spirit. The first cause, of course, was abatement of the original zeal. Unless there could have been a regular succession of new recruits imbued with the same fervor as the founders, there was no possibility of keeping the passion for perfection at white heat. Age does something even to fanaticism; there is no such thing as steady and undiminishing fervor. Besides, who was to inspire these new torchbearers? Mother Ann had the power to kindle hearts; so, to a lesser degree did Father James Whittaker. Richard McNemar of Ohio and Kentucky was another such. But the zealous prophets who can kindle a continuing flame in others are among the rarest of human beings. It was natural that the ardor should cool. Even so, if the Shakers had been willing and able to make some compromise with the absolute to which they were dedicated, they might have endured for another century. But in so doing they would have diluted still further the essence of their mission, and would have become just another more or less logical and ineffective sect. Their way, they are still in the line of the small dissenting groups of the whole Christian era, and indeed of all religious history.

The course the Shakers chose led to disaster by another route. In 1837 there were striking manifestations of spiritual phenomena in many of the societies. The leaders encouraged these in the idea that here was the germ of a reawakening and a revivifying of the early faith. The Believers had always experienced contacts of one kind or another with the world of the spirit. Shakerism began with a vision of Mother Ann's in the prison cell at Manchester. The crossing of the Atlantic was memorable for the help given by two visible "angels of God" standing by the mast; it was a common thing in many of the Shaker meetings to converse with the spirits of Noah and the prophets. And many of the early songs and dances were directly inspired from above. But this new awakening was different. It was less spontaneous, more calculated and planned from New Lebanon. It went to extremes that even the Shakers themselves later disavowed. It had obvious ill effects on certain of the Shaker communities; it made a bad impression on neighbors who were beginning to understand and even admire these fanatics in their midst; it alienated some of the more thoughtful of the Believers.

There were two ways in which this new spiritualism made itself felt: in a renewal and elaboration of the symbolic element in worship, and in the use of mediums by the different societies for the testing and proving of members. The symbolism brought much that was picturesque and colorful into the ritual, but it also brought uncontrolled emotionalism in physical expression (so that the doors of the churches had to be closed to "the world") , and an extreme of artificial mysticism. It was responsible for the cleansing rites in which happy bands of singing Believers went forth in the fall of the years to cleanse "every building, every apartment, every lane, field, orchard and pasture of all rubbish and needless encumbrance," and for the dedication of the land in the spring when the sisters "commenced sowing the east lots with the seed of Blessing, Protection, Dependance."

But it was also responsible for the publishing of the *Holy, Sacred and Divine Roll and Book, from the Lord God of Heaven to the Inhabitants of Earth,* and for the laying out of Holy Hills for outdoor worship. *The Holy Roll* was "revealed in the United Society at New Lebanon" to Philemon Stewart and published at Canterbury in 1843. It was obviously inspired by the Book of Mormon (discovered in 1827, printed in 1830), and its style is reminiscent of the book of Revelation. The Shakers believed at the time that it was a new revelation of the will of God made to them and through them to the world. They ordered copies of it to be sent to all the kings and rulers of Europe and of such other parts of the globe as they could reach, and to the President and other leaders of the United States government, including heads of Departments. Only the king of Sweden was civil enough to acknowledge its receipt. Later on the Ministry decided that the book was not a true revelation and withdrew it so far as possible from circulation. But it was widely read by the Shakers at the time of publication.

The Holy Hills of Zion are faintly reminiscent of the Groves of Ashtaroth or of early druidical worship. Great secrecy and mystery were observed in the laying out of these Holy Hills. Each society had a special name for its newly established place of worship which became the intimate, mystical name by which the community was called. New Lebanon was *Holy Mount;* Watervliet, New York, *Wisdom's Valley;* Enfield, New Hampshire, was *Chosen Vale;* Harvard, Massachusetts, was *Lovely Vineyard;* Pleasant Hill, Kentucky, was *Holy Sinai's Plain,* etc. The procedure was the same everywhere: suspicious uniformity in a supposedly inspirational affair. A site was chosen somewhere on the

Shaker land, and a square of about three-fourths of an acre was cleared, leveled off and fenced in. Then a stone was mysteriously "discovered" and set up by the elders bearing an inscription which was jealously guarded from the eyes of the "world's people." So sacred did the Shakers consider this stone that years later when the Holy Hills were abandoned, the stones were buried or otherwise made safe from possible sacrilege by unsympathetic eyes.

The site of the Holy Hill in Enfield, New Hampshire, is about a mile above the Shaker buildings on the side of Montcalm Mountain. In the exact middle of its three-fourths of an acre square, is still to be found a stone pediment from which a slab has been removed. The Shakers used to go by cart-path, on foot if they were able, otherwise by carriage to worship in this place. Sometimes the meeting would last all day. The dancing and the singing were more extreme and uncontrolled than in the regular Sabbath day services. Ex-Shakers who have left accounts of them do not attempt to explain the compulsion which they admit seemed to be laid on the participants, any more than McNemar tried to explain the Kentucky Revival. Yet from these meetings, the Believers drew comfort and exaltation. "The world," however, felt no sympathy for them; rather, indeed, scorn, ridicule—even fear. After 1848 or 1850 the ritual became less frenzied, but the Enfield hill was used for worship as late as the eighteen-eighties.

Extreme and artificial as these practices may have been, they were far less harmful than the second way in which this spiritual revival manifested itself. The employment of mediums in the different societies for the testing of members put both temptation and a powerful weapon in the hands of ambitious leaders. Elisha Pote, leader of the Maine Shakers, who seem to have kept their heads in most emergencies, came out flat-footedly against the use of this technique at the start. But he was in the minority.

The outstanding example of its injurious results was in Union Village, Ohio, in 1838. Freegift Wells had been sent down there from New Lebanon in 1836 to fill the place vacated some years before by the death of David Darrow. The post had been offered to Richard McNemar who had refused it on account of his many duties to other communities of the Southwest. Apparently Freegift was jealous of Richard from the first. After trying in many unsuccessful ways to undermine Richard's popularity with his own people, Freegift decided to pull a few spiritual wires. In 1837 a young medium named Margaret O'Brian testified through her contact with the spirit world that Richard was wholly puffed up in his own conceit and guilty of insubordination to his superiors. When even this revelation failed to swerve the Believers from their loyalty to Richard, she had another more circumstantial vision to clinch the matter.

Sorrowfully Richard's old friends voted to expel him from the society which he himself had made. Richard appealed to the Central Ministry who upheld him, cross-questioned and discredited the medium, and ruled that henceforth all revelations must be passed upon by them before acceptance. Richard returned in triumph and was reinstated. But the journey and the shock of his treatment had been too much for him. He died during the year. He was the last of the great ones of the early Believers. He had the fervor, the unselfish consecration, the larger outlook, the common sense in the handling of practical problems that were so characteristic of Mother Ann. It was ironic that he who was always so selfless and so charitable to others, so scrupulous about the truth, should have been sacrificed to the personal ambition of a small-minded sectarian in the name of a false and exaggerated spiritual revival that some of the leading Shakers were themselves questioning.

Another reason given by some of the present day Shakers for the decline of their church concerns the quality of latterday leadership. At worst it was feeble and ineffectual; at best it had become too rationalistic. Or perhaps they would state it the other way around. Some of the outstanding leaders of the second half of the nineteenth century were intellectual men: Frederick Evans, Giles Avery, Daniel Fraser. Frederick Evans was sometimes accused by his own people of being a deist and therefore a bad influence on the membership at large. Deism was ever a bogy to the majority of the Believers. The revivals out of which most of the Shaker communities had drawn their membership were the weapon the churches of a hundred and fifty years ago set up to combat deism. The Shakers were not an intellectual group as a whole. It was easy for the simple "hand-minded" members to charge men of intellect with deism.

Cultivation of the intellect was regarded as almost equally dangerous and sinful with indulgence of the flesh. The pleasure these keen-minded leaders found in consideration and discussion of world problems or theories of economics and government, was in any case a waste of time according to Shaker standards, if it were not actually a dangerously near approach to intercourse with the world and the devil. This is not as farfetched an attitude as it may appear. Singleness of purpose and directness of aim were the characteristics and the safeguards of the founders. The minute they turned aside in any direction from the path they had marked out for themselves, they were in danger of losing their way. The few survivors feel confident that they, at least, have not lost their way, though they are leaderless, but for comradeship they must look increasingly now toward their friends who have preceded them to that spirit world which is the goal of their hopes and the fulfillment of their dreams.

Another cause, at the opposite extreme, for the dying out of the Shakers—not listed by them but always mentioned first by the "world's people"—is their celibate way of life. Obviously a society based on celibacy could not long endure. Yet there are celibate orders in the Roman Catholic and other churches that have endured for centuries. Why should this way of life prove fatal to the Shakers and not to other groups? In the first place, celibacy as practised in the Roman church, for instance, is admittedly for a few chosen individuals only; it does not apply to the general membership of the church. The whole Shaker church, on the contrary, practised it and advocated it. In the second place, celibacy in most monastic orders is mainly a matter of self-imposed personal discipline, and implies no criticism or disapproval of normal sex relations in the outside world.

The Shakers, on the contrary, while admitting the right of every human being to live his own life as he chose and saw fit, believed that the celibate life was not only the highest and purest but the most expedient as well. Communal ownership of everything was much safer when there were no children to inherit. Communal industry was steadier and more dependable when the disturbances of sex attraction were absent. Self-discipline of the physical body was easier when the thing which the "world's people" called love between man and woman was discredited and ruled out of existence. All this was on the practical side. Its wisdom was shown by its results—up to a certain point.

It is unfair to the Shakers, however, to infer that the practical reason was the principal one. The mystical and the practical were ever interwoven in the fabric of Shaker life, and the mystical provided more color and pattern than the practical. Celibacy was a cornerstone of their spiritual life, a proof that the body could be conquered by the spirit, that the flesh could be ruled by the will. Yet the Believers were probably farthest from the essence of celibacy when they were most fervently worshipping. For the more devout and inspired the ritual, the more emotional its effect. Shakers who held themselves rigidly repressed in all their workaday human relationships gave way to such emotional excesses in their worship that they were even suspected by hostile "world's people" of breaking all their weekday rules of conduct on the Sabbath day.

This spiritual abandon had in it, of course, some of the elements of sex excitation and was, to that extent, creative in its effects. From it the Believers drew renewed inspiration. When, however, the zeal of the early converts began to abate, when the religious services grew more restrained and (from the worldly point of view) decorous, the knell of Shakerism had sounded. Celibacy is perhaps an ideal conquest of life, but sterility, its logical successor, is a surrender to death. Life cannot be put into a mold and kept there, however perfect and beautiful the mold. It spills over or ferments and explodes. If it does not it has ceased to be life. This is how life went from the Shakers. This is the real reason that Shakerism could not last.

In the beginning most of the new converts to Shakerism had been young men and women in their early twenties. In embracing celibacy, their normal sex instincts were sublimated in ecstatic devotion to the new religion and its founders. The hero-worshipping instinct found satisfaction in devotion to Mother Ann and the Elders; the creative urge found an outlet in the building—both material and spiritual —of the Millennial Church. Later, when the communes were fully established and the new religion had become stabilized and formalized, increasingly fewer young men and young women were attracted to join. And of the many children cared for and educated by the Shakers, only about one in ten remained to become a member and sign the covenant.

The middle-aged, however, who had tasted the life of "the world" and had found it bitter, turned to the Shakers for the peace and security they craved. It was refuge rather than struggle or adventure that they sought. Some of them were intellectuals, some were purely "hand-minded." Many of them were sincere. But most lacked the early fervor. They were content to accept celibacy as a condition of peace and security. They did not, perhaps, feel it much of a sacrifice. The personnel of the Shakers changed gradually—imperceptibly. Of course there were still devoted leaders like Evans, Eads, and Blinn, who tried to keep Mother Ann's torch burning, and lesser known, obscurer members who proved by the saintliness of their daily lives that the Shaker way was still a consecrated and a practical way of life. But the logic of rapidly decreasing numbers was unanswerable. The tide was going out too fast.

The first of the Shaker communities to be discontinued was that ill-fated society of West Union at Busro where Busseron Creek flowed into the Wabash River just north of Vincennes, Indiana. Busro had struggled from the beginning against such odds as Indian attacks, roving bands of marauding soldiers in the War of 1812, flood, fire, hostile neighbors and—worst of all—that scourge of early settlers in the river bottoms of the middle west, malaria. It was abandoned in 1827—so early in the century that to many of the later Shakers it was only a name. The brethren and sisters were apportioned between Pleasant Hill, Kentucky, and Union Village, Ohio. All the Shaker property in Indiana was sold by 1837, though the last house there was not torn down till 1882, and the last survivor of the Busro society lived on into the twentieth century. Sister Sarah Pennybaker's life, which ended at Pleasant Hill in 1916, had spanned the years between Monroe and Wilson, linking the oxcart era to the automobile age.

The remaining eighteen societies found themselves able to cope with such disasters and discouragements as befell them until late in the nineteenth century. Tyringham was the next to succumb in 1875. The few remaining members joined the Enfield, Connecticut, and the Hancock, Massachusetts, societies; and the property was sold to a Stockbridge man who resold it a little later to be run as a summer and winter resort under the name of the Tyringham Forest Association. Since then it has gone into private hands, the church having been bought and remodelled for a dwelling by the late Sidney Howard.

The eighteen-eighties and nineties saw the passing of five more Shaker colonies. The Lower Canaan Family of Mt. Lebanon was disbanded in 1884 and the property sold to the Berkshire Industrial Home. The Gorham, Maine, family, really a part of the Sabbathday Lake society, was given up and the members moved to the latter place in 1887. On October 24, 1889, the North Union, Ohio, society was dissolved and its 1,366 acres of land sold to a real estate company for $316,000. Of the twenty-seven surviving members, eight went to Union Village and seventeen to Watervliet, Ohio. At present none of the Shaker buildings remain. The land, chosen originally for its high situation, its fertility and its water supply, as most of the Shaker home farms were, is now one of the attractive residential parts of the city of Cleveland and keeps a reminder of its origin in the name Shaker Heights. In 1892 the Groveland, New York, society, founded and gathered latest of all the northern ones, followed the example of North Union. Its surviving members went to Watervliet, New York—the earliest community.

It is a point of interest that in most cases the societies last founded were first to go. The Shakers sold their Groveland property to the state of New York to be used as an institution for persons afflicted with epilepsy. It is now called Craig Colony; one of the buildings has been given the name House of the Elders in honor of its former occupants. In 1897 the Upper Canaan Family was moved to Enfield, Connecticut, further reducing the number of families at Mt. Lebanon from the eight it once had to four. All the other Shaker societies were undergoing similar reductions and retrenchments.

With the beginning of the new century, it was only too evident that the Shaker day was drawing to a close, in spite of spurts of activity here and there, as at Canterbury. "The Manifesto" ceased publication: along with the old century it went out of existence in 1900. That same year, the Watervliet, Ohio, society was dissolved and its members sent to Union Village. By 1903, there were only ninety Believers left in Ohio. In 1907 the Mt. Lebanon ministry ordered the dissolution of Whitewater. Three years later, in 1910, Union Village followed its three predecessors; the members were distributed among the other societies, some going to South Union, Kentucky, and some to the northern societies of Watervliet and Mt. Lebanon, New York, and Canterbury, New Hampshire. The Shaker property went into the hands of a receiver; later on, the lands and buildings were bought by the United Brethren to be used as a home for their aged and also as a Children's Home. Today the Lebanon State Prison Farm uses the eastern half.

The Pleasant Hill, Kentucky, community came to the end of its earthly existence that same year of 1910. The leading trustee, Dr. W. F. Pennybaker, gave a deed of the Shaker property including eighteen hundred acres of land to George Bohon of Harrodsburg *in trust*, with the condition that Bohon was to care for the twelve Shakers resident at Pleasant Hill so long as they lived, and then use the property to found the Pennybaker Home for Girls. It was not till 1925 that sister Mary Settles, the last Shaker in Kentucky, died there at the age of eighty-seven. The South Union, Kentucky, society was given up in 1922 and the estate sold at auction for $229,000. Seven of the ten survivors went to Mt. Lebanon, New York, and the other three accepted $10,000 each as their share of the property and moved to Auburn, Kentucky. Two of these forsook the Shaker tradition to become man and wife. Shakerism in Ohio and Kentucky, for which the dauntless Issachar and Richard had pled and worked and suffered, was now only a memory and a few groups of buildings. Two thousand of the South Union acres, now owned by Oscar S. Bond of Louisville, have become one of the outstanding stock farms of Kentucky, and the central dwelling house is to be used as an inn. The former Guest House of the Shakers at Pleasant Hill is now a Shaker Museum. In 1936 Colonel James Q. Isenberg of Harrodsburg was urging a revival of Shaker industries with emphasis on the Shaker high standards of workmanship. By the summer of 1940, the Pennybaker School had been turned over to the Goodwill Industries for their rehabilitation work, and members of the Pennybaker family were bringing suit for recovery of the property since it was being used for other than the stipulated purposes. Inasmuch as the lands and buildings were Shaker property, this lawsuit sounds like a reversion to the old habit of the "world's people" of trying to get back family property that had been given in good faith to the Believers.

In Massachusetts and Connecticut, meanwhile, the work of dissolution was continuing. The society at Shirley, Massachusetts, was given up in the late summer of 1908 and the property sold to the state. The one Shaker brother went to Hancock, and the three sisters stayed at Shirley until January 1909, when the state of Massachusetts took possession and established the Shirley Industrial School for Boys, after which the sisters joined the Harvard society. In 1917 the Enfield, Connecticut, society was dissolved, and the eight survivors apportioned between Hancock, Watervliet, New York, and New Lebanon. The last elder, Walter Shepherd, died in the North family at New Lebanon. One survivor is still living at Hancock.

The property was bought by a Boston man, John C. Phillips, who operated it for a time as a tobacco farm, then sold it in 1931 to the state of Connecticut for a prison farm. The prisoners are cultivating the fields, and canning fruits and vegetables for winter use just as the Shakers did. Harvard, Massachusetts—the place seen in vision by Mother Ann before ever she left England and beloved by her in spite of her sorrows and injuries at the hands of the Harvard mobs—was the next to go. The few Believers who were left went to New Lebanon, and the buildings were sold about 1920 to Fisk Warren, a single tax enthusiast who wanted to experiment practically with his theory by renting the buildings on ninety-nine year leases. Several of them are now in private hands, the church having been adapted for a dwelling by Dr. Louis C. Cornish. One of the smaller houses was acquired by Clara Endicott Sears and moved to the Harvard hillside where Alcott's Fruitlands stood, to be used as a Shaker Museum.

The northern New England societies were also surrendering to the relentless diminution of numbers. In 1918 the Enfield, New Hampshire, community regretfully closed its doors and moved its seven survivors to Canterbury. There was one brother, Elder Franklin Young and six sisters. The South Family possessions had already been sold to a local farmer. When the North and Church Family buildings and lands were known to be for sale, the Ministry at Canterbury received an offer from a New York Sport Club of $100,000 for the entire property which included eleven hundred acres of land. While they were hesitating over this, not quite wanting to accept because they distrusted the use that might be made of their dedicated community, representatives from the Roman Catholic Brotherhood of La Salette in Canada came to see them with a view to opening negotiations for its purchase.

The Shakers felt more favorably disposed to them than to the New York Club because under a monastic order the buildings would again be used for communal life and educational purposes, and because, as they said, "We would like to have our fields cultivated again." They finally sold it to La Salette in 1923 for $25,000—one-fourth of the New York offer. The most cordial relations have obtained between the Canterbury Shakers and these Catholic brothers who conduct a school and a seminary for training priests, cultivate the Shaker lands, raise garden vegetables and can them for winter use and own a herd of ninety cows. The new owners have tried so far as possible to care for everything as the Shakers did. They even made a special effort to match the granite of which their new chapel is built to that used in the Shaker stone dwelling a hundred years before.

In 1931 the fifteen remaining members of the Alfred, Maine, society left their home on the high plateau above the lake to join forces with the Sabbathday Lake community at New Gloucester. The town of Alfred gave a farewell party for these departing Shakers who had dwelt among them for nearly a hundred and fifty years. Elder Henry Green, then eighty-seven, was the nominal head, having been with the Shakers since he was left there, a boy of fourteen, by his father. He had succeeded Elder John B. Vance in the leadership of the colony.

It was Eldress Harriet Coolbroth, however, who made the Shaker speech of appreciation on that occasion. She gave a brief history of the Alfred community; then, with usual Shaker directness, and in the consciousness that she was facing an audience of friends, summed up the reasons for the closing of the Alfred society. "But after a while it became necessary to sell a piece of land here and there; the members died one by one and there were no converts to take their places; those who remained were getting older and less vigorous; year by year there was less income, and so it is at last the Shakers have got to a place where they can neither keep the buildings in repair or till the land as formerly." The Alfred property was sold in the same year to Notre Dame Institute—a Roman Catholic school for teachers. Here, as at Enfield, New Hampshire, the relations between the old and the new owners have been friendly and pleasant.

In 1933 the New Lebanon society sold its Church Family buildings and land to the founders of the Lebanon School for Boys—lately reorganized and renamed the Darrow School in honor of the early Shaker, George Darrow, upon whose homesite the first church was built. The present church, standing on the same ground, is used by the school as a gymnasium—a not wholly inappropriate use, since the Shaker services were often termed by themselves "exercising," or "being exercised." The Center Family, which has also become the property of the Darrow School, still houses two of the Shaker sisters, Emma and Sadie Neale, who will continue to occupy their old home as long as they live, giving, meanwhile, friendly and helpful counsel to the new owners.

261

In 1938 the one remaining family of the oldest community in Shakerdom gave up the hopeless struggle. Watervliet, New York, formerly Niskayuna—the "wilderness tract" that was John Hocknell's gift to the Believers, the fulfillment of Mother Ann's visions, the answer to the prayers of the earliest Believers for a home of their own—closed the doors of its South Family. The last survivors turned their backs sorrowfully on the buildings and the grounds they had known so well and so long, and went to New Lebanon. There were only three of them left to go, all women. The occasion for their departure was the death of sister Anna Case, an outstanding personality who had been promised that she should live her life out at Watervliet. The West Family had been sold to farmers some years before. The Church Family had been bought by the County of Albany in 1928 to found a home for the poor and infirm—the *Ann Lee* Home. It would have pleased Mother Ann whose grave is nearby in the little Shaker cemetery where the bodies of all the early leaders are buried. Some of the Shaker fields are now used as an airport; airplanes take off where Mother Ann, dying, saw "brother William coming in a glorious chariot" to take her home.

Four Shaker communities still remain open today: New Lebanon, New York, Hancock, just across the line in Massachusetts, Canterbury, New Hampshire, and Sabbathday Lake in Maine. New Lebanon, the former home of the Ministry, last summer (August 1940) sold its Second Family dwelling house, and moved the few survivors to the North Family where visitors are received and where Shaker articles are sold. Shaker chairs may still be ordered, for Robert Wagan's business is even today being carried on by Eldress Sarah Collins and Sister Lillian Barlow, but the entire membership is probably well below twenty. Hancock, just over the mountain, likewise has a gift shop where small Shaker-made articles such as pincushions, sewing-boxes, baskets, etc., are sold, as well as maple sugar and candy. Some of its farm lands are still being cultivated, but with hired labor.

The Maine and New Hampshire societies—Sabbathday Lake and Canterbury—have perhaps the most favorable situations for survival, since they are really isolated, on good country roads, but several miles from the nearest highways, whereas Hancock is directly on a busy highway and New Lebanon is only a few rods from one. Yet, in spite of their seeming remoteness, neither Canterbury nor Sabbathday Lake is too far from markets such as Concord and Portland, nor too difficult of access to tourists who care to make the effort to find them. Canterbury seems the more active and prosperous of the two. It sells food-stuffs such as baked beans and brown bread in Concord, has a good gift shop in its office building where many small articles of Shaker make are sold, and an antique shop in the old schoolhouse.

Sabbathday Lake has a similar gift shop in its office building, and it now uses its church for an antique shop. In the upper story ,where once the elders used to dwell, is a museum containing exhibits from most of the different Shaker communities. "But nothing from Enfield, New Hampshire," a sister remarked regretfully. "When the Enfield community was given up the best things went to the Cleveland, Ohio, [Western Reserve Historical Society] museum. No one in New Hampshire was interested." One of the most significant exhibits is Lucy Wright's saddle given by her to Hannah Goodrich in 1792 on the occasion of Hannah's going—a bit reluctantly—from her home in Hancock into the wilds of New Hampshire to help "gather" the Canterbury society. She remained there eventually as leading eldress in New Hampshire, and she made much use of Lucy Wright's saddle on her many journeys of encouragement to the other young

societies. The leather of the saddle looks as strong and new
as if recently tanned.

Today the spirit of even these two most active societies is
backward-looking rather than forward-looking. It cannot be
otherwise when they review their recent past. Three or four
years ago the membership of each was put at about forty; it
is less today. In all four of the surviving societies there are no
elders now. There is no longer a central Ministry to direct
the Millennial Church. The only men left are very old. Most
of the sisters are past sixty. The Shakers themselves admit
quite frankly that their course on earth is nearly run. They
are proud of their past, resigned to the present, and confident, even now, of the future. For themselves, their faith in
the supremacy of spirit over body makes for serenity. For the
world which they are leaving in spiritual darkness, they believe that some day—somewhere—somehow—a resurging of
the spirit will come. And perhaps next time the "world's
people" will be more ready to believe, more ready to accept.

On August 22, 1940, an interesting ceremony took place
in Enfield, New Hampshire. It was the dedication of a new
bridge over Mascoma Lake. The plaque on it reads as
follows:

> Shaker Bridge Built by the Shakers in 1848. Was de-
> stroyed by hurricane in 1938. Rebuilt by the State
> Highway Department in 1940. Dedicated to the
> Shakers for their many services to the town of Enfield,
> N.H. Truly Industrious—Always Helpful—A Kindly
> People.

The Canterbury Shakers had been invited to be present at
the dedication ceremony. They sent Sister Margaret Apple-
ton who had formerly been a member of the Enfield society.
With a pair of old Shaker shears she cut the ribbon that for-

mally opened the new Shaker bridge to traffic. Governor Murphy of New Hampshire and other state notables were present for the exercises. All the speakers paid tribute to the Shakers as good neighbors and good citizens of the town. But the governor in his brief address which emphasized the large part religion had played in the building up of this country, made special mention of Mother Ann, coupling her name with that of Elder Franklin [Young]. Most of the audience looked puzzled, but Sister Margaret's eyes lighted up with surprised pleasure that the last ranking elder in Enfield was still remembered. Even more poignant was her remark to the governor when on his arrival a little late he had apologized to her for keeping her waiting. "Oh you didn't keep me waiting," said Sister Margaret gently. Bridges and governors might come and go; the Shaker spirit was free of the bonds and bounds of time.

XV. THE SHAKER LEGACY

A CHURCH is judged by its leaders. If any way of life can produce great men and women, or even moderately adequate and integrated human beings, it is worth studying. The United Society of Believers has, during its century and a half of existence, developed its quota of men and women with unquestioned qualities of leadership. They were not all equally competent; some would never, perhaps, have risen to eminence in "the world." The fact that they deliberately chose a small vineyard in which to rove removed them automatically from the kind of competition they would have met in a larger social group. But it is possible to pick out several who would have been outstanding figures in any parish or town, and there are at least two who have the outlines of real greatness. Perhaps the size of the field does not matter.

Mother Ann, the founder, stands outside such a list. It is not altogether sure whether Shakerism produced her or she Shakerism. The spirit of Shakerism in her undoubtedly made her what she was, and her claim to be the founder of the Shaker church has never been questioned. She belongs in the line of those mystics like Joan of Arc and St. Francis of Assisi whom the world has never been able to explain. She was great in that she was able to rouse in others her own passion for spiritual perfection; she was great in that she practised what she preached and never used her power of influence for her own personal gain. Therefore she was able to inspire a number of lesser leaders to follow her example.

The Believers have many names to which they can point with justifiable pride. There were William Lee and James Whittaker who loyally supported Mother Ann and encouraged, comforted and upheld the first converts through all the hardships of those early years. There was Joseph Meacham, the first American leader, who left his position as a respected Baptist minister in New Lebanon to "gather" this wild sect of "Shakeing Quakers" into some kind of Gospel Order. There was Lucy Wright who, as the "first leading character in the female line," followed Father Joseph in the Ministry and guided the United Society well on its way toward the summit of its adventure. There was Issachar Bates—that hard-bitten soldier of the Revolution, that merry singer of ballad tunes—who gave up everything to join the Shakers, becoming their most indefatigable missionary to the "Southwestern territory." It was he who travelled thirty-eight thousand miles in ten years, most of it on foot, converting eleven hundred people to Shakerism. It was he who wrote from Busro, Indiana, in 1811, "My health is not very good, probably in consequence of having to travel seven miles every day to and from my work at the mill, sometimes in mud and water up to my knees, but my faith is everlasting and I mean to keep it."

There was Benjamin S. Youngs, author of *The Testimony of Christ's Second Appearing*, and John Dunlavy and Malcham Worley, scholars and preachers in that sparsely settled southwestern territory. There was Matthew Houston, cousin of Sam Houston of Texas and a slave holder who freed all his slaves when he joined the Shakers and helped found the Kentucky societies. In Ohio there was Daniel Baird, the inventor, and Richard Pelham, the scholar, and James S. Prescott, historian and last eminent leader of the North Union community. There was David Parker of New Hampshire, respected throughout the state for his integrity and business acumen, and Caleb Dyer, known in New York business circles.

There was the gentle Otis Sawyer of Sabbathday Lake, Maine, who made a collection of Shaker literature, the kindly Elijah Myrick of Harvard, Massachusetts, Daniel Fraser the social reformer, Giles Avery of Mt. Lebanon, beloved throughout Shakerdom. There was Henry C. Blinn, editor of "The Manifesto," and Harvey L. Eads, eloquent preacher and writer from South Union, Kentucky, during the middle years. And there was Richard McNemar—founder, almost, of the Shaker church in Ohio and Kentucky. And about forty years later there was Frederick W. Evans, ranking elder of the Believers at the peak of their power.

Richard McNemar was a great man judged by any standards: one of those supermen who seem to be endowed with the energy to undertake anything and the ability and courage to carry out whatever they have undertaken. He was born in Tuscarora, Pennsylvania, November 20, 1770—the year of Ann Lee's vision in the Manchester prison. Richard's family were a part of the wave of Scotch-Irish migration that settled western Pennsylvania. His mother was a Knox. They were restless pioneers, ever moving westward and southward. Richard came honestly by his questing nature.

He was given such opportunities for education as there were and improved them all, becoming proficient in the classics, able to read Latin, Greek and Hebrew with ease. He and Malcham Worley were early friends and schoolmates. In 1797, four years after Kentucky had been admitted to the Union, Richard was licensed by the Presbyterian church to preach at Caneridge, Kentucky. In the next two years he was connected with various churches on both sides of the Ohio River, which seems to have been easily overpassed in matters ecclesiastical. His most important ministerial charge was at Turtle Creek, Ohio, about thirty miles northeast of Cincinnati. Under his leadership this church became the largest and most influential in the state, with the possible exception of that at Cincinnati. Other ministers in that area were John Dunlavy, Matthew Houston, John P. Campbell and Barton W. Stone. In 1799 this group of men was instrumental in starting the Kentucky Revival of which Richard became the leading spirit and the outstanding preacher. It is told that audiences of thirty-thousand persons gathered to listen to him.

In March of 1802, however, the Presbytery of Cincinnati became alarmed by the liberal doctrines that were being expounded at the revival meetings, and charged Richard and his four fellow preachers with heresy. Yet, although it declared Richard's teachings "hostile to the interests of all true religion," he was allowed not only to go on preaching, but to divide his time between six or more places, giving half of it to his own congregation at Turtle Creek and apportioning the rest among the others. In 1803—the year Ohio was admitted to the Union—Richard and his friends withdrew from the synod of Kentucky (to which the Presbytery of Cincinnati belonged) and set up a presbytery of their own called the Presbytery of Springfield. The Turtle Creek congregation, which had previously petitioned to be given *all* of Richard's time, joined this, and other societies of Schismatics, as they were called, sprang up in both Kentucky and Ohio. Richard was the outstanding figure in the movement.

It was natural that the three Shaker missionaries from New Lebanon—Bates, Youngs and Meacham—should have tried to enlist his interest. It was natural, too, that once Richard decided to throw in his lot with the Shakers he brought all the enthusiasm and vigor of his nature to the new cause. Virtually the whole of his Turtle Creek congregation followed their leader into this new faith. They had been led by him from Presbyterianism into New-Light, or Schismatic, doctrines; they trusted his guidance wherever it took them.

From this point on, Richard's history is that of the Shaker communities in the Southwest. It was on March 23, 1805 that the three Shakers came to Richard's house. On June 29 of the same year, David Darrow was sent from New Lebanon to assume charge of this new colony, this "opening of the gospel in the Southwest," which Mother Ann had foreseen in a vision. Richard became David's chief advisor. Never half-hearted in anything, he contributed his all to the new adventure. His farm which he had bought in 1802 became the East Family. His wife—John Dunlavy's sister—joined the Believers. So did all but one of their seven children.

For the next two years there was plenty to do in the way of acquiring land, putting up buildings, dwelling houses, sawmills, etc., but Richard found time not only to write his celebrated *Kentucky Revival*, but also to help Youngs in that monumental work, *The Testimony of Christ's Second Appearing*. The *Kentucky Revival* was published in 1807 and *The Testimony* in 1808. Richard was the father of Shaker journalism, being a firm believer in the power of print. Indeed it is possible that the project of writing and publishing *The Testimony* may have originated with him. Certainly his own book, the *Kentucky Revival*, laid the groundwork for such an undertaking.

Besides Richard's supervision, in an advisory capacity, of the founding and gathering of the Union Village society, he found time to visit and encourage other newborn societies of that section. He helped found the Watervliet, Ohio, society in 1806. He did some proselyting among the Shawnee Indians in 1807. In 1809 he went on that difficult journey by foot to Busro, Indiana, with Issachar Bates and

Benjamin Youngs—certainly a change, if not a rest, from the arduous work of authorship. A year later he made a second visit to it in company with Archibald Meacham. He helped organize the Whitewater society in 1820 and that at North Union two or three years later.

All this time the various communities were having continuous trouble from unfriendly neighbors who, singly or in mobs, expressed their fear and hatred of these new religionists by deeds of violence and destruction of property. The worst mob attack came in 1810, but there were many others, in 1813, 1817, 1819, and 1824, besides lawsuits, incendiary fires and minor annoyances. Yet Richard found time in between for a horseback trip to New Lebanon, New York, in 1811, and for work on the hymn book, *Millennial Praises*, which appeared in 1812.

In 1817 Richard and Francis Bedle pronounced the famous Shaker curse over Lebanon, Ohio, by order of David Darrow. In 1823 Richard was again busy writing, this time on a revision of *The Testimony* for the printing of which a press was brought to Union Village from Cincinnati. From 1826 to 1827 he was involved in the moving of the Busro society and the disposal of the Shaker property there. He made his second trip north in 1829, visiting the communities in New York, Massachusetts, Connecticut and New Hampshire. The reason for this visit was the adoption of the newly revised covenant—a revision made to protect the Believers against lawsuits for the recovery of property by "the world."

After his return, he was continuously occupied during the next six years with visits to all the Ohio and Kentucky societies in an effort to insure their adoption of the new Covenant—not so different from the old, but tighter legally. In fact, he was so busy getting the signatures of all the members

271

that he forgot to add his own. It was during this same period that he prepared the speech delivered by Wickliffe in the Kentucky senate in defense of the Pleasant Hill Shakers against charges brought by seceding members. In addition to these duties, he took charge, for a time, of the White-water and the Watervliet, Ohio, communities, which were about a day's horseback journey apart. He was very happy at Watervliet. That society was particularly sympathetic toward his interest in printing. Many of the early hymns and other Shaker publications were printed there. The individual members at Watervliet contributed out of their personal savings to buy Richard a printing press of his own, with cases and type which he took back to Union Village with him.

Richard's days were well filled during the eighteen-twen-ties and thirties. Wherever there was trouble there he was sent to soothe, to straighten out, to persuade or to defend. He was unable to remain for long in any one place. He had scant time to spend with his beloved tools for which he had so painstakingly built himself a tool-cabinet in earlier, less hectic years, though he superintended the printing done at Watervliet. The responsibilities that mounted steadily, as the communities of Ohio and Kentucky grew, gave him less and less time to spend on the work with his hands which, theoretically, all Shakers were expected to do. When he was asked in 1836 by the New Lebanon Ministry to assume charge of Union Village (which meant being the official "lead" of all the Ohio and Kentucky societies), he declined the honor, feeling that his duties in the field would call him away too much. The Ministry thereupon appointed Freegift Wells of Watervliet, New York, in Richard's stead. And Richard, with his customary directness, kept on with his work among the scattered societies.

But things were never to be the same. In fact, although nobody realized it for many years to come, Union Village had already reached the peak of its influence and prosperity. The leadership of Freegift Wells marked the beginning of the long, slow decline. Freegift was a man of small caliber— a sectional sectarian who looked upon these southwestern communes as narrowminded Easterners have often regarded frontier regions, and upon Richard with jealousy that increased in proportion to his realization of Richard's popularity. Almost the first thing he did was to set about undermining this. First he accused Richard of "feeling above taking orders," making much of the fact that Richard had, for some time, done very little work with his hands. Then he discovered that Richard himself had not signed the last Covenant: that Covenant for the adoption of which he had spent himself so unstintingly! These things Freegift brought before the membership who remained stubbornly loyal to Richard. He even used forged letters to try to discredit Richard, but to no avail.

Then Freegift had a stroke of good fortune: the coming of the spiritualist revival to Union Village. The medium, Margaret O'Brian, proved a willing tool in Freegift's hands. She began to have visions for testing the members: information from the spirit world as to the worthiness or unworthiness of various brothers and sisters. Her revelations proved pointedly that Richard was unworthy. Even so, it was only after repeated testimonies of this sort, and then most reluctantly, that the Believers finally voted to expel Richard. In the spring of 1839, Freegift gave orders that he should be set down in the streets of Lebanon with only his clothes and his printing press with which to earn his living.

Richard was sixty-nine years old, and he had spent thirty-four of those years in the service and for the glory of

Shakerism. And now the Believers had turned against him. But even in this extremity he was not without resources. He turned his wheel-barrow with the printing press on it, toward the home of his old friend, Judge Francis Dunlavy, who had helped the Shakers against the mob attack twenty-nine years before. The judge took him in gladly and advised him to report what had happened to the Ministry at New Lebanon, New York. Richard made the trip there in June, was vindicated and returned home to be reinstated by a suavely apologetic Freegift who was conveniently able to blame and disavow the medium. But Richard's heart was broken. He died the following autumn, September 15, 1839. Incidentally, the departure of the printing press from Union Village was symbolic. With it, and with Richard departed the Shaker printing interests from Ohio.

One who knew Richard has said of him that he had "native endowment, toilsome acquirement, studious training. . . . His mind was ever open for more light. He accorded to others the same rights he reserved for himself." He was the eternal adventurer, the practical frontiersman, the honest thinker, unafraid to follow his convictions wherever they might lead him—the prototype of all that was best in the Shaker church. If he, with his talents and his courage, had continued on the main highway of American life, his name would undoubtedly have been better known than it is now. But he chose a bypath, and he followed it undeviatingly. For him it was the way to eternal life.

Frederick Evans was also a great man. He was a mystic and a theorist, while Richard was on the practical side. Yet, paradoxically, it was Richard who came to Shakerism through religion, while Evans reached it by way of freethought, economics and socialism. The two men were different at every point; they belonged to two different schools of thought, two different eras, two different nationalities and environments. And yet they were both attracted to the same small unpopular sect, and they were both men who might have gone a long way in the wider world. What did they have in common that attracted and bound them to the faith of Mother Ann?

Frederick W. Evans was born in Leominster, Worcestershire, England, on June 9, 1808, of a middle class family. His mother was of higher birth than his father, which made for disharmony in the family. Frederick lost her when he was four years old, and he was brought up by her relatives, passing the years between eight and twelve at Chadwick Hall, where he spent most of his time with the farmers and the servants, having been given up by his uncles and aunts as a poor educational risk. However, the self-education he received learning about rotation of crops, sheep raising, fruit culture, etc., and the profound interest he developed in the less privileged classes of society proved to be exactly what he needed to fit him for the life he was later to live. In 1820 his father and brother decided to go to America, and the young Frederick was given a choice of staying with his relatives at Chadwick Hall or accompanying his father and brother to a strange land of which he knew almost nothing. He chose America.

Evans was one of those intellectuals who develop slowly. As a child he was the despair of his teachers, seeming wholly uninterested in the studies he was expected to pursue. But when his mind was once awakened and his curiosity roused, as happened soon after his arrival in America, he read everything he could lay his hands on. Voltaire, Tom Paine were both grist for his mill. His brother George was a socialist and a friend of Horace Greeley. Frederick met men who were thinking and talking about such matters as land reform, labor problems, freedom of the press and of speech: very different matters from those that had engrossed his attention at Chadwick Hall. Or perhaps they were just a theoretical exposition of conditions he had come to know on the practical side in England. At any rate, he was soon thinking for himself along these lines.

One thing he felt certain of in this early period: that religion was *not* a major factor in his life. For a time he considered himself a complete materialist. But like Richard McNemar he was ever a seeker after new light, keeping his mind open for new truths, examining them honestly when they presented themselves, hungering for something he could not find in any of them. He made trial of divers utopian communes before he was led to visit New Lebanon. The mystic element in the Shaker faith satisfied the lack he had felt in all other religions, and he saw that he had reached the end of his quest. In 1830 he entered the North Family at New Lebanon where he remained till his death.

The Shakers, on their part, recognized Evans as a kindred soul. He was soon promoted to be one of the elders, and eventually became the "lead" in the New Lebanon Ministry, which meant official head of the whole Shaker church. He was singularly well fitted for the exercise of such a charge. On the material side, his practical knowledge gained as a boy from watching the orderly seasonal procedure of sowing, cultivation, reaping, selling, etc., in a farm run in the best tradition of English landowners, had trained him for the management of the Shaker agricultural units. His early experience of a not too happy family life, both in his own family and among his uncles and aunts where he certainly had reason to feel that he was not wholly wanted, his loss of his mother in childhood, and the unsettled life with his father and brother, all combined to keep him from feeling the need or importance of family ties. His love for humanity, fostered both by his friendship with the under- lings at Chadwick Hall and by the theories of social equality which he had been imbibing since his arrival in America, found a perfect outlet among the Shakers. This Society, dedicated to a search for the ultimate goal of spiritual per- fection through the development of an earthly utopia, wholly satisfied his mystical cravings.

Evans threw himself into the work of expounding and disseminating Shaker ideas to all who would listen to him. He preached to large congregations of "the world" in the big meetinghouse at New Lebanon every Sunday. He visited other Shaker societies; he wrote articles on Shakerism. Soon his articles began to be reprinted in newspapers and maga- zines. His opinion was asked and received with respect. He went to Washington to meet Lincoln and to convince him of the sincerity of the Shakers as pacifists. In 1868 he spoke at a two-day Shaker convention in Boston, after which James T. Fields asked him to write his autobiography for the "Atlantic Monthly." In replying, Evans said, "I see great importance in a principle, very little in an individual." How- ever, he did as Fields requested, with scant stress on bio- graphical details and a full statement of the Shaker beliefs. The article was published in book form by the Shakers the following year, with additional doctrinal material.

This was only one of Evans's many books and pamphlets and articles. Like Richard McNemar, he was a good publi- cist for the cause he had espoused, and a firm believer in the sacredness of freedom of speech. One of the points made by him again and again was that the free-thinkers and so- called infidels often had more of the truth than could be found in the established churches. He felt that the Amer- ican government, to which he was always loyal even when

277

criticizing its flaws, owed nothing at all to the church, declaring that all the Founders (except Carroll of Virginia) "were infidels to the existing so-called Christianity of the world. . . . Jefferson, Thomas Paine, Franklin and Washington (who has been somewhat whitewashed by the sectarian priesthood) were Materialists, Deists, Unitarians, etc." There was murmuring among the Shakers against some of Evans's radical statements—notably by Eads of Kentucky and Blinn of New Hampshire—but Evans was not the sort of man who could be muzzled. He continued the free expression of his opinions when and where and as he saw fit.

His writing was not wholly along religious lines. He produced a great many articles urging limitation of land ownership, woman suffrage, improvement of health through diet and regular hours, better housing and working conditions for the laboring classes, pacifism, etc. He protested energetically against the closing on Sundays of the World's Fair (Centennial) in Philadelphia in 1876, and again of that at Chicago in 1892, arguing that it was not fair to working men who could go on no other day. Besides, said Evans, each day of the week was a holy day for *some* sect. He received letters which he answered, from inquirers all over the world. In 1890 he carried on a correspondence with Tolstoi. He met and talked with visitors to Mt. Lebanon. Of all the Shaker leaders, except possibly Richard McNemar, Frederick Evans was given the most opportunities for contact with "the world." He was the Shaker Front, so to speak, during the middle and latter part of the nineteenth century.

Even across the Atlantic Evans's name was known. He made two visits to England to preach Shakerism there: the first in 1871, the second, when he also visited Scotland, in 1887. On both visits he was well received, speaking in

many places at meetings arranged for him by friends who
had either met him in America or had corresponded with
him. Hepworth Dixon, who had visited Mt. Lebanon while
in America gathering material for a book he was writing,
was the chairman of one of the London meetings. In con-
cluding, he said: "We in England, whatever we may think
about the special marriage dogma proposed to us tonight,
will always have a kindly regard for a community which
has made of a rugged mountaintop a kind of garden, and has
converted the daily lives of men and women into a religious
service."

Evans was seventy-nine years old when he made his second visit to England. He looked like a prophet with his deep-
set eyes, his serious, intent gaze that had always sought out
the truth wherever it might be found. His tall figure had the
same slight stoop it had worn for years, not from age or
weariness, perhaps from overwork in his early days. He gave
the same impression of energy and alertness that he had
always shown; his brown eyes were still bright and kindly.
He was active and well up to the end, which came six years
later. It is recorded of him that he died "without sickness
and without pain."

Evans was luckier than McNemar in his last days. Or was
he? Perhaps the distrust that some of his radical ideas called
forth from other Shaker leaders hurt him as much as Freegift's treatment did Richard. Perhaps his consciousness
that Shakerism, as such, was on the wane—for he could not
help recognizing this fact—was as bitter to him as was
Richard's knowledge that the Shakers had repudiated him.
Richard, at least, had never failed *them*. Although Evans
died full of years and honors, he was all too conscious of
the many evils in the world that the Believers had not been
able to help. Richard could have drawn some comfort from

the fact that he was leaving the Shaker church much stronger for his labors in it. Evans had been watching it slip, watching it lose members and close the doors of empty buildings.

But both of them knew that the spirit cannot be killed. Perhaps they were not so different after all. They were both honest, courageous thinkers; they had the same passion for perfection; they were both uncompromising in their determination to find or make an ideal world. Neither of them could bring himself to turn back to an imperfect society and accept the conditions he saw there. This Shaker church offered them a chance to create a utopia on earth, during their years of probation before entering the utopia of the spirit. It was an adventure worth embarking on. They were both gallant adventurers who never even looked back.

A century and a half has gone since Mother Ann brought her little band of adventurers to the shores of this continent. Then the country was new—new, at least to the English and Europeans who began settling it, blocking out home sites where forests still stood uncut and swamp lands lay yet undrained. The old growth pine trees of which northern New England and New York Shaker records make frequent mention had started as seedlings on those New York and New England hillsides anywhere from a hundred and fifty to three hundred years earlier; the oldest and biggest about the time Columbus discovered America, the youngest, before the Revocation of the Edict of Nantes drove the protesting Camisards toward a faith that flowered in Shakerism, before William of Orange established liberty of conscience in England.

These pines were all hard, fine wood which had taken its time about growing, having yearly rings often of less than one-sixteenth of an inch in width. By 1880 these trees were practically gone. The latest to be cut down showed a rotting beneath the bark. There were no more of them. Their generation had passed. Yet some of the logs cut from them a hundred years ago were used again in the foundation of the New Shaker bridge at Enfield, New Hampshire. Shingles split from them have kept Shaker roofs tight for a century; the boards sawed by the early sawmills from the widest part of the big trunks still endure in the Shaker buildings.

The Shakers are almost gone too. Yet certain material things that they made are still in existence, still in use. Other institutions have found shelter and security in the Shaker dwelling houses whose foundations were laid so solidly years ago that in all but a few of the Shaker communities many of the original buildings are still standing, as firm, as plumb as when they were finished. At Busro, Indiana, no trace is left; at Shaker Heights, Ohio, where North Union once stood, there is only the name to tell that the society Richard McNemar labored to found once lived and flourished there.

But in the others, there are still some buildings left to show that when man builds with honest care, his work endures. One of the Mt. Lebanon families is used for a school; the Alfred, Maine, and Enfield, New Hampshire, dwellings now house Roman Catholic brotherhoods; Pleasant Hill, Kentucky, shelters a home for girls; Shirley, Massachusetts, and Groveland, New York, are used by state institutions. The brick house for the Elders at Tyringham, built in 1823, is being used today as a family dwelling. The stone barn at Harvard, Massachusetts, looks strong and enduring. The stone machine shop at Enfield, New Hampshire, could be put into use today, as regards the condition of its foundation, its walls and its interior finish. Even wooden churches built by Moses Johnson in the seventeen-nineties are still standing.

Shaker chairs and tables are being collected both by specialists in early American furniture and by private owners. They are influencing modern trends. The Shaker built-in cabinets are being studied and copied in modern interior construction. Two or three years ago a New York store opened "Shaker House" with "a whole line of sharp, smart, functional furniture in the Shaker tradition," as an advertisement reads. The following year they presented dresses that derived their inspiration from Shaker costumes, using a paragraph descriptive of Shaker style to advertise them. "The plain simple functionalism and austere spirit smash straight into the core of today's silhouette—the fitted bodice and full rhythmic skirt. . . . In smooth, plain serges like the serges in the brethren's trousers. In silks and cottons as fine as those the Shaker sisters wove. . . . Shaker-fine workmanship. . . . Colors like those the Shakers crushed from vegetables and the neighboring hardhack trees. Plum like fruit of Lebanon orchards, etc."

The Shakers made many inventions which they did not patent, but from which others profited. Their ingenuity in discovering new ways of doing old things, or of improving old ways, added much to the fund of common knowledge into which their neighbors dipped freely. They made many contributions to agricultural practice, from horse rakes and rotary harrows to Frederick Evans's experiments with ensilage. They improved the breed of domestic livestock. They invented clothespins and matches. They set standards of quality and workmanship by which buyers living in their neighborhood judged the products of others. In countrysides where the Shakers once dwelt, one finds in the older houses today Shaker clothes baskets, Shaker sewing baskets

Shaker boxes and sieves; and in the barns, Shaker grain measures, Shaker buckets, Shaker hay forks and rakes. It is a long time since any of these were made, but they are still strong, still being used.

Besides the inventions, the furniture, the buildings—all the material things that one can touch with one's hands—the Shakers left records that other pioneers could use as blueprints for conquering other wildernesses: working models of a shared community life. They left examples of business cooperation, of motion-saving devices in shop and barn, of flexible handling of working groups, of an ordered management that kept everybody employed without any being overworked and made it possible for improved modes of living to be afforded and enjoyed equally by all. They contributed probably more than neighboring farmers' wives realized to a wider understanding of the relation between diet and health. They were among the first to advocate a greater use of vegetables and fruit, the use of the whole grain in making flour; their simple, wholesome fare in which there was no waste pointed the way to health as well as to thrift. And they gave a conspicuous proof of the wisdom of their way of life by their prosperity and their longevity.

The Shaker adventure offers an interesting disproof of the claim made by modern big business that the profit motive underlies all progress. The Shaker communities were a practical demonstration that competition is not necessarily the motivating force either of business success or of improved standards of living. Nothing they made was made primarily for profit. If they built up a good chair business at Mt. Lebanon in the middle and latter part of the nineteenth century, if they found ready markets for the livestock raised in Ohio and Kentucky, the flannel manufactured in New Hampshire or the garden seeds and brooms put out by most of the societies, it was not because they had consciously striven for markets, or had produced for profit. Their first aim in any kind of production had been to supply their own needs—make themselves self-supporting and independent of "the world." That was why they had raised and manufactured so many different kinds of things.

Their second aim had been to achieve as nearly perfect an article as possible. They were building a kingdom of Heaven on earth and they could not defile it by inferior material furnishings. When they found themselves turning out a little more than they needed, they applied the same standard to everything they sold to "the world," lest the Shaker name should be dishonored. This was the reason their products sold at a good price: the buyers knew they could depend on them. They knew too, that the Shakers never short-weighted a customer. Frederick Evans felt that the Shakers made a mistake in producing for sale rather than wholly for consumption; he thought they were dissipating their efforts in doing this, spending time and labor on what was of doubtful spiritual value to them. Time has perhaps proved him right. But the success, from a purely worldly point of view, of their outside business proves once again the truth of paradoxes, proves that a total disregard of the profit motive may, and does, build a profitable business.

On December 27, 1887, the "New York World" published an editorial about the Shakers which is here quoted in part. "Just one hundred years ago Sunday, this people organized at Mount Lebanon, New York, the first and only success-ful attempt at Communism known in history. . . . The Shakers have a keen appreciation of the necessity and dignity of labor, but they never hire halls to talk about it nor rush about the country exhorting each other to strike for short hours and long pay. Everyone of them has some useful work to do, according to age, sex and strength. Perhaps no class of people has done more for the country than they, when it is remembered how few they are in number." This was written during the time of Elder Frederick Evans's leadership; a tribute from a metropolitan newspaper in one of America's largest cities to an obscure and dwindling sect administered from a remote hilltop in rural New York. The Shakers accepted the tribute gravely without undue gratification. They were a dignified people and a humble people. Perhaps what the world needs today is more people who are both dignified and humble.

In order adequately to evaluate the Shaker experiment from the point of view of its intangible influence on its own time or on the future, one must stop and wonder what one means by influence. At any given period of history it is possible to say the influence of such a one is dead—ended. A visitor from some other planet, looking at our world of today with the detached attitude of an utter outsider might well feel that the influence of Jesus Christ was negligible if not wholly gone. The influence of any real prophet or leader fluctuates, having its ebbs and flows of enthusiasm, not steady and dependable like tides, but irregular, unpredictable.

The Shakers say that whatever is of the spirit must endure because it is indestructible. They have always been content to belong to the line of small, earnest, often persecuted and so-called heretical sects, believing that these sects *alone* carried the torch of pure Christianity. They say today of their gradual extinction: "Never mind. The spirit will make itself felt again—sometime, somewhere." Perhaps that is just what influence means: the flowing in from time to time of a spiritual current emanating from a soul strong enough to give it its initial impulse. That the people of any generation are insensible to it is no denial of its potential power. This idea alone is something for purposes of bequeathal to the "world's people."

One of the intangible legacies the Shakers left to the world is their demonstration that it is possible for man to create the environment and the way of life he wants, *if he wants it enough.* Man *can* choose. In a world of defeatism, this is a cheering thought. The Shakers were a small society of never over six thousand members, divided between less than twenty small communities that averaged about three hundred members apiece. In all of these they were surrounded by neighbors who, if not actually hostile in the beginning, were at least unsympathetic.

Their plan of life was communistic in a nation that has always looked askance at socialism and communism. Their theology was on the deistic, non-trinitarian, humanistic side in the midst of churches that still held to the old Jonathan Edwards ideas of theism, the Trinity and predestination. Their celibate practice often had the result of breaking up families, when family life was considered more sacred than it is now. Yet, in spite of all these things, the Shakers went about their business of building a utopia on earth in order to prepare themselves for an eternal utopia in Heaven. They knew what they wanted; they planned intelligently for the accomplishment of it; they carried their plans through to fruition.

As soon as the United Society was established, no Shaker ever felt economic insecurity; no Shaker ever knew unemployment; no Shaker ever had reason to envy a brother or sister for that of which he felt a lack. The Shakers were practical idealists. They did not dream vaguely of conditions they would like to see realized; they went to work to make those conditions an actuality. They wasted no time or energy in raging against competitive society, or in complaining bitterly that they had no power to change it; instead, they built a domain of their own, where they could arrange their lives to their liking. And that domain has lasted well over a century.

Another Shaker legacy to the world of today is the example of self-control, practised by them throughout their history. External pressure from the elders—even coercion at times—was undoubtedly exercised in regulating the daily living and working conditions of the group. But in the matter of individual conduct, every man was his own ruler. This was a requirement for membership in the order. The Shakers truly believed that "he who conquereth himself is greater than he who conquereth a city." Elder Harvey L. Eads, the bishop of the Kentucky societies, said, "The fact is, the true-souled and obedient Shaker is the freest person on the foot-stool of God, because all his bonds are self-imposed."

It was something to prove by a century of communal life that men and women *could* live and work side by side, if they chose, in freedom from the physical compulsions of sex. If it is a matter of pride to a savage to endure walking barefoot over hot coals or cutting himself with knives without whimpering, man's ability to deprive himself of some of the elemental satisfactions of life is an equal reason for pride. Whether or not one agrees with the type of mind that requires such a sacrifice, one has to respect the courage and singleness of purpose that carries it through. Self-control stands midway between self-indulgence and external coercion. Society has always condemned too great a degree of self-indulgence by the individual as hostile to the best interests of the group. Man as an individual has always rebelled instinctively against too much external compulsion, either by the group or its chosen leader. The middle course of self-government—the inner control of impulse and action—is the practical, self-respecting way. The Shakers knew this, preached it and practised it.

The Shakers practised tolerance. In spite of the fact that they had been ill-treated by bigots from other sects, and in spite of the fact that they were inflexibly exacting with themselves, they never tried to coerce others into adopting their beliefs. The word never is used with due allowance for the fact that in the early days a few over-zealous Believers did attempt methods of over-persuasion with some of their friends and relatives, but these instances were few and individual. The United Society as a whole has preached and practised tolerance for all faiths and for all individuals during the entire course of its existence. It has taken up the cudgels for oppressed minorities with which it did not always agree, both in this country and in others. The Shakers realized that in another age or another country they would have been less free to practise this tolerance in which they so firmly believed. They were grateful to the American government for giving them protection in their experiment. They were grateful to the Quakers for their struggles to achieve and protect liberty of conscience. Tolerance is perhaps the most adult virtue of an adult civilization. "The world" has not yet grown up to it, but the Shakers understood it.

Another Shaker contribution—one that stems straight from Mother Ann and is flowering today more vigorously than for many years—is their insistence on the necessity for confession of sin. In common with the Roman Catholic Church, the Shakers believed that spiritual progress is impossible where there has been no clearing away of the dead wood of past sins. Modern psychoanalysts are turning more and more to this method of moral and mental rehabilitation. The Shakers required of every applicant for membership that he or she confess all past misdeeds and make reparation, if possible, for such evils as could be repaired.

They further ruled that no Believer might participate in the religious services when holding a grudge or unkind thought against any other. There was no way of checking up on such sins as this; it was squarely the responsibility of the individual conscience. But the Shaker life was not planned for the insincere. There was no advantage to be gained, no satisfactory life there, for the Believer who was not honest with himself. And it is becoming more and more evident in the world that no satisfactory life can be built anywhere without personal honesty and personal integrity.

Perhaps the best legacy the Shakers left to the world is their serene confidence and courage in the face of difficulties. At every step they needed both; in the beginning, during mob attacks and other persecutions, in relations with unbelieving families and friends, in calm acceptance of the fact that they were a small minority going in a direction contrary to that taken by most of the world. Always they moved unflinchingly toward their chosen goal.

They did not bluster nor use violence; their courage was quiet, calm and unyielding. They could not prevent wars, but they could and did keep out of them. They could not prevent fire and flood, but they could and did remake on a firmer foundation what had been lost thereby. They could not abolish poverty from the world, but they could and did abolish it from their communities. They could not save their bodies from the wastage of disease and ill-health, but they could and did build a régime in which a sane mind in a healthy body was the rule rather than the exception. They could not prevent death, but they could and did prolong life into a happy and productive old age that accepted death as only another phase of the real life of the spirit. They built their own practical utopia in an imperfect and impractical world. They had the confidence to undertake a hazardous experiment and the courage to carry it through.

And now, when the end of the adventure seems to be in sight, they are still clear-eyed and confident; they are still courageous and they have no regrets. If one is fortunate enough to have a chance really to talk to one of the few remaining Shakers, one gains an impression of serenity, of a life that has found earthly satisfactions in simple pleasures and real happiness in the wider world of the spirit. The adventure is nearly over, but it blazed part of a trail toward the summit of the long-awaited Millennium. There are many trails leading toward the highest peaks, and none of them is easy. But mankind is never content to leave a peak unconquered. There will be other courageous climbers who will blaze other trails.

CONCLUSION

THE Shaker Adventure began in an era of wars, of economic discontent, of agnosticism; it is nearing its end in a time of such world-wide bloodshed, such economic distress in many lands, such openly proclaimed atheism as make past periods of unrest and turmoil seem comparatively peaceful. In the early years the blaze of religious fervor kept the Believers warm; the few of them who are left must now draw close to the dying embers to ward off the gathering chill. The pessimist, looking out at the world today, questions whether the religion of even Jesus has made a mark on the brutishness of human nature. The spiritual descendants of Jesus have numbered billions; those of Mother Ann, who claimed to be the reincarnation of his spirit, a scant six thousand. The tides of destruction seem to be engulfing all Christendom. How can one small island like the Millennial Church hope to leave even a trace after the flood has subsided?

In times of turmoil new religious sects always arise. Always they offer the hope and the prospect of a millennium. Most of them either die quickly or grow slowly into churches that tend more and more to conform to the existing pattern of already established churches. The difference between a sect and a church is that a sect keeps to itself and makes no effort to conform to worldly conventions, nor to conciliate worldly opposition. A church, on the contrary, tends more and more to fit into the social and economic pattern of its locality and its nation, usually becoming desirous of disarming opposition.

In other words, the fervor of a religious group burns brightest and best when the group stands most completely outside the life of the world. The more it seeks to warm and quicken that life, the more it loses its own first fire. This is one of the many paradoxes of religion. Perhaps paradox is an essential part of religion, as it seems to be of human history. When the night is darkest, the dawn begins to come. When the European world seemed deepest sunk in ignorance, the Renaissance began. And now that days of unsurpassed gloom and despair are upon the world, perhaps some other revelation of the power of man's spirit over his physical nature and the physical world about him will come, to light a new torch for groping mankind. There is always some up-springing of the spirit of God in the soul of man, always small groups of fanatics who claim to be divinely led.

It is a question how much the fanatic—the crank—contributes to progress. The odd child of the family sometimes grows up to be the family pride. Eccentricity, whether group or individual, is hard to live with. Those who conform un-thinkingly and pleasantly to their environment are so much in the majority that we like to call them normal. Yet, as the old saying states it, it is the crank that makes the world go around. In future days of humanity it may appear that the small, unpopular groups which stood deliberately aside, kept steadfastly apart from the course of normal, organized churches and political and economic systems, were the groups which contributed most in the long run to the mental and spiritual side of human progress. They are the experimenters, the adventurers.

It is possible that most established religions, as well as most entrenched economic systems, have made a mistake in stressing security rather than adventure. To youth, at least, spiritual adventure should make more of an appeal than spiritual security. When a race, a civilization or a religion turns its back on adventure, it has indeed made its final surrender. Man must have security, a home to come back to at night after the stress of the day, but his need of an adventure to look forward to in the morning is even greater.

Today there are many confused people in the world. There is a widespread tendency toward rationalization and wishful thinking. Men and women who started out as idealists feel cheated because life has forced compromise upon them, has not brought them what they have wanted and what they *think* they have been seeking. But wishful thinking is not seeking. Ideals are not toys to be played with; utopias are made not through high-minded wistfulness, but through hard work. What idealists and reformers of today need—what they have always needed—is to give ear to the American colloquialism "Put up or shut up." Most of us do neither. We keep on talking, but we make no personal sacrifices, take no chances. The Shakers "put up." They staked everything they had on their adventure. "The world" regarded them as reckless gamblers. No adventure, said "the world," could be worth the loss of family life, children, personal possessions, fame. But the Shakers felt that the adventure was worth much more than they had given up for it. They believed they had proved the truth of Christ's saying, "He that loseth his life for my sake shall find it." The Shaker story is the story of an adventure which, by worldly standards, failed. But perhaps this judgment is not the final one.

SOURCES

THE Shakers have always been interesting to the "world's people." They were deliberate publicizers of their own peculiar culture and theology, and they were inevitably "news" to their inquisitive and sometimes worried neighbors. There is no lack of primary source material available about them, whether written by themselves, by ex-Shakers or by observers from "the world." The Shaker beliefs, their membership requirements, their laws of government and their social regulations are set forth clearly and adequately in their own authorized publications which also include factual accounts of their early beginnings in England and America. Informal records of Shaker daily life with its varied seasonal occupations were kept in most of the Shaker societies by unofficial, self-appointed, sometimes anonymous scribes.

Although a large part of these writings still remain in manuscript, some few were published by the Shakers in their magazine "The Manifesto," and some others have been quoted in books by writers from "the world." Other purely Shaker sources are catalogues of such Shaker products as seeds, chairs, herbs, etc., and advertisements of Shaker inventions. Many accounts of life among the Shakers were written and published by ex-Shakers—usually at their own expense—but these are not uniformly dependable since they were sometimes actuated by a spirit of vindictiveness. The non-Shaker sources include descriptions by visitors from "the world," statistical materials such as town records of taxes and of sales of property, county and state records and histories, official reports of lawsuits involving the Shakers, and so on.

This bibliography makes no claim to completeness. It includes only such books as are of unquestioned authority or seem necessary to present divers phases of Shakerism. Most of them are easily available to the reading public. Fuller bibliographies may be found in the appendix to Nordhoff's *Communistic Societies of the United States*, listing seventy-two titles; in MacLean's *Bibliography of Shaker Literature*, listing 523 titles, and in the "Grosvenor Library Bulletin" for June 1940 which lists the 388 titles on its own shelves and reports the number of Shaker items found in other libraries in various parts of the country.

In the list that follows, I shall make use of letters to show the character and source of each book mentioned. D means that the subject matter is doctrinal or theological; F, that it is factual. SH indicates Shaker authorship; W, authorship by "the world"; X, ex-Shaker authorship. In the case of those books which seem to me peculiarly indispensable, I have added a short descriptive note.

D—Doctrinal   SH—Shaker author
F—Factual   W—Author from "the world"
X—Ex-Shaker author

Andrews, Edward Deming.
The Community Industries of the Shakers. Albany, 1932.   F W
  Issued by the University of the State of New York as Handbook 15 of the New York State Museum. Gives a comprehensive picture of the industrial activity that was carried on in the different Shaker societies. Lists and describes various articles of manufacture and processes used.
The Gift to be Simple. New York, 1940.   F W
  A sympathetic study and evaluation of Shaker music, giving its probable origins, its development by the Believers, and its essential place in the Shaker ritual. Lists names of songs and includes words and music of many. Has section on Shaker dances.

Shaker Furniture, the Craftsmanship of an American Communal Sect,
by Edward Deming Andrews and Faith Andrews. New Haven, 1937.

F W

A careful and authoritative history of Shaker craftsmanship as illustrated in Shaker furniture. Many illustrations. The most complete
and scholarly work on the subject.

These three books by Dr. Andrews illumine three different aspects of
Shakerism: their practical communal economy, their spiritual esthetics
and their manual craftsmanship.

[MACE], AURELIA [G.]
The Aletheia. Farmington, Maine. 1899.   D F SH
Valuable because of the many illustrations.

BLINN, HENRY CLAY.
Advent of the Christ in Man and Woman. East Canterbury, N.H. 1896.

D SH

BROWN, THOMAS.
An Account of the People Called Shakers. Troy, N.Y. 1812.   F X

COOMBS, ELIZABETH.
Brief History of the Shaker Colony at South Union, Kentucky. The Fil-
son Club History Quarterly, Louisville, Ky. July 1940.   F W
Darrow School Prospectus. New Lebanon, N.Y. 1940.   F W
With illustrations of Shaker buildings.

*A Declaration of the Society of People (Commonly Called Shakers),
Shewing their Reasons for Refusing to Aid or Abet the Cause of War,
etc.* Albany, N.Y. 1815.   D F SH

DOOLITTLE, MARY ANTOINETTE.
Autobiography of Mary Antoinette Doolittle. Mt. Lebanon, N.Y. 1880.

D F SH

DUNLAVY, JOHN.
*The Manifesto, or a Declaration of the Doctrines and Practice of the
Church of Christ.* Pleasant Hill, Ky. 1818.   D SH

DYER, MARY MARSHALL.
A Portrait of Shakerism. Concord, N.H. 1822.   F X
Of interest as an example of the virulence of some of the charges and
attacks made by ex-Shakers. The early history of the author showed
emotional instability, and the fact that the book was published at her
expense seems to suggest that she could find no publisher willing to
sponsor it.

EADS, HARVEY L.
Shaker Sermons. Shakers [Watervliet], N.Y. 1879.   D SH

SOURCES

ELKINS, HERVEY.
Fifteen Years in the Senior Order of Shakers. Hanover, N.H. 1853.
                                                                                 D F X

EVANS, FREDERICK WILLIAM.
Autobiography of a Shaker, etc. Albany, N.Y. 1869.   D F SH
    The story of how the best known of the Shaker elders came to Shaker-
ism, and his interpretation of Shaker theology. Was first written as
an article for the "Atlantic Monthly," at the solicitation of the editor;
republished later, with additions, by the Shakers.
Religious Communism. A lecture by F. W. Evans. London, 1871.
                                                                                D F SH

Gentle Manners: A Guide to Good Morals. New Lebanon, N.Y. 1899.
                                                                                           SH

Gazetteer of Grafton County, New Hampshire. Syracuse, N.Y. 1886.
                                                                                     F W
    Contains statistics about the Enfield, N.H., Shakers.

HASKETT, WILLIAM J.
Shakerism Unmasked. Pittsfield, Mass. 1828.   D F X

HUTTON, DANIEL MAC-HIR.
Old Shakertown and the Shakers. Harrodsburg, Ky. 1936.   F W
    A short history of the Pleasant Hill, Ky., community.
*Investigator, or, a Defence of the Order, Government and Economy of
the United States Called Shakers, Against Sundry Charges and Legis-
lative Proceedings.* Lexington, Ky. 1828.   F SH

LAMSON, DAVID RICH.
Two Years' Experience Among the Shakers. West Boylston, Mass.
1848.   F X

MACE, FAYETTE.
Familiar Dialogues on Shakerism. Portland, Me. 1838.   D SH

MACLEAN, JOHN PATTERSON.
*A Bibliography of Shaker Literature, with an Introductory Study of the
Writings and Publications Pertaining to Ohio Believers.* Columbus, O.
1905.   F W
    More than a bibliography because it contains important factual ma-
terial about Shaker publishing and Shaker authorship in Ohio and
Kentucky, with valuable details about the circumstances under which
some of the earliest books were issued.
Shakers of Ohio: Fugitive Papers Concerning the Shakers of Ohio, etc.
Columbus, O. 1907.   F W

A Sketch of the Life and Labors of Richard McNemar. Franklin, O. 1905. F W

The Society of Shakers. Rise, Progress and Extinction of the Society at Cleveland, O. Columbus, O. 1901. F W

MacLean made the history of the Shaker societies in the Southwestern Territory peculiarly his by the care and the interest he took in collecting factual material while most of the Ohio and Kentucky communities were still open and active. His life of McNemar gives a vivid and dramatic picture of one of the greatest of the Shaker leaders.

McNEMAR, RICHARD.

The Kentucky Revival. Cincinnati, O. 1807. D F SH

The first bound book to be published by the Shakers. It remains the best and most authentic account of that still unexplainable upsurging of religious emotionalism known as the Kentucky Revival. Valuable, besides, for the insight it gives into Shaker psychology, and the self-portrait of a great religious leader.

THE MANIFESTO, see THE SHAKER.

The Memorial of the Society of the People of Canterbury, in the County of Rockingham, and Enfield in the County of Grafton, Commonly Called Shakers. 1818. D F SH

A protest against bearing arms.

New Hampshire Gazetteer. Concord, N.H. 1874. F W

Contains statistics about the Canterbury and Enfield, N.H., Shakers.

NORDHOFF, CHARLES A.

Communistic Societies of the United States. New York. 1875. pp. 115-256. D F W

The most complete single history of the Shakers that has yet been written. To the detached and impartial attitude of a trained observer and reporter, the author added a sympathetic understanding. The book has a peculiar value because Nordhoff wrote it at a time when all of the eighteen Shaker societies were still in operation, and he gathered his facts and his impressions from personal visits to all but the four least active of them.

O'BRIEN, HARRIET E.

Lost Utopias. Boston, Mass. 1929. D F W

The Other Side of the Question. Cincinnati, O. 1819. F SH

In three parts. I. An explanation of the proceedings of Eunice Chapman and the legislature, against the United Society, called Shakers, in the State of New York. II. A refutation of the false statements of Mary Dyer against the said society, in the State of New Hampshire.

298

III. An account of the proceedings of Abram Van Vleet, esq., and his associates, against the said society at Union Village, O.

[Compiled by Eleazer Wright—*pseud.* of Richard McNemar—Calvin Morrell, Matthew Houston, Samuel Sering.]

PLUMER, WILLIAM.

The Original Shaker Communities in New England. New England Magazine, May, 1900.   F W

From letters written by Plumer in 1782.

Report of the Examination of the Shakers of Canterbury and Enfield, Before the New Hampshire Legislature, at the November Session, 1848. Concord, N.H. 1849.   F W

ROBINSON, CHARLES EDSON.

A Concise History of the United Society of Believers Called Shakers. East Canterbury, N.H. c1893.   D F W

Of importance because, though written by one of the "world's people," it was approved and republished by the Shakers who appreciated the honesty and sympathy of the author's treatment.

SEARS, CLARA ENDICOTT.

Gleanings from Old Shaker Journals. Boston and New York. 1916.
D F W

A sympathetic and well documented account of the Shaker society at Harvard, Mass. Illustrations and extracts from manuscript Shaker journals in the author's possession.

THE SHAKER.

Published as *The Shaker,* Jan. 1871-Dec. 1872; as *Shaker and Shakeress,* Jan. 1873-Dec. 1875; as *The Shaker,* Jan. 1876-Dec. 1877; as *The Shaker Manifesto,* Jan. 1878-Dec. 1883; as *The Manifesto,* Jan. 1884-Dec. 1899. At Shakers, N.Y. [Watervliet] and Shaker Village, N.H. [Canterbury].
D F SH W

This magazine, issued by the Shakers during the last thirty years of the nineteenth century, contains valuable factual material in its society records, letters, obituaries, historical notes and reprints of published accounts of the Shaker way of life, besides articles on Shaker theology, spiritualism, theories of economics, etc. A few illustrations and many Shaker hymns with music are also included.

Shaker Heights Then and New. Publication committee of the Shaker Heights board of education. Cleveland, O. 1938.   F W

Shaker Music. Albany, 1875.   SH

SMITH, JAMES.

Remarkable Occurrences Lately Discovered Among the People Called Shakers. Paris, Ky. 1810.   F X

The Story of Shakerism. By one who knows. East Canterbury, N.H. 1907.   D F SH

    A pamphlet which is still being sold by the Shakers.

A Summary View of the Millennial Church, or United Society of Believers (Commonly called Shakers) etc. [by Calvin Green and Seth Y. Wells]. Albany, 1823.   D F SH

    "Published by order of the ministry in union with the church," this book devotes most of Part I to the early history of Shakerism and of Mother Ann and the English founders, and it outlines, in Part II, the Shaker covenant of membership, the Shaker system of government, education of children, religious ritual, etc. The remainder of the book is theological.

STEWART, PHILEMON.

A Holy, Sacred and Divine Roll and Book; from the Lord God of Heaven, to the Inhabitants of the Earth, Revealed in the United Society at New Lebanon. Canterbury, N.H. 1843.   D SH

Testimonies Concerning the Character and Ministry of Mother Ann Lee and the First Witnesses of the Gospel of Christ's Second Appearing; Given by Some of the Aged Brethren and Sisters of the United Society. Including a few Sketches of their own Religious Experience, Approved by the Church. [Edited by S. Y. Wells.] Albany, N.Y. 1827. D F SH

    This is one of the most important of the early sources of information about the founders of Shakerism. In it, some of the first American converts tell of their individual contacts with Mother Ann and the Elders.

WHITE, ANNA.

Shakerism, Its Meaning and Message, Embracing an Historical Account, Statement of Belief and Spiritual Experience of the Church from its Rise to the Present Day, by Anna White and Leila S. Taylor. Columbus, Ohio. 1904.   D F SH

    This is the most complete factual history of the Shakers published by the Shakers.

WINTER, ESTHER C.

Shaker Literature in the Grosvenor Library. Buffalo, N.Y. June 1940.   F W

Gives a short sketch of Shaker history and valuable information about Shaker books and pamphlets available at the Grosvenor and other libraries in the United States.

WOODS, JOHN.
Shakerism Unmasked. Paris, Ky. 1826.   F X

[YOUNGS, BENJAMIN SETH.]
The Testimony of Christ's Second Appearing, etc. Lebanon, O. 1808.
         D F SH

This has sometimes been called by "the world's people" the *Shaker Bible*. It was the first bound book (except the *Kentucky Revival*) to be issued with the sanction of the United Church. It contains less factual material about the beginnings of the Shaker communities than is found in *A Summary View*, but it gives the completest statement of Shaker theology, following a masterly analysis of Christian ecclesiasticism before the coming of Ann Lee, that can be found anywhere. It is *the* most important single book issued by the Shakers.

LIST OF SHAKER SOCIETIES

| | | | Number of Members | | |
| | | | At | In | |
Society	Begun	Families	Peak*	1874†	Ended
Alfred, Maine[1]	1793	2	200	70	1931
Canterbury, New Hampshire[6]	1792	3	280	145	
Enfield, Connecticut[3]	1792	5	200	115	1917
Enfield, New Hampshire[1, 5]	1793	3	350	140	1918
Groveland, New York[3]	1826	2	200	57	1892
Hancock, Massachusetts[6]	1790	3	300	98	
Harvard, Massachusetts[5]	1791	4	200	90	1919
Mt. Lebanon, N.Y.[1, 2, 5, 6]	1787	8	600	383	
North Union, Ohio[4] (Cleveland)	1826	3	200	102	1889
Pleasant Hill, Kentucky[1]	1814	8	490	245	1910
Sabbathday Lake, Maine[6] (New Gloucester)	1794	3	150	70	
Shirley, Massachusetts[3]	1793	3	150	48	1909
South Union, Kentucky[5]	1811	4	350	230	1922
Tyringham, Massachusetts[5]	1792	3	100	17	1875
Union Village, Ohio[1, 3]	1812	6	600	215	1910
Watervliet, New York[3, 5]	1787	4	350	235	1938
Watervliet, Ohio[5] (Dayton)	1813	2	100	55	1900
West Union, Indiana[4] (Busro)	1810	3	200		1827
Whitewater, Ohio[5]	1824	3	150	100	1907

* Numbers of members at peak are approximate.

† This date is just a century after Mother Ann's coming to America, and the figures are from Charles Nordhoff's survey of the Shakers published that year in his *Communistic Societies of the United States.*

[1] Property now used for religious or charitable purposes.

[2] Property now used for private schools.

[3] Property now used for state institutions.

[4] Site built over; no Shaker buildings left.

[5] Property owned by private individuals.

[6] Survivals in 1940.

INDEX

INDEX

307

INDEX

Elders, *see* Ministry

Enfield, Conn., birthplace of Joseph Meacham, 24; missionary journeys to, 29; society founded, 35; death of William Lee at, 41; society gathered, 53, 96; industrial growth of, 131, 134; church built, 196; decline, 234; accession of Upper Canaan Family, 257; dissolved, 258-60; statistics, 302

Enfield, N.H., New-Light revival of 1781, 35-6; visit from Shaker missionaries, 36; gathered, 53; visits, 79; site of, 121; agricultural and industrial growth of, 123, 125, 131-2, 134, 141, 230-3, 236; families of, 147-8; relations with town, 160, 232; Shaker Bridge built at, 163-6; contributions to charity, 174; building program, 198, 199, 202, 230-2; peak reached, 163, 228; coming of railroad to town, 229-31; Caleb Dyer trustee at, 230-3; lawsuit with A. Conant & Co., 233; Henry Cumings trustee at, 246; "Holy Hill" at, 250; dissolution, 259; New Shaker Bridge dedicated, 264-5; use of property, 281; statistics, 302

Esthetics, 191-3

Evans, Frederick, theories of health, 157, 158; head of Shaker church, 179, 255, 276; as economist and socialist, 177-9, 284; Lincoln visited by, 179-80; as theologian, 209, 297; as pamphleteer, 214-16; preaches in London, 279, 297; life of, summarized, 274-80

Ex-Shakers, attacks on Shakers by, 77, 83, 93, 99-100; charges by James Smith quoted, 168-9; accounts of Shakers by, 211, 246

Farrington, John, 33; testimony of, about Ann Lee, 44-7; 108

Farrington, Nathan, 33

Father James, *see* James Whittaker

Fields, James T., Evans's autobiography written for, 277

Founding, defined, 34

Fourier, François Marie Charles, 177, 182

Fraser, Daniel, Shaker leader and economist, 177-8

"Fruitlands," 185, 259

Functionalism, 191-3

Furniture, 201-6; built-in cabinets, 202; cabinetmakers, 203; Robert Wagan's chairs, 205, 262; collected today, 282

Gates, Benjamin, trustee from New Lebanon, visits Lincoln, 171; sent to Florida to found Shaker colony, 239

Gathering in gospel order prophesied by Ann Lee, 25; defined, 35; early, in New York and New England, 53; early, in Southwest, 73-4; later, 82; need for regulation of, 100

George II of England, 7

Gold Rush of 1849, 229

Goodrich, Daniel and Elizabeth, of Hancock, Mass., 24

Goodrich, Hannah, sent to New Hampshire from Hancock, 56, 263

Gorham, Me., revival of 1781 at, 35, 36; society founded, 37; gathered by John Cotton, 53; voyage to Niskayuna, 37-9; moved to New Gloucester, 256; *see also* New Gloucester

Government (Shaker), centered at New Lebanon, 56; ministry, 95-6; bishopric, 96; elders, 96-7, 140; trustees (office deacons),

INDEX

tion with Lafayette, 184; prophecy of, concerning end of Shakerism, 244-5; Ann Lee Home in Albany County, 262; evaluation of life of, 25, 40, 43-7, 266

Lee, Nancy (niece of Ann), goes to America, 16

Lee, William, brother and disciple of Ann, 6, 13; voyage to America, 14-17; early leader, 18; missionary journeys, 24; beaten by mob, 29, 32; imprisoned at Albany, 27; death of, 41, 42; as artisan, 17, 133

Lexington, Ky., 74, 125, 172, 297

Lincoln, Abraham, visited by Shakers, 171, 179; visited by Evans, 277

Literature, utilitarian and inspirational, 207, 240, 241; theological, 102-6, 111, 208; historical, 103, 107-8, 110, 115-16, 210-11; hymns, 211-13; journalistic, 214-16; keynote of Shaker literature, 216

Liverpool, England, Shakers sail from, for New York, 14

Localities of Shaker influence, in England, 6, 7, 14-15; in New York and New England, 15, 20, 24, 30, 35, 53; in Southwest, 70, 71, 74

London, England, visited by Evans, 279, 297

Losses of members, through illness, 71, 240, 255; by backsliding, 241

Losses of property, through trustees, 233, 234, 238, 239, 246; by fire, 234, 238, 239; by war, 171, 234, 238, 246

Louisville, Ky., 258, 296

McNemar, Richard, Presbyterian preacher, 59; historian of Kentucky Revival, 59; leading

New-Light dissenter, 64; associated with Barton Stone in forming Presbytery of Springfield, 64-5; break with Stone, 66; joins Shakers, 68-9; missionary journeys, 69-74; assists in gathering of Union Village, 74; handling of mobs by, 77; visits to New Lebanon, 80-2, 271; as craftsman, 98, 150, 203; as coauthor with Youngs, 103, 106; as organizer, 136, 141, 270-2; as "trouble shooter," 144-6, 298-9; relations with Indians, 176; as writer of verses, 207, 221; of theology, 207-9; of history, 210, 216; of pamphlets, 214; trial and death of, 239, 251, 273, 274; life of summarized, 268-74; as printer, 270-2; MacLean's Life of, 297

Mace, Aurelia, 155, 296

Maine, early converts from, 23; opening the gospel in, 35-40; societies founded in, 35, 37; Shakers well treated in, 40, 166, 167; Elisha Pote, 250

Manchester, England, 6; birthplace of Ann Lee, 7; Toad Lane in, 7, 9, 11, 12; persecutions in, 11-14; home of John Hocknell, 15

Manifesto, The, by John Dunlavy, 106-7

Manifesto, The (Shaker magazine), 157, 181, 210, 214, 240, 294, 298

Mann, Horace, 229

Mariah, the, Shakers embark on, at Liverpool, 14

Mascoma Lake, N.H., site of Shaker community, 37, 121, 131; Shaker Bridge over, 163-6, 264

Massachusetts, revival in, 21-2; converts from, 23-4; first mob

311

INDEX

career, by Ann Lee, 183; of ending of Shakerism, by Ann Lee, 244-5

QUAKERS, as spiritual ancestors of Shakers, 6, 114, 115, 267; similarity between ideas of Shakers and Quakers, 31, 170, 288

RAND, ELEAZER, sent to gather Harvard and Shirley, 56

Relations with "the world," early, in England, 11-15; early, in America, 24, 26-34, 75-8; attitude of "world" gradually changing, 78; respect of "world" for Shakers, 160, 167; Shaker business relations with "world," 162-4; Shaker attitude changing, 230

Rensselaer van, Stephen, Esq., Niskayuna "leased in perpetuity" from, 19

Revivalism, Cavalier, 6-7; Wesley, 7; Whitefield, 7; the Wardleys, 12; New Lebanon revival, 20-2; Edwards, 20; in New Hampshire and Maine, 35-6; Kentucky Revival, 57-65; Shaker revival under Lucy Wright, 80; spiritualistic revival of 1837, 248-51

Ricker, Jabez, 130-1; 166

Ritual, 151-2; organization of, 218, 221; early songs, 219, 221; teachers of music, 220; characteristics of, 222-3; as drama, 223-5; public admitted to religious services, 223-6; in revival of 1837, 248, 250; on "Holy Hills of Zion," 250; *Millennial Praises* published, 271

Roman Catholic Church, as owners of Shaker lands and buildings, 260, 261; celibacy of, compared with Shakerism, 253; Shaker agreement with, on confession of sins, 288

Ruskin, John, Shaker agreement with, 178

Russell, Ralph, founder of North Union at Warrensville, 136

SABBATHDAY LAKE, see New Gloucester

St. Gaudens, Augustus, Shaker church bought by, 197

Schismatics, precursors of Shakers and Campbellites in Southwest, 65, 69, 269; receive Shaker missionaries, 68, 69; schismatic churches magnets of Shaker influence, 70

Second Coming of Christ, announced by Wardleys, 6; announced as in form of a woman, 9, 10, 13; prophecies of, at New Lebanon revival, 21; Shaker belief in reality of, 155, 290

Separation from the "world," cardinal principle of Shakerism, 10; put in practice, 19, 25; achieved, 48, 51, 52, 87, 195

Shaker, meaning and history of word, 117

Shaker Bible, see *The Testimony of Christ's Second Appearing*

Shaker Bridge, built at Enfield, N.H., 163-6; rebuilt, 166; dedication of New Shaker Bridge, 264-5; old logs used in new bridge, 281

Shakerism, beginnings in France, 5-6; beginnings in England, 6-11; announced to world, 9; beginnings in America, 19-20, 22-3, 59; founding and gathering defined, 35; founding of societies in America, 34-7; cardi-

315

INDEX

Stone, Barton W., active in Kentucky Revival, 64; breaks with McNemar, 66; meets Shaker missionaries, 68; denounces them, 69, 75; persecutes Shakers, 75

Summary View of the Millennial Church, A, 83, 300

Survivals (of Shaker communities in 1941), 262-4; 281, 282

Sweden, Shaker interests in, 194; influence of on craftsmanship, 194; receipt of *Holy Roll* acknowledged by king of, 249

TAXATION, examples of, 162-3; willingness of Shakers to pay, 171; protest against over-taxation, 173; Enfield's taxes at peak, 232

Testimonies Concerning the Character and Ministry of Mother Ann Lee, etc., 107-10; as history, 210, 300

Testimony of Christ's Second Appearing. etc., The, 102, 103-6; summarized, 111-19; as literature, 207-8; 270, 301

Testimony withdrawn from the world, 52, 183, 186-7, 226

Thombs, Dana, vision of Ann Lee seen by, 39

Toad Lane, Manchester, home of Ann Lee, 7, 9, 11, 12, 14

Tolerance (shown by Shakers), 175-6; support of, in Bennett vs. Comstock, 180-1; in regard to Oneida Community, 181-2; in regard to dissenters, 216, 288

Tolstoi, correspondence with, by Evans, 180, 278

Townley, John, member and patron of Wardleys' Society, 14-15

Transcendentalists, 177; visits to Shakers, 185

Trustees, system of, 56; duties defined, 94; appointment of, 97; importance and functions of, 133, 137-40; David Parker, 141-3; Benjamin Gates, 171; Caleb Dyer, 230-4, 246; Nathan Sharp, 234, 239, 246

Turtle Creek, Shaker missionaries visit, 68; David Darrow sent to, from New Lebanon, 69; lands bought at, for site of Union Village, 70; McNemar's congregation at, 75; McNemar at, 268, 269; see also Union Village

Tyringham, Mass., society founded, 35; gathered, 53; site, 122; barn, 128; backsliding, 242; dissolution of, 256; property in private hands, 256; statistics, 302

UNION VILLAGE (Turtle Creek), founded, 70; assumes leadership in Southwest, 72, 96; gathered under David Darrow, 73-4; persecutions at, 75-8; mob of 1810 at, 77, 299; site of, 122; stock farming, 128; industrial growth, 132, 135, 136, 138; early records of, 138-9; contributions to charity, 174; visited by Henry Clay, 184; peak of prosperity, 227; losses, 234; industries after peak, 236; spiritualistic revival, 251; dissolution of, 257; statistics, 302

Unitarians, 112, 278

United Society of Believers (commonly called Shakers), see Shakerism, Shakers

VANCE, JOHN, as craftsman, 150

Vegetarianism, practised, 152, 283; favored by Evans, 157

317

members, 241; dissolution, 257; statistics, 302

Wells, Freegift, sent to Union Village, 251, 272; hostility of, to McNemar, 251, 273, 274

Wesley, John, 7, 20

West Union, Ind. (Busro), founded, 71; gathered, 73; early history of, 71-4, 136; removal of, during War of 1812, 74; abandoned, 136, 255; losses from war with Indians, 171; disposition of property, 255-6, 281; statistics, 302

Whitcher, Benjamin, early convert at Canterbury, 36; donation of property by, 53; testimony in vindication of Ann Lee and the Elders, 108

White River Junction, Vt., 163; logs for railroad bridge at, supplied by Shakers, 231

Whitefield, George, 7, 20

Whitewater, Ohio, founded at Darby Plains, 136; gathered by Issachar Bates at Whitewater, 82, 136; bookbinding at, 135; put in charge of McNemar, 145; dissolution of, 257-8; statistics, 302

Whittaker, Daniel, 13, 14

Whittaker, James, disciple of Ann Lee in Manchester, 12-13; goes to America, 14-17; as artisan, 17, 98, 133, 150; imprisoned at Albany, 27; beaten by mob, 29, 32; visit to Maine and New Hampshire, 39-40, 50; begins work of organization, 41; becomes spiritual head of Shakers, 48; ministry and character of, 48-52, 166, 266; death and last words, 52; publication of letter from, 103

Wickliffe, Robert, Shakers in Kentucky defended by, 145

"Wilderness Tract," option taken on, by Shakers, 18; purchase of at Niskayuna, 19; described, 54-5

Wilds, Elijah, land donated by at Shirley, 53; testimony of, in vindication of Ann Lee and the Elders, 108; as farmer at Shirley, 157

William of Orange, 114, 280

Wood, Aaron, 29, 55, 108

Wood, Jonathan, 29

Woods, John, Shakers attacked by, 93; author of Shakerism Unmasked, 99; on education, 160; 300

Worley, Malcham, Shaker missionaries to the Southwest received by, 68, 221; converted to Shakerism, 68; as preacher in Turtle Creek, Warren County, 70; as scholar and theologian, 103, 208

Wright, Eleazar, new name given to McNemar by Lucy Wright, 81; used as pseudonym by McNemar, 299

Wright, Lucy, leading Shaker eldress, 52; gives saddle to Hannah Goodrich, 56, 263; successor to Meacham as head of Ministry, 56, 79, 267; revival encouraged by, 80; visited by McNemar, 80-2

Young, Franklin, last elder at Enfield, N.H., 260, 265

Youngs, Benjamin Seth, as missionary to Southwest, 67, 70, 72, 73, 221; as leading elder of South Union, 74; opposed by Barton Stone, 76; as writer, 103-6, 207-8, 301; as theologian, 104-5, 267, 301

Youngs, Isaac N., clockmaker, 204; author of treatise on music, 220

3 IS41·M48